MUSIC VIDEO AND THE POLITICS OF REPRESENTATION

U.
LIBRARY

D1465277

BARNSLEY COLLEGE

00135229

30001037

Music and the Moving Image

Series Editor
Kevin Donnelly, University of Southampton

Titles in the series include:

Film's Musical Moments
by Ian Conrich and Estella Tincknell (eds)

Music, Sound and Multimedia
by Jamie Sexton (ed.)

Music Video and the Politics of Representation
by Diane Railton and Paul Watson

Visit the Music and the Moving Image website at
www.euppublishing.com/series/MAMI

MUSIC VIDEO AND THE POLITICS OF REPRESENTATION

Diane Railton and Paul Watson

EDINBURGH UNIVERSITY PRESS

© Diane Railton and Paul Watson, 2011

Edinburgh University Press Ltd
22 George Square, Edinburgh

www.euppublishing.com

Reprinted 2012

Typeset in 10/12.5 Adobe Sabon
by Servis Filmsetting Ltd, Stockport, Cheshire, and
printed and bound in Great Britain by
CPI Antony Rowe, Chippenham and Eastbourne

A CIP record for this book is available from the British Library

ISBN 978 0 7486 3322 7 (hardback)
ISBN 978 0 7486 3323 4 (paperback)

The right of Diane Railton and Paul Watson
to be identified as authors of this work
has been asserted in accordance with
the Copyright, Designs and Patents Act 1988.

CONTENTS

ACKNOWLEDGEMENTS

Just as there is more than one way to skin a cat, there's more than one way of co-authoring a book. One of these is to agree on its subject, purview and structure, carve up the job of writing it, and then stitch it together when the words are in the bag, so to speak. This book was not written in that fashion. From first to last, what follows is the product of a different model of collaboration, the result of a process of genuine co-authorship. Put simply, what you read here is the upshot of many hours of two people sitting in front of a computer hatching thoughts and trying to find the words to record them. Indeed, it's not just the nature of the argument we put forward here, or the style in which it is expressed, that is the product of this working method, but the very substance of each sentence. We hope that the book benefits from this approach. While that is, of course, for others to decide, what is true is that this book would never have reached fruition without the support of a whole range of people to whom we would like to express our gratitude. Firstly, we have received unwavering support from both the School of Arts and Media at Teesside University and its Institute of Design, Culture and the Arts. Just as important has been the support, advice and friendship offered by our colleagues in the English Studies Department – thanks to you all. In a similar vein, this book would never have seen the light of day without the guidance and patience of all those at Edinburgh University Press who have been involved in coaxing this project into fruition. Thanks to Vicki Donald, Esme Watson, Sarah Edwards and Rebecca Mackenzie. On a related note, thanks also to Kevin Donnelly, the editor of Edinburgh University Press's Music and the Moving Image series, of which this book is part. Not only did he help us secure the commission in the first place, but more recently his comments on earlier drafts of the book have been invaluable in helping us address its shortcomings. One of the potential drawbacks of the working practice we employed here is that it is sometimes very time-intensive. This is, of course, most acutely felt at home. As such, our most significant debt of gratitude is to our respective partners, Ian and Alex, who have not only had to endure untold moods, whines, moans and whinges over the years, but who have had to do so while listening to some pretty eclectic (some might say weird) background music.

'Don't mind doing it for the kids'

for

Ben

Callam

Ellie

Jude

Marcel

Oliver

Roy

INTRODUCTION: THE KLEENEXES OF POPULAR CULTURE?

Music video is a significant and interesting form of contemporary popular culture, one which is widely circulated, complex and important. This claim is, however, a potentially controversial one. For it is easy, as many critics have done, to either dismiss music video as a worthless by-product of capitalist business practice or, worse, to ignore it all together. Graham Fuller spells out this situation in 'A Good Music Video is Hard to Find' in claiming that 'the search for the art and artistry of the music video goes on but the consensus is that El Dorado or Santa Claus will turn up first'. He goes on to say that, since the inception of MTV in 1981, 'what critical evaluation of music video there is relegates it to the trash can of popular culture'.[1] This kind of reaction to such a fascinating subject is, however, both predictable and perplexing. It is predictable in that the instrumental logic of music videos serves to direct attention towards a range of secondary commercial products and away from their own formal and aesthetic qualities, yet also perplexing in so far as the recent resurgence of academic interest in popular culture might have been expected to embrace the vibrancy of such a ubiquitous cultural product. These responses, to either dismiss or ignore, are, of course, the recto and verso of long-standing discourses concerning value and distinction, two sides of the same coin which continue to define music video as a kind of 'throwaway art ... the Kleenexes of popular culture'.[2] It is the contention of this book that they warrant much more sustained and detailed consideration.

Music video's *raison d'être* as a promotional device has had a number of significant consequences for the way it has been studied and conceptualised.

I

All music videos have an avowedly commercial agenda: they are first and foremost a *commercial* for an associated but distinct consumer product, the music track itself. Indeed, many directors of music videos also make advertisements for other products – Hype Williams, who has directed videos for artists such as Beyoncé, Ashanti, Janet Jackson and Pharrell, has also made commercials for Nike; Little X has made commercials for MacDonald's and directed videos for Akon, Sean Paul, Rihanna, and Korn; Jake Nava has directed commercials for HSBC and Del Monte as well as videos for Robbie Williams, Britney Spears and the Rolling Stones. As Peter Wollen has argued, music videos represent the 'breakdown of the distinction between programme and ad'.[3] The fact that music video is always already a secondary product, an advertisement for another cultural form, tends to short-circuit discussion of music video itself by re-routing critical energies towards putatively more valuable objects.

This critical elision is mirrored in the practices of cultural journalism, to the extent that music video falls outside of its institutional norms which privilege the music and the performer as the key sites of creativity and meaning. So, while reviews of albums, singles and live performances now regularly occupy a significant number of column inches in both dedicated music magazines and the review sections of the press more generally, reviews of the latest video releases are notable only by their absence. And in many ways this is understandable if we think of music videos *only* as advertisements. You wouldn't expect a review of the latest perfume or mobile phone to make reference to the television commercial which was used to advertise it. However, when we consider that music videos have a life of their own – with television channels and websites dedicated to screening them – which other commercials do not, this critical neglect becomes difficult to understand. For music videos are not simply advertisements; they are, rather, as Thomas Doherty suggests, both 'promo and product' and, as such, have 'revised the nature of contemporary music'.[4]

And yet, to a significant extent, this deficit, this lack of interest, is replicated in the institutional practices of academic writing and research. That is to say, despite Roy Shuker's claim that 'the analysis of MV clips has been one of the major growth areas in both television studies and the study of popular music', academic work on music video is not common.[5] Indeed, with the exception of the recent publication of Carol Vernallis's *Experiencing Music Video* and Roger Beebe and Jason Middleton's *Medium Cool*, there has, over the years, been little sustained work on the subject.[6] For the most part, discussion of music video is subsumed under other topics and foci. So there may be, for instance, one or two essays about music videos in a collection about popular music: both Angela McRobbie's *Zoot Suits and Second Hand Dresses* and Andrew Blake's *Living Through Pop*, for example, each include one chapter on the subject. There may also be passing reference made to music videos in discussions of genres or artists: Imani Perry's article on women and hip hop, for example, mentions them, as does Robyn Brothers in her article about U2.[7] However, there is, and has been, little dedicated work on music videos themselves. Indeed, despite the fact that critical interest in music video emerged soon after the launch of MTV, from today's vantage point this period appears to be, if not a false dawn, then certainly a half-forgotten moment of enthusiasm and vitality. For the 1980s, and, indeed, the early 1990s, saw a spate of articles in journals dedicated to film studies, television studies, media studies and cultural studies, discussing both the new phenomenon of music television and the videos that constituted its content. The range and scope of these articles was broad, stretching from Deborah H. Holdstein's discussion of music video as a part of the music industry's star machinery, to Joan D. Lynch's discussion of the influence of surrealist art on music video aesthetics, via articles critiquing the ideologically gendered messages of MTV or numerous pieces celebrating its postmodernism.[8] This nascent critical interest promised not only to elucidate the formal and political properties of music video, but also to provide a space in which many of the tenets of film, media and cultural studies could be rethought. Although scattered in its distribution and piecemeal in its interests, there seemed to be a new field of study arising, a new interest for academics concerned with the study of the popular. However, rather than growing and developing its own institutional presence, it quickly became subsumed into precisely those paradigms it promised to recast and, ultimately, petered out almost entirely. The desire to understand and explain music video *qua* music video rapidly gave way to a range of other priorities. Perhaps the most noticeable of these was the desire to read music video, or more precisely music television, as variously a symptom of, a product of, or synonymous with postmodern culture. Kaun-Hsing Chen, for example, conceives MTV as 'a schizophrenic simulacrum ... a simulacrum of multiplized originals', that absorbs a whole range of other cultural forms and 'abandons the ideology of the reality principle'.[9] Here, if postmodernism is the theory, and Jean Baudrillard is invoked as its High Priest, then MTV is the practice. Peter Wollen suggests that music videos are 'a hybrid and technologically sophisticated form', 'replete with quotation and allusion' which push us to rethink our ideas and question our critical concepts – they demand 'new concepts and new attitudes'.[10] They are exemplars of what Andrew Darley terms 'displayed intertextuality', hybrid forms that happily play with and manipulate images from the past and the present and in doing so 'frustrate attempts at categorisation along traditional lines'.[11] For critics such as these, then, music videos are important because they are radically different to what has gone before and, thus, make us re-evaluate contemporary art, aesthetics, and ideas of creativity, representation and originality. The analysis of music video, therefore, is put to work for broader theoretical ends as the site where both the economics and the aesthetics of postmodernism condense into palpable evidence of the logics of postmodernity.

While postmodernism's preoccupation with notions of semiotic excess, assemblage, self-reflexivity and fragmentation provided the *lingua franca* for discussing music television, music video was being co-opted elsewhere. Not only were music videos being incorporated into the study of popular music generally, but, more specifically, they were being used as a way of interrogating the relationship between music and cultural politics, and in particular the cultural politics of race and gender. As with most other areas in the study of the popular there are two key strands in this body of work, those which seek to warn against the negative aspects of music video and those which ferret out positive aspects to celebrate. The former consists of work which discusses both MTV and individual videos in relation to the potential damage that can be done by the production and perpetuation of stereotypical images. Whether based on statistical content analysis, as with Steven A. Seidman's or Rita Sommers-Flanagan et al.'s analyses of gender roles, the close textual analysis of Sheri Kathleen Cole, or the ethnography and autoethnography of Jennifer Hurley or Elizabeth Ellsworth et al., this type of work focuses on the limited, distorted, often sexualised ways in which women, especially black women, are represented in music videos.[12] The latter strand, by contrast, sets its sights on unearthing positive, transgressive, and potentially progressive representations. So from this position, gangsta rappers in music video are 'organic intellectuals', Queen Latifah produces afrocentric feminist videos, Cyndi Lauper 'appropriates the image of the street' for girls.[13]

It is here that the study of Madonna is significant. This has to do, in the first instance, with the sheer quantity of work dedicated to discussion of Madonna and her videos.[14] But it is also to do with the privileged place that Madonna has within discourses of both postmodernism and feminism, discourses which have figured her variously as a feminist role model, a postmodern artist, the embodiment of a queer politic, or, more rarely, as the epitome of the exploitative logics of the culture industry. For Kaplan, for example, she 'embodies the new postmodern feminist heroine', and it is in this respect that videos such as LIKE A PRAYER (1989), 'an enlightened work that emphasizes positive aspects of the black community', JUSTIFY MY LOVE (1990), with its 'shocking violation of conventional sexual representations', EXPRESS YOURSELF (1989), in which 'Madonna is constantly inverting relations of gender power and domination', or VOGUE (1990), with its 'queer camp effect' are lauded for their critique of normative values and challenge to conventional prejudices.[15] What is important, however, is that the study of music video, once again, is either an afterthought to another project or organised around the analysis of a certain few performers, Madonna being principal amongst these.

The result of these tendencies is that the study of music video has been half buried beneath the clamour to write about other, albeit related, products, and half submerged in the intellectual trends and preoccupations of a range of academic disciplines. It is in this respect that 1993 seems to represent both the life and death of music video as a form of popular culture capable of sustaining serious scrutiny on its own terms. For this year saw the publication of two books that can be seen as both the culmination of the burgeoning critical interest in music video and as a beacon of hope for the future development of music video as a specific field of study. Despite its titular concern with music television, Andrew Goodwin's *Dancing in the Distraction Factory: Music Television and Popular Culture* not only provided a history of MTV and a discussion of its specificity as a televisual format, but also paid real attention to the structure, form and narrative style of the videos themselves.[16] Goodwin's wide-ranging discussion, which covered economic and commercial issues, close textual analysis, cross-textual analyses and examination of the pleasures afforded by watching music videos, seemed not merely a culmination of what had gone before but a potential blueprint for subsequent inquiry. Similarly, Simon Frith et al.'s *Sound and Vision: The Music Video Reader*, provided an interdisciplinary collection of ten essays that covered both music television and analyses of specific videos and in so doing claimed the study of music video for popular music studies by hooking the analysis of video up with key concerns of that field, providing genre-specific work on heavy metal and country music, and grounding theoretical debate in the history of rock. Both books, with their mixture of socio-cultural and textual analysis, their concern with issues of gender and cultural politics, and their focus on music video as a distinct cultural form in and of itself, could have marked the beginning of an institutionalisation of music video studies. Unfortunately they did not. For what is clear is that there has been very little work since the mid-1990s which either discusses music video in terms of its formal qualities and cultural importance or takes up the texts of specific music videos as sites of meaning symptomatic of broader socio-political concerns in the same way that the textual operations of films, television programmes and other popular media have been taken up. In their own ways, then, both cultural journalism, in absenting it from its purview, and the academy, in making its analysis dependent on something else, replay and confirm the idea that music video is, in itself, a weightless, trivial phenomenon, that either exists beneath intellectual scrutiny or is incapable of sustaining it.

This narrative of critical atrophy is all the more surprising, and all the more ironic, when recounted alongside a parallel narrative, a narrative which tells of music video's unbridled success as a popular cultural form. It is perhaps obvious, but nevertheless important, to say that music video has never been so culturally visible and accessible as it is in this historical moment. In terms of form, content, style and the experience it offered its viewers, MTV was new and exciting in the 1980s. It did not remain unique for long however, and there has been a considerable growth in the number of dedicated music televi-sion channels over the past three decades. These new channels – for example CMT (Country Music Television), BET (Black Entertainment Television), VH1 (Video Hits 1), TMF (The Music Factory), the growth of nationally specific MTV channels, not to mention the explosion of niche-based and jukebox channels – have broadened both the generic scope and target audience of music television. But while the proliferation of music television channels since the mid-1980s is important here, it is not all important. For it is on and through the computer screen that the distribution and redistribution of music video takes on added levels of complexity. The internet has provided the music industry with new ways of broadcasting music videos to its consumers with sites licensed to screen music videos on demand. Perhaps more interestingly, however, the same technological infrastructure that allows record companies to promote their products more widely has enabled consumers to circumvent these official channels of broadcast and, instead, redistribute the music videos which they deem significant. The main point here, of course, is that even if the former scenario seems unproblematically to confirm the notion of music video as a secondary product designed to maximise revenue from the music as primary product, then the same does not apply in the latter case. In select-ing from the general catalogue of music videos which specific works are to be fed back into the system – that is to say, simultaneously re-circulated and archived – the relationship between video and song is reversed. For this enter-prise implies that it is the video itself which has become the primary product, something which is valuable on its own terms. The significance of this is not simply to do with the fact that, like popular music, music videos now have a life outside of their official institutional existence. It also has to do with their cultural longevity. Put simply, music videos now no longer, if they ever did, come and go with the release schedule of the song they promote. Indeed, the new and the old, the classic and the contemporary, increasingly circulate, and are re-circulated, alongside one another in the present moment of the screen. The proliferation of music video charts ('the best rock videos ever', '100 sexiest videos', 'the greatest videos of all time') produced by web-based magazines, music forums, blogs and other websites, feature classic 1980s videos along-side contemporary ones as well as everything in between. As the practice of list-making develops and grows it serves to produce an informal canon of videos that appear on list after list: a canon which cuts across both time and genre. This situation undercuts the commonplace, yet misplaced, assumption that music video is an intrinsically ephemeral, disposable form, one whose lifecycle is determined solely by the economics of capitalist business practice. Moreover, this informal canon is being accompanied by the development of a more formal, institutionalised process of canonisation as a number of major galleries now collect music videos. For example, the Museum of Modern Art in

New York and the British Film Institute in London archive and exhibit music video as part of their remit. This is not only significant in terms of the canonisation of the form and the emerging sense of artistic respectability which is part and parcel of this process of institutionalisation; it is also significant precisely to the extent that the storage and preservation of music videos belies the idea that they are transitory and worthless.

However, it is not simply this process of archiving and canonising, be it formal or informal, that makes music video such a pervasive cultural form. For videos are now distributed and accessed in a range of formats, and through a range of media, in ways which similarly serve to uncouple them from their status as secondary products and thus vastly expand their cultural reach in space and time. Indeed, music videos are now clearly primary products in their own right. They are available for purchase in a number of ways: as part of a 'special edition' CD single package; on DVD (in collections of the work of a performer or an individual director); or as downloads for use on portable media (phones, mp3 players, iPads, etc.) on which they can be stored, transported and privately consumed. This process of becoming products in their own right is not simply reducible, however, to the emergence and development of personal mobile media but is, rather, a part of the more general penetration of screens and screen technology into virtually all aspects of contemporary life. In other words, screens are no longer the prerogative of the cinema auditorium and the home but are now increasingly essential features of the street, the architecture of building facades, and the interior design of public leisure spaces. Indeed, in the planning and organisation of the social environment the design and management of screen light is often seen to be every bit as vital as the design and management of natural light. Whether in the shopping mall or the gym, bar or bowling alley, the airport lounge or the bus shelter, it is music video that is often to be found populating these screens, if not forcing us to watch then at least making it increasingly difficult to ignore. So, music videos, often uncoupled from their soundtrack, are now a significant feature of our leisure time. And this uncoupling gives them yet another life as stand-alone visual imagery, not merely as commercials for the (unheard) song.

In a number of ways, then, the story of music video's cultural life stands in sharp contrast to the story of the decline of academic interest in it. To acknowledge the irony of this situation, however, is to also acknowledge the need to scrutinise music video in this cultural moment, that is to say, to subject it to the same kinds of rigorous analysis which have proved so illuminating in the study of other forms of audio-visual popular culture. For music videos are not only important because of their ubiquity or the increasing perception of them as valuable products in their own right. They are also important because the visual aspect of music video impacts upon not only the pleasure we can get from any given song but also on the meanings we can attach to it and by extension how we can analyse and understand it. One brief example will suffice here. The lyrics for Shanice's 'Take Care of U' (2006) and Destiny's Child's 'Cater 2 U' (2005) evince a remarkable similarity. Both are an expression of a woman's devotion to 'her man' and detail not only her admiration for him but also her desire to demonstrate her love precisely by caring for him and catering to his needs. For instance, both songs open by acknowledging the man's hard work and their respective appreciation and admiration. In the case of the former, Shanice then goes on to instruct the subject to 'lay back a while, take off your shoes / relax yourself, I'm going to take care of you'.[17] This involves, amongst other activities, cooking his dinner, washing his clothes, and running his bath. Similarly, the Destiny's Child song asks its subject to 'Sit back' and 'Let me help you / take off your shoes / . . . let me feed you / let me run your bathwater / . . . [because] anything you want, I want to cater to you'.[18] Moreover, these two songs do not just display a high degree of lyrical equivalence but are also generically similar in so far as they both operate within the recognisable musical conventions of R&B. However, despite these lyrical and generic similarities, and despite the fact that both Shanice and Destiny's Child are clearly attributed authorship of the songs' sentiments, a quite different version of femininity is produced by each video.

The video for 'Take Care of U' begins with scenes of an informal meal with four couples sitting around a table drinking wine, eating and chatting. Shanice's partner asks 'have y'all heard my wifey's new song?', switches on the media player and the song begins. The video then cuts between three separate scenarios: the dining table, where the couples laugh, chat, and exchange glances with each other; the candlelit pool, where Shanice stands unaccompanied in the water and lip-synchs to camera; and the interior of the house where Shanice and her partner are shown together in a number of different settings – the kitchen, the bathroom and the bedroom. Both the dinner party scenario and the scenes within the house serve to situate the video in the natural, the real, the everyday and thus give legitimacy to the story they tell. In this respect the latter scenes are perhaps the most interesting because they depict Shanice and her partner performing the actions of the song's lyrics. So there are close-ups of Shanice's bejewelled hands untying her partner's trainers, holding a slice of pizza to his mouth while he bites into it, massaging his head as he sits in the bath, and, ultimately, kissing him passionately as he sits on the bed. And these images are intercut with images of the dinner party where the couple gaze longingly at each other across the table as their guests look on approvingly. The apparent naturalness of the behaviour depicted as well as the sense of verisimilitude of the situation is further enhanced by the fact that the role of Shanice's partner in the video is played by her real-world husband, Flex Alexander. Taking care of your man, then, is depicted not only as the willing performance of acts of servitude but, simultaneously, as a form of sexual foreplay.

Moreover, it is also depicted as something Shanice, herself, does and chooses to do.

The video for 'Cater 2 U', by contrast, is set in a fantasy world where the desert setting does not preclude the presence of a swimming pool or the wearing of figure-hugging fishtail evening dresses. The video begins, and indeed ends, with the three members of the group huddled together naked in the desert, their modesty preserved by carefully positioned hair and limbs. The rest of the video consists of a series of tableaux of the members of Destiny's Child performing individually and together. So we see Beyoncé Knowles dancing alone and unobserved on the diving board of the swimming pool; Kelly Rowland lip-synching as she gets out of, and then poses sensuously with, a silver car; and Michelle Williams reclining languorously on a sun-lounger while proclaiming her desire to 'cater 2 u'. These scenes are intercut with scenes of the three women dancing together for both the camera and, apparently, an audience of three men. The men, however, are seen only fleetingly, gazing wistfully at the women, and never in the same shot as Destiny's Child's highly choreographed dance routine. Indeed, it is only towards the end of the video that the men are allowed to encroach upon the women's space and briefly share the frame with them before the video closes with the three women once again naked together in the desert. The presence of these men seems utterly superfluous to the video's spectacle of female bodies and female pleasures.

If on the one hand then, TAKE CARE OF U literalises the acts of servitude detailed in the lyrics and in doing so positions Shanice as the author of her own subjection, on the other hand the imagery and performance of Destiny's Child in CATER 2 U largely proceeds without reference to the lyrics. Indeed, the abstracted emptiness of its desert spaces, the posed tableaux of the women's bodies, and the noticeable lack of attention directed to its male subjects by both the camera and the group, does not simply jar with the lyrical narrative of female subordination but in fact reinforces the image of Destiny's Child as independent women who are in control of their own lives. That is to say, the video (re)establishes an image of women who are in control of their own bodies, their own desires, their relationships with men and their friendships with women, and it thus stands in sharp contrast to Shanice's portrayal of someone dependent on the approval of her friends and husband.

Two videos, then, which accompany very similar songs, songs whose lyrics may make our feminist hackles rise, but videos which present us with very different stories of how to be a woman. And it is the many different stories contained within music videos and the specific ways that they are told that is the topic of this book. The book takes as its focus the notion of representation and the political implications bound up with the complex practices of representing within music video. As Richard Dyer has argued, cultural representations 'have real consequences for real people, not just in the way they are treated . . .

but in terms of the way representations delimit and enable what people can be in any given society'.[19] And it is in this sense that the theoretical approach we pursue here is concerned with the ways in which the practices and conventions of representation in music video both constrain and make possible ways of thinking about ourselves as individuals within contemporary society. We consider music video, on one level, as a distinct media form with its own patterns of production, codes and conventions of representation, and complex modes of circulation, and, on another level, as a key site through which cultural identities are produced, inscribed and negotiated. Our approach is, broadly speaking, a feminist one inasmuch as its principal concern is with the production and reproduction of normative gendered identities. It is in this way that we take music video to be a site in which and through which identities are represented in specific and restricted ways – ways which, politically speaking, delimit the real options available to real people for being and acting in the world. In other words, we want to address, even if we cannot always answer, the complex questions raised by videos such as TAKE CARE OF U and CATER 2 U – questions to do with the relationship between popular culture, raced and sexed identity, pleasure and politics.

The book is organised into two parts. In the first of these we explore some key critical concepts in relation to music video. The first chapter serves to situate the research in the rest of the book both theoretically and politically. In it we consider the often heated debates about the concept of postfeminism and how we may usefully define a postfeminist approach to the study of music video, a popular form which is, at least chronologically, a post second-wave feminism phenomenon. We argue for a feminist approach that is informed by poststructuralism, recognises the successes of second-wave feminism without dismissing the continuing need for a feminist politics, and is aware that young women today live in a very different world to that of a generation ago. In Chapters 2 and 3 we discuss two important aspects of the study of music video – genre and authorship. Both concepts are of critical concern to the study of visual images, whether they come in filmic or televisual forms, as well as to the study of popular music. We argue, however, that it is not possible to simply transpose these ideas from the study of music, film, or television onto the study of music video in any straightforward manner. Indeed, authorship and genre have very different and complex relationships to music video. Even if they clearly have an impact on the content of specific music videos, music genres do not simply map onto music video genres. Music videos do, however, have their own generic formations that serve a number of key legitimating functions. So, while it is certainly possible to talk of, say, the 'hip hop video' or the 'rock video', we suggest that it is not enough to leave it at that. In Chapter 2 we discuss four genres of music video – the pseudo-documentary, the 'art' music video, the narrative music video and the staged performance video – identifying their key generic codes and the differing legitimating functions they perform. In Chapter 3 we move on to discuss some of the complex ways in which authorship can be considered in relation to the study of music video, a situation in which performer, director and songwriter may all have genuine claim to an authorial voice. However, we stress that this topic cannot be adequately grasped without taking into consideration the notion of authenticity, a concept that is central to both academic and popular criticism of popular music. We argue that there is no simple answer to the question of who authors a music video and that the authentic authorial voice does not necessarily lie with the person we can see mouthing the words of the song. Moreover, precisely who can be seen as the authentic voice of any given video has an impact on how we understand and interpret that video and the politics of images it contains.

The second part of the book is devoted to the examination of music video as a site where normative constructions of race, gender and ethnicity are put on display, confirmed, reinforced and, sometimes, challenged. As such, we explore the ways in which music video presents us with a range of ways of being in the world. In Chapter 4 we focus on the ways in which long-standing tropes of blackness and whiteness are utilised to produce different femininities for black and white women. Using the videos of Beyoncé Knowles and Kylie Minogue as exemplars of this process, we argue that the presentation of the female body is raced, and raced in ways that can be traced back at least to the Victorian era and the colonial discourses that were in circulation at the time. Moreover, this situation seems to lead to different levels of choice for the presentation of the self, with white women having more scope than black women to 'play with' different identities and images, more ways to present themselves to the world. We develop this idea further in Chapter 5 with a discussion of ethnicity. Here we consider the way that ethnic identity can be produced on and across the female body. Focusing primarily on the videos of Christina Aguilera and the controversies sparked by her claim of Latina identity, we explore the differences between the videos produced to promote both the Anglophonic and Hispanic versions of two of her early singles: 'Genie in a Bottle' / 'Genio Atrapado' (1999) and 'Come on Over' / 'Ven Conmigo' (2000). By looking closely at the construction of these videos we can see the ways in which ethnicity is transcribed across the female body, how the body is decorated, displayed and framed to produce both the 'all-American girl' and its exotic other. In Chapter 6 we argue that not only is gender raced in its representation, but that the representation of race is also gendered. More specifically we explore the very different status and function of the body in the construction of masculinity and suggest that, very often, it is precisely the absence of the sexualised male body that not only comes to define masculine subjectivity in music video but is also an important process through which hegemonic masculinity maintains its power. Indeed, music videos employ a number of strategies to variously displace, disguise and disavow the sex of the male body, or even delete it from the field of vision entirely. It is these strategies which we discuss here.

Throughout the book, then, we take music video seriously not only as a distinct form of popular culture with its own complex set of structures and conventions but also as an important site for the representation of cultural identities. Notwithstanding their undoubted commercial agenda, indeed, to some extent because of it, music videos are an important and significant part of the contemporary cultural terrain.

A Note on Examples and Referencing

Examples

Given both the significant number of music videos that are now in existence and the enormous amount of titles that continue to be produced on an annual basis, the examples discussed here cannot pretend to be exhaustive. Indeed, while we often reference a number of titles which evince a particular property of the discussion, the approach we adopt is to examine a few videos reasonably thoroughly instead of a lot of videos in a more cursory manner. The specific examples pursued here have been chosen on the basis that they illuminate an area of interest or concern that extends beyond the particular case and informs thinking about music video more generally. It is our view that the theoretical and political arguments we seek to make in this book are better articulated and substantiated through precise analysis than through generalised claims. Indeed, when generalisations are made they are more likely to stand up to scrutiny if they are founded in precision and the particular rather than being merely general.

Referencing

As Andrew Goodwin pointed out some time ago in *Dancing in the Distraction Factory*, there are no generally recognised academic conventions for citing titles of music video.[20] This remains the case. The key problem, of course, is that music videos share their title with another product (the song they promote) for which there are suitable and recognised conventions. This presents both an academic and stylistic problem: how to refer to and distinguish between these different, but related, works. As such, where we refer to a song we follow standard procedures and enclose the title within quotation marks. Where we refer to titles of films, albums and video collections we italicise their name. However, in instances where we make specific reference to a music video we follow Goodwin's lead and present the title in small capitals. For example: the video AMERICAN IDIOT promoted Green Day's song 'American Idiot' which featured on their 2004 album *American Idiot*.

NOTES

1. Graham Fuller, cited in Steve Reiss and Neil Feineman, *Thirty Frames Per Second: The Visionary Art of the Music Video* (New York: Harry N. Abrams, 2000), p. 23.
2. Barbara Ellen, 'Up Front', *Observer*, Magazine, 4 March 2007, p. 5.
3. Peter Wollen, 'Ways of Thinking About Music Video (and Post-Modernism)', *Critical Quarterly*, vol. 28, nos 1–2 (1986), p. 168.
4. Thomas Doherty, 'MTV and the Music Video: Promo and Product', *Southern Speech Communication Journal*, vol. 52, no. 4 (1987), p. 349.
5. Roy Shuker, *Key Concepts in Popular Music* (London: Routledge, 1998), p. 203.
6. Carol Vernallis, *Experiencing Music Video: Aesthetics and Cultural Context* (New York: Columbia University Press, 2004); Roger Beebe and Jason Middleton (eds), *Medium Cool: Music Videos From Soundies to Cellphones* (Durham, NC: Duke University Press, 2007).
7. Angela McRobbie (ed.), *Zoot Suits and Second Hand Dresses: An Anthology of Fashion and Music* (Boston: Unwin and Hyman, 1988); Andrew Blake (ed.), *Living Through Pop* (London: Routledge, 1999); Imani Perry, 'Who(se) Am I?: The Identity and Image of Women in Hip-Hop', in Gail Dines and Jean M. Humez (eds), *Gender, Race, and Class in The Media*, 2nd edn (London: Sage, 2003); Robyn Brothers, 'Time to Heal, "Desire" Time: The Cyberprophesy of U2's "Zoo World Order"', in Kevin J. H. Dettmar and William Richey (eds), *Reading Rock and Roll: Authenticity, Appropriation, Aesthetics* (New York: Columbia University Press, 1999).
8. Deborah H. Holdstein, '*Music Video: Messages and Structure*', *Jump Cut*, vol. 29 (1984); Joan D. Lynch, 'Music Videos: From Performance to Dada-Surrealism', *Journal of Popular Culture*, vol. 18, no. 1 (1984); Joe Gow, 'The Relationship Between Violent and Sexual Images and the Popularity of Music Videos', *Popular Music and Society*, vol. 14, no. 4 (1990); Robart Pahlavi Bowie, 'Rock Video "According to Fredric Jameson"', *Continuum: The Australian Journal of Media & Culture*, vol. 1, no. 2 (1987).
9. Kuan-Hsing Chen, 'MTV: The (Dis)Appearance of Postmodern Semiosis, or the Cultural Politics of Resistance', *Journal of Communication Inquiry*, vol. 10, no. 1 (1986), p. 66.
10. Wollen, 'Ways of Thinking About Music Video (and Post-Modernism)', p. 169.
11. Andrew Darley, *Visual Digital Culture: Surface Play and Spectacle in New Media Genres* (London: Routledge, 2000), pp. 115–16.
12. Steven A. Seidman, 'Revisiting Sex Role Stereotyping in MTV Videos', *International Journal of Instructional Media*, vol. 26, no. 1 (1999); Rita Sommers-Flanagan, John Sommers-Flanagan and Britta Davis, 'What's Happening On Music Television?: A Gender Role Content Analysis', *Sex Roles*, vol. 28, nos 11–12 (1993); Sheri Kathleen Cole, 'I am the Eye, You are my Victim: The Pornographic Ideology of Music Video', *Enculturation*, vol. 2, no. 2 (1999), http://enculturation.gmu.edu/2_2/cole/index.html (10/02/2010); Jennifer M. Hurley, 'Music Video and the Construction of Gendered Subjectivity (Or How Being a Music Video Junkie Turned Me into a Feminist)', *Popular Music*, vol. 13, no. 3 (1994); Elizabeth Ellsworth, Margot Kennard Larson and Albert Selvin, 'MTV Presents: Problematic Pleasures', *Journal of Communication Inquiry*, vol. 10, no. 1 (1986).
13. Lynda Dee Dixon and Patricia A. Washington, 'Rap Music Videos: The Voices of Organic Intellectuals', *Transcultural Music Review*, no. 4 (1999), http://www.

sibetrans.com/trans/trans4/dee.htm (15/12/2005); Robin Roberts, ' "Ladies First": Queen Latifah's Afrocentric Feminist Music Video', *African American Review*, vol. 28 (1994); Lisa A. Lewis, 'Being Discovered: The Emergence of Female Address on MTV', in Simon Frith, Andrew Goodwin and Laurence Grossberg (eds), *Sound and Vision: The Music Video Reader* (London: Routledge, 1993), p. 137.

14. See, for example, Karlene Faith, *Madonna: Bawdy & Soul* (Toronto: University of Toronto Press, 1997); Santiago Fouz-Hernández and Freya Jarman-Ivens (eds), *Madonna's Drowned Worlds: New Approaches to her Cultural Transformations 1983–2003* (Aldershot: Ashgate, 2004); Lisa Frank and Paul Smith, *Madonnarama: Essays on Sex and Popular Culture* (San Francisco: Cleis Press, 1993); Georges-Claude Guilbert, *Madonna as Postmodern Myth: How One Star's Self-construction Rewrites Sex* (London: McFarland, 2002); Fran Lloyd (ed.), *Deconstructing Madonna* (London: Batsford, 1993); Cathy Schwichtenberg (ed.), *The Madonna Connection: Representational Politics, Subcultural Identities, and Cultural Theory* (Boulder: Westview Press, 1993); Adam Sexton, *Desperately Seeking Madonna: In Search of the Meaning of the World's Most Famous Woman* (New York: Delta, 1992).

15. E. Ann Kaplan, *Rocking Around the Clock: Music, Television, Postmodernism and Consumer Culture* (London: Methuen, 1987), p. 117; Ronald B. Scott, 'Images of Race and Religion in Madonna's Video *Like a Prayer*: Prayer and Praise', in Schwichtenberg (ed.), *The Madonna Connection*, p. 73; E. Ann Kaplan, 'Madonna Politics: Perversion, Repression or Subversion? Or Masks and/as Mastery', in Schwichtenberg (ed.), *The Madonna Connection*, p. 157; Douglas Kellner, *Media Culture: Cultural Studies, Identity, and Politics Between the Modern and the Postmodern* (London: Routledge, 1995), p. 278; Pamela Robertson, *Guilty Pleasures: Feminist Camp From Mae West to Madonna* (Durham, NC: Duke University Press, 1996), p. 131.

16. Andrew Goodwin, *Dancing in the Distraction Factory: Music Television and Popular Culture* (London: Routledge, 1993).

17. Shanice, 'Take Care of U' (Play Tyme Music, 2006).

18. Destiny's Child, 'Cater 2 U' (Columbia, 2005).

19. Richard Dyer, *The Matter of Images: Essays on Representations* (London: Routledge, 1993), p. 3.

20. Goodwin, *Dancing in the Distraction Factory*, p. xiii.

PART I

TOWARDS A CRITICAL VOCABULARY

1. SITUATING MUSIC VIDEO: BETWEEN FEMINISM AND POPULAR CULTURE

The video for Pink's 'Stupid Girls' (2006) is organised around a series of pasquinades of fellow female pop stars and other famous women. Some of these are direct parodies of music videos while others satirise images from popular culture more generally. So, for instance, in one of these vignettes Pink lampoons Jessica Simpson's fetishised performance of car washing in THESE BOOTS WERE MADE FOR WALKING (2005) as, dressed only in a skimpy denim miniskirt, bikini top and cowboy boots, she gets (in)appropriately soaked with suds and (over)plays to the camera's voyeuristic gaze. Similarly, a different scenario shows Pink mimicking Fergie from the Black-Eyed Peas in both appearance and performance as she dances for the pleasure of a stand-in 50 Cent. Other vignettes, such as references to the notorious Paris Hilton sex tape, parody well-known images of feminine celebrity, while yet others, such as sequences which deal with body-obsessed culture (getting 'San Tropezed', vomiting out excess calories, or toning up at the gym), take as their target a more general notion of contemporary idealised young womanhood. Either way, however, the video deploys parody to critique normative definitions of sexualised female identity, that is to say, a culture which equates idealised femininity with 'stupidity'.

This critique is reinforced by a set of equal and opposite images of women which, in their putative challenge to normative femininity, are offered up as positive role models. This is realised through Pink's performance of what are traditionally male roles: she enacts the role of US president and plays running back on an American football team. Indeed, the video is structured around the

Manichean conceit of a fight for the heart and mind of a young girl whereby an angel on her left shoulder shows her the virtues of physical strength and intellectual acumen and a devil on her right shoulder encourages her into a life of commercialised femininity. The video, of course, ultimately resolves this dilemma between being strong and being stupid when in the closing moments the girl switches off the TV and rejects her Barbie doll and Girls World in favour of her keyboards and football. In this way, the video's parodic strategies are mobilised not merely to attack the apparent vapidity of a celebrity culture which defines women in terms of the cut of their bodies and notions of sexual attractiveness but also as a counterpoint to the positive images of female agency it promotes.

As such, the video can be seen to have much in common with the bulk of feminist academic work on music video, and, indeed, popular culture more generally, in that it is concerned, on the one hand, to identify and critique images in which women are variously misrepresented, falsely represented, negatively represented, or simply not represented at all, and, on the other, to celebrate positive images of women, that is to say, images deemed valuable in promoting a broader range of possibilities, opportunities and capabilities for women. In terms of music video, negative images and misrepresentations are often those that are identified as sexually exploitative – images in which women are depicted simply as bodies or body parts to be observed and desired rather than social agents who have complex desires and drives of their own. In this respect, Sheri Kathleen Cole discusses the 'pornographic ideology of music video'; Imani Perry condemns hip hop videos in which women 'are often presented as vacuous, doing nothing but swaying around seductively'; and Julie L. Andsager and Kimberley Roe criticise country music videos which 'often trivialise women' or in which women 'portray themselves in traditional ways, mostly as sex objects'.[1] Conversely, positive images of women are those in which women are identified as providing good role models for their audience by, for example, producing videos which celebrate 'female resourcefulness and cultural distinctiveness' or 'in which the privileged experiences of boys and men are visually appropriated'.[2] For many critics Madonna is exemplary in this respect inasmuch as she is seen to variously defy, challenge and redefine hegemonic representations of femininity. E. Ann Kaplan suggests, for instance, that in combining 'unabashed seductiveness with a gutsy kind of independence' she represents 'the postmodern feminist heroine', while David Gauntlett argues that she 'made it possible to articulate feminist ideas in an accessible (or indeed sexually provocative) way' and thus 'paved the way' for, and empowered, a younger generation of female performers.[3] Either way, this type of research is predicated on a threefold premise: firstly, and most obviously, 'the notion that the recurring images of women in popular media have some influence on how people think of women in real life'; secondly, that these images of women are simply *either* positive *or* negative, good or bad, progressive or reactionary; and lastly, that it is possible to know which is which and, by implication to adjudicate on the respective politics of the image by measuring it against external reality, that is to say, the way real women are, or could/should be, in the real world.[4]

Despite more nuanced versions of this brand of criticism – which acknowledge that music videos 'can operate in multiple ways' that 'allow for a range of interpretations and uses' that 'can be read as either subversive of patriarchal constructions of femininity' or as a site where dominant discourses are reinforced and reinscribed – it nevertheless inevitably operates within a realist paradigm in so far as it turns upon a distinction between real women and images of women.[5] If, however, reality and the real world are seen as inextricably bound up with, indeed produced through, forms of representation, then feminine identity, like all cultural identities, is neither interior to the body nor anterior to representation but only knowable and transformable through its discursive articulation. Indeed, in this respect, perhaps the most powerful image of STUPID GIRLS (2006) depicts Pink lying naked from the waist up on an operating table with her body already marked-up for modification, enhancement and improvement by a surgeon's knife. The political import of this image emerges not simply from the implied relationship between mutilation and perfection, but more importantly from the way it signals the plasticity of identity. In other words, despite the rather crude binarism which STUPID GIRLS establishes between vacuous femininity and female enlightenment, the video consistently draws attention to the idea that gendered identity and the sexed self cannot be reduced to, or fixed within, the fact of the biological body. For in the end it is, of course, Pink herself who performs the video's various incarnations of both 'stupid' and empowered femininity. As such, STUPID GIRLS visualises both the body and sexed/gendered identity as contingent and malleable, or, more precisely, as selected, produced and performed within specific discursive formations. One implication of this is that the ontological imperative to locate identity in the facticity of the sexed body is suspended and attention is instead redirected towards the historical realm of social and cultural production. On this account, gendered being is not an inevitable state of embodiment but, more complexly, is understood as a range of possibilities for being in the world instigated by the various ways the fact of the body is (re)presented in discourse and becomes meaningful within specific historical conditions. A second implication, therefore, is that the field of cultural representation becomes situated not only as the locus of the production of identity formations, but also as perhaps the key site for political analysis and intervention.

One of the most important tenets of postmodern and poststructural theories is the notion that the self is not an essential self rooted in genetic make-up or formed in early psychological development but, rather, a discursively constructed self produced and maintained through the workings of a multi-plicity of cultural institutions and practices. In other words, our identity is not something that comes from within, something to be revealed in its truth or concealed in its denial; it is a product of our specific social, cultural and histori-cal situation. Moreover, this discursively constructed self can be understood as a self-construction in that, given the range of discourses on any given topic circulating at a particular time, there are always choices to be made between complementary or competing ways of being in the world. Cultural products, therefore, have political significance not because they conceal the truth of the world or misrepresent the truth of the self, but because they provide us with the bricks and mortar from which we construct ourselves and the world around us. It is in this sense, then, that the products of popular culture are a key means by which the discourses through which we understand ourselves, through which we *are* ourselves, circulate and become legitimate in the society in which we live.

Given this, if music videos do not reflect or distort reality but are part of the discursive field in which it is produced, then it becomes necessary to consider what resources they provide for the construction of the self and the ways in which these resources both enable and delimit ways of being in the world. In other words, criticism which is directed towards separating out good images from bad ones in order to promote the former and critique the latter only gets one so far. For not only does it tend to imply a rather crude model of com-munication in which images deemed distortive of reality are seen to have a negative effect on either society or the individual and those deemed progres-sive are, conversely, said to produce positive effects, it also, perhaps more problematically, rests on the idea that reality itself is singular, veridical and knowable independently of its articulation through forms of language. Indeed, as Charlotte Brunsdon argues, to search for, or call for, 'realistic images of women is to engage in the struggle to define what is meant by "realistic"'. And, of course, this kind of quarrel over how the world really is, 'is always an argument for the representation of "your" version of reality'.[6] So, in terms of Pink's STUPID GIRLS, this would mean that the young girl ought to make the choice to leave her girly toys alone – conceived as tools of a patriarchal culture which socialise her into 'feminine stupidity' and subservience – and instead pick up the football and play with the boys. However, within the narrative economy of the video, this is not a choice at all since there is no value afforded to the markers of femininity. Moreover, the very fact that it is presented as an either/or choice negates the possibility of engaging with and finding value in the multiple identity positions which are possible within the overarching categories of femininity and womanhood. Indeed, whatever else the analysis of the representation of women in music videos reveals, it throws into stark relief the possibility of embodying a range of feminine identities and demonstrates that there are a range of ways of inhabiting a female body. And while, as we discuss in the following chapters, this multiplicity is often circumscribed by long-standing discourses of both patriarchy and (hetero)sexuality, it nevertheless remains the case that the images of women produced by music video are too various and complex to be reduced to a simple either/or game.

THE POLITICS OF POSTFEMINISM

It is of course precisely these kinds of question – questions to do with the relationship between liberation, consumption and mass-mediated images of both feminism and femininity – that are central to much contemporary feminist debate. Moreover, the term increasingly being mobilised in such debates is 'postfeminism', a label which is, as Yvonne Tasker and Diane Negra suggest, simultaneously both troubling and compelling.[7] For some critics, it is troubling in so far as the prefix itself all too literally announces the end of feminism by signalling that we have entered an historical period that succeeds it.[8] Indeed, in this respect 'postfeminism' is used critically and derogatively by some feminists to describe the position of other writers, who may or may not claim to be feminist, who argue that feminism's battles are won. Perhaps the most controversial of these writers is Katie Roiphe. Described as an 'antifeminist feminist postfeminist' by Sarah Projansky, both Roiphe's name and her work have become synonymous with a naive conservatism variously branded as retro-sexism, lipstick feminism, new sexism, and 'do-me-feminism'.[9] At the heart of this position is the contentious claim that a feminist critique is no longer needed precisely because its political project has been realised. In a recent interview, Roiphe herself sums up this position in claiming that:

> The revolution has succeeded . . . The feminists of the Seventies should be happy. They should kick back and have a giant Scotch as they survey the world and see that they have won. There is nothing better for the feminist movement than looking in the face of its own extinction.[10]

While agreeing that the term may signal the end of a distinctly feminist politics and critique, other critics interrogate their putative demise along different lines. Easily the most cited example of this is Susan Faludi's book, *Backlash: The Undeclared War Against Women*, which squarely equates post-feminism with antifeminism. For her, the emergence of postfeminist discourse in America in the 1980s was part of a neo-conservative response to the political changes brought about by the achievements of second-wave feminism, a response which, on the one hand, claimed that women had achieved equality while, on the other hand, argued that feminism had let women down. On this view, the notion of postfeminism became bound up with a much broader backlash against feminism which was 'set off not by women's achievement of full equality but by the increased possibility that they might win it'.[11] In other words, it became a key weapon in the 'pre-emptive strike' that prevented feminism reaching its political terminus. Indeed, for Faludi, the incursion of antifeminist discourse into the feminist cultural sphere itself is proof positive of the insidious nature of the backlash. The media's co-option and popularisation of the brand of feminism expressed by, amongst others, Roiphe, Christina Hoff Sommers, Naomi Wolf and Camille Paglia, not only serves as a distraction from the 'proper' foci of feminist critique, but worse, is part of the process by which it is repudiated. Taking her metaphor from the film *Invasion of the Body Snatchers* (1956) she argues that postfeminism is 'a media-assisted invasion of the body of the women's movement: the Invasion of the Feminist Snatchers, intent on repopulating the ranks with Pod Feminists'.[12] The irony of this reading, of course, is that the 'stars' of postfeminist publishing and lecturing become the strongest and most vocal advocates for antifeminist ideas.[13]

More recently, Angela McRobbie has offered what she calls a 'complexification' of this backlash thesis.[14] Whereas Faludi focuses on concerted antifeminist strategies she identifies in the media that either adopt a negative view towards feminism outright or encourage women back into traditionally feminine roles within the home and family, McRobbie suggests that it is precisely the media's appropriation of feminist issues that contributes to the undoing of feminism. She argues that postfeminist culture 'positively draws on and invokes feminism as that which can be taken into account, to suggest that equality is achieved, in order to install a whole repertoire of new meanings, which emphasize that it is no longer needed, it is a spent force'.[15] For McRobbie, the very fact that feminist ideas and concerns are articulated and disseminated through popular mediated forms, the very fact that they are taken into account, means that feminism as a political movement is deferred and displaced onto the media itself. In this respect, it is the very 'taken into accountness' that permits 'an all the more thorough dismantling of feminist politics'.[16]

Even though McRobbie does not entirely reject the notion of postfeminism she is nevertheless deeply concerned about the way in which its assimilation into popular discourse naturalises it and transforms it into a form of Gramscian common-sense. Indeed, a number of critics argue that it is precisely the commodification of feminism, its increasing collocation with capitalist practice, that recasts the image of the modern feminist from a political identity into a consumer choice. Put simply, postfeminism becomes equated with, or worse reduced to, images of successful women. That is to say, stories of women's educational and professional success, images of empowered female sexuality, and even accounts of women who 'choose' to return to domesticity are seen as mileage markers on the road to women's liberation. McRobbie refers to this as 'female individualisation', a process by which the language of

collective activism is replaced by a language of personal choice and respon-
sibility for not being successful is displaced from the social structure onto
individual women.[17] As Susan J. Douglas suggests, the clear implication of this
is that 'whatever challenges women face in juggling work and family are their
individual struggles, to be conquered through good planning, smart choices,
and an upbeat outlook'.[18] This is a version of feminism which celebrates individual female agency, economic independence and the emancipatory powers of
consumption. It is feminism defined as a kind of project of the self, a process
of achieving freedom and autonomy through retail choices, a situation in
which 'a woman's right to choose' no longer refers to abortion and control
of the reproductive process but, rather, to whether to decide to buy Jimmy
Choos or Manholo Blahniks. Imogen Tyler has called this 'narcissism as liberation', arguing that a 'new culture of pampering' has emerged that encourages
'women to compensate themselves for sexual inequality, and the difficulty of
lives spent juggling the competing priorities of work and motherhood, through
the consumption of scented candles and bubble-bath'.[19]

Of course, it is not difficult to see why many critics find this definition of
postfeminism troubling. In denying collectivity and focusing on discourses of
individual ambition and self-improvement, and by eschewing a macro-politics
of social change in favour of a micro-politics of personal lifestyle, the image of
sexually empowered, professionally successful and economically independent
women functions as a synecdoche for all women. Indeed, this model of postfeminism ignores evident economic disparities between women as well as those
between men and women and thus tends to emerge as a white middle-class
discourse by default. In other words, the privileging of personal success and the
pleasure of consumption runs the risk of glossing over very real axes of socio-
economic difference which continue to not only limit women's potential to
succeed and ability to consume, but also constrain the 'choices' that even economically successful, independent women are able to make. For this reason,
postfeminism, at least in some critical quarters, is shorthand for the depoliti-
cisation of feminism and the latest in a long line of attempts to dupe women
into thinking that equality has been achieved and that feminism is therefore
no longer relevant. That is to say, the popularisation of feminist issues and
concerns through the media has led to a slippage between the notions and
practices of postfeminist culture and (post)feminist politics where the former
term has come to stand in for the latter. The process of taking feminism into
account has thus ironically produced feminism as, in Kathleen Rowe Karlyn's
phrase, 'a structuring absence' in postfeminism, something that dare not be
spoken of, in fact something that must be disavowed in order to be a 'good'
postfeminist.[20]

If the notion of postfeminism is troubling then it is simultaneously compelling. Indeed, a significant part of its allure lies in the same ground that people

find troubling. For even if the relationship between feminism and popular culture is often an uneasy one, and even if the link between the mediation of feminist issues and the actual experience of real women is unclear, the idea of postfeminism nevertheless impels us towards trying to understand precisely the nature of these imbrications. In other words, whatever else the term implies, and regardless of whether one accepts it or treats it with caution, postfeminism does at least direct critical attention towards the now: towards a situation where it is no longer practical or possible to separate out discourses of feminism from the way in which those discourses are produced, negotiated, and defined through popular culture. Perhaps most obviously, but not unimportantly, it acknowledges the fact that 'rather than coming to consciousness through involvement in feminist movements, most people [now] become conscious of feminism through the way it is represented in popular culture'.[21] And of course, this partly explains why the generations of women born in the aftermath of second-wave activism tend not to identify themselves as feminist while at the same time articulating particular concerns which are clearly central to feminist debates. As such, it is precisely through an engagement with the media and consumer culture that young women now construct their identities and understand themselves as social subjects. Indeed, within global capitalism there is little alternative to this. Instead of bemoaning this state of affairs, or simply pointing out its more obvious limitations, it seems more productive to use our energies in an attempt to understand this process at the level of both representation and self-representation.

It is at this point, where feminism intersects with forms of cultural representation – in particular the forms of representation that constitute popular culture – that postfeminism most clearly chimes with a range of other 'posts', most notably poststructuralism and postmodernism. Notwithstanding some important differences between the terms, all three posts nevertheless point towards a particular understanding of reality, history and identity, and their relationship to language and representation. Indeed, above all else, the post-ing of these terms problematises the idea that there is an exterior to representation, a position outside or above language from which it is possible to know the truth of the world. In dispensing with the idea that there is a way that things are in themselves, and the idea that it is ever possible to discover or 'know' this, the self becomes uncoupled from either biology or psychology and instead emerges as a product of discourse. In other words, there is no one, authentic, essential self that lies at the root of one's being, but rather being one's self is constituted from the more or less self-conscious presentation of identity or personality through and within the available discursive structure. It is, of course, the work of Michel Foucault which clears the ground for the articulation of this position. One of Foucault's key interventions is to locate the question of individual identity within a broader consideration of the relationship between truth, power and self. In developing what he calls a 'hermeneutics of technologies of the self', he resists the idea that individual selfhood is simply determined and controlled by either ideology or regimes of power.[22] For Foucault, technologies of the self are:

> those intentional and voluntary actions by which men [*sic*] not only set themselves rules of conduct, but also seek to transform themselves, to change themselves in their singular being, and to make their life into an *oeuvre* that carries certain aesthetic values and meets certain stylistic criteria.[23]

One clear implication of this is that subjects are active in the process of constituting and presenting themselves. In defining it alongside a series of other technologies – of production, of sign systems and of power – each of which is associated with certain types of domination, technologies of the self can be seen as the specific repertoire of methods and techniques which allow individuals to simultaneously work on themselves and police themselves within the totality of the prevailing discursive structure. The political rub of this position is that power is not simply repressive, and, moreover, individual identity is not simply the result of power's impress. So while, on the one hand, who we are, what we do, and what we are able to do is clearly shaped and constrained by regimes of power, on the other hand it is precisely those regimes of power that provide us with the raw materials from which we shape ourselves and come to understand who we are. And it is in this sense that Foucault's work impels us to pose the question of social subjectivity as not only one of how an individual is acted upon, but also one of how an 'individual acts upon himself [*sic*]'.[24]

The cash value of this position for feminist theory, and in particular feminist studies of the media and culture, is twofold. Firstly, it not only short circuits the idea that postfeminism is simply a backlash against proper feminism, it also offers us a way of explaining how an individualised, popular feminism need not be a depoliticised one. Foucault's work on the history of domination, and how that history always informs the present, offers up a much more complex framework for understanding both historical and contemporary manifestations of feminism and feminist practice. For instance, much criticism which sees postfeminism as either antifeminism or part of a backlash against feminism turns on a rather crude opposition between a putatively authentic feminist position and an inauthentic feminine one. On this view, the authentic feminist critic plies her wares by identifying and criticising images of women from popular culture that apparently resuscitate normalised and/or nostalgic femininities, even if those images seemingly trade in postmodern irony, in order to reinscribe gender relations from a previous era. However, if, following Foucault's line of thinking, feminism itself is seen as a specific product of discourse with its own associated regimes of truth, knowledge and power then there can be no single authentic feminism but only a continuous process of negotiating what feminism means. One implication of this, therefore, is that postfeminism can be understood as one term which describes a feminism of now, which is, of course, also a product of discursive practice. It is in this sense that Charlotte Brunsdon argues that the term postfeminism not only attributes an historical specificity to second-wave feminism but also suggests that contemporary feminism is 'post-1970s feminism in ways that are not simply chronological'.[25] So while on the one hand, the prefix 'post' does perform a periodisation function in so far as it designates a moment of feminist history that succeeds the women's movement of the 1960s and 1970s, on the other hand it signals a particular relationship to second-wave feminism that is not straightforwardly contiguous, antagonistic or dismissive.

By the same token, if we consider femininity as something which is discursively produced, it cannot be only ever the bad Other to feminism, something to be resisted on the path to becoming an enlightened feminist. In this respect we should approach the question of contemporary femininity as something which also stands in a particular historical and discursive relation to second-wave feminism. For contemporary femininities take shape and are lived in a context where second-wave feminism is, as McRobbie says, taken into account, that is to say, a situation in which the gains made by the feminist movement have been installed as part of, and have informed, everyday discourse. As such, these 'new femininities' may on one level appear anachronistic and nostalgic yet they do come *after* second-wave feminism and thus come *with* both the rhetoric of independence and liberation used by the women's movement and the political advances it achieved. One way of conceptualising postfeminism, therefore, is as 'the coming together of "traditional" feminist values with a historically and materially different experience of being young and female'.[26]

It is, of course, the friction generated by this coming together that makes postfeminism such a controversial term. The place where these issues most often meet, indeed the place where they often seem fused together, is in the sphere of popular culture, and, more specifically, in the increasing number of images of apparently successful young women who seem to have benefitted from growing up in the wake of second-wave feminism. Indeed, images of strong, sexually liberated and economically independent women now regularly fill our cinema, television and computer screens: whether it is the characters in much-discussed shows such as *Sex and the City*, *Ally McBeal* and *Buffy the Vampire Slayer*, the increasing number of weapon-wielding, karate-kicking, 'action babes' in the cinema, the proliferation of Lara Croft-influenced digital heroines, the type of post-Madonna pop star who is able to change sexual identity as often as hairstyle, or even the *Desperate Housewives* who live behind the white picket fences of Wisteria Lane, there is now an identifiable and emerging canon of postfeminist culture which, in various ways, trades on the idea that contemporary women can be both powerful and feminine at the same time. The theoretical and political dilemma is, of course, how to read these images, how to distil their significance not only *for* feminism and but also *from* a feminist position.

One response might be to pick these texts off one by one, index their representational content against feminist analytical criteria, and adjudicate on their relative progressive or regressive nature. This is an approach which has a long-standing tradition in feminist cultural criticism and which turns on the idea that challenging negative images of women and promoting positive ones is a key strategy in exposing institutional sexism and levelling up the life opportunities of women to those of men. It is this method that produces a particular brand of postfeminist criticism, one which engages in analysis of this or that image of modern empowered femininity in order to either a) chart the distance travelled in gender politics in direct proportion to the degree of liberation the critic finds in the text; or b) to claim that we have in fact not come very far at all and that women continue to be defined by the same old sexual stereotypes. This is why a show such as *Sex and the City* can, on the one hand, be seen as 'revolutionary . . . a great study of female friendship' and on the other hand dismissed as 'soft-vanilla feminism' where 'the characters just come across as the same sort of air-brushed, be-make-upped, bland women, no different to all the women on TV before'.[27] Each response, however, is really only the opposing side of the same coin which sets out to 'discover' whether a particular text or a particular heroine is good or bad for women. And while this kind of approach has been instructive in terms of pointing up the limited ways in which women have been represented historically, and continues to bear fruit in the hands of certain critics, there nevertheless remain a number of theoretical and political problems associated with it.

Firstly, it runs the risk of setting up feminism as a simultaneously censorious and prescriptive discourse – outlawing certain texts, pleasures and behaviours while celebrating others as promoting appropriate and useful feminist messages. This is often laced with a recruitist or pedagogic strategy which attempts to highlight the virtues of the latter over the former, one which critiques bad feminism in order to throw good feminism into relief. The dilemma here is not only that such disagreements over the definition of authentic feminism are politically self-refuting, but also that they tend to ignore the very women on whose behalf they are apparently conducted. The idea, for instance, that the history of feminism can adequately be understood as, or reduced to, metaphors of generational conflict or distinct waves belies the fact that there is far more continuity and connection between feminism's various incarnations than there is rupture and disjunction. Moreover, one thing that has changed over the past forty years or so is the way that women are now able to live their lives.

Contemporary feminism, if it is to remain relevant and effective, needs to be able to account for, and to take into account, these changes much more than it needs to agree on a singular definition of itself. By the same token, feminist cultural criticism might do well to avoid the temptation to simply use the texts of popular culture as a pretext for spinning its own tales of resistance, recuperation, revolution and recontainment. This is not to say that some mainstream texts do not demand to be subjected to feminist criticism – that is, squarely criticised for their restrictive, reactionary, or just downright offensive representations of women. Rather, it is to suggest that this brand of feminist cultural criticism perhaps needs to be complemented by a more nuanced approach to the politics of representation, one which forestalls the desire to simply pass judgement on a text's politics and instead locates its representations within a broader cultural repertoire of images, meanings and discourses from which we construct a sense of who we are. In other words, it is one thing for feminist criticism to intervene in popular culture in order to make itself heard, but quite another to accept that popular culture itself intervenes not only in the process of constructing our individual identities, but also in the process of understanding certain identities as being feminist. If, as Richard Dyer argues, the way in which a social group is treated in representation bears fundamentally not only on how members of that group are able to see themselves and others like themselves but also on how others perceive that group, then that is as true for the social group we call feminists as for any other social group.[28]

One implication of this, therefore, is that popular culture is a site where definitions of both women and feminists are *produced*, not simply reproduced. This impels us towards a more complex understanding of the relationships between reality and the way that reality is manifested in representation. This is not simply to rehearse the now well-worn postmodern idea that representation can never capture the full extent of unruly reality, nor the idea that reality itself is entirely reducible to an endless chain of representations. Rather, it is to say, with Dyer, that 'the analysis of images always needs to see how any given instance is embedded in a network of other instances' and thus cannot be pinned down to definite and final meanings.[29] It is to say, in other words, that the tension between the world and the textuality of representation is usually too complex, too messy, too elusive and, in the end, too interesting to be explained by recourse to an either/or logic, a logic which positions texts as either one thing or another: good or bad, positive or negative, enabling or constricting, feminist or not. Representations don't work like this so we shouldn't analyse them as if they do. Moreover, even if this kind of either/or analysis tells us something about its author's politics it often does so at the expense of telling us very much about the difficult business of how representations work politically.

PINK POSTFEMINISM

How then is it possible to understand Pink's STUPID GIRLS as distinctly post-feminist and what is the intellectual and political value in doing so? Moreover, what is it, if anything, that constitutes postfeminist analysis, and how does this meet with and depart from feminist analysis? Firstly, and perhaps most obviously, STUPID GIRLS is postfeminist inasmuch as it is a product of a postfeminist moment. In other words, if we take Charlotte Brunsdon's historically specific, 'relatively neutral' notion of postfeminism as a marker of periodisation, 'a way of differentiating second-wave feminism from what came subsequently', then the video's articulation of feminine identities can be considered postfeminist in the sense that they are clearly informed by second-wave feminism but are produced and circulate in a cultural time that comes after it.[30] However, while this approach to defining postfeminism is, relatively speaking, uncontroversial and does serve to take the sting out of the debate, its apparent neutrality often belies the textual and political complexity of the specific cultural products it periodises and classifies. Specifically in terms of STUPID GIRLS, it is significant that its representations include not only the strong can-do girls of second-wave feminism, but also the 'girls with ambition' who dream of being president, and the powered-up consumer babes so often associated with postfeminism – the ones you'll find in Fred Segal 'with their itsy bitsy doggies and [wearing] their teeny-weeny Ts'.[31] It is also significant, moreover, that despite being a product of postfeminism in the historically specific sense, the video engages in a forth-right attack in its parodies of celebrified, brand-driven girliness, those images of what Rosalind Gill has identified as 'the sexually autonomous heterosexual young woman who plays with her sexual power and is forever "up for it"'.[32] And, of course, this is precisely the kind of commercialised hyper-femininity that is variously reclaimed, dismissed, recuperated and resisted in postfeminist debates. Gill's analysis is concerned with what she calls the 're-sexualisation and re-commodification of women's bodies' in forms of contemporary media culture and suggests that images of putatively independent women are often 'endowed with agency' only in so far as 'they can actively choose to objectify themselves'. Moreover, she argues that this shift towards women's 'freely chosen' self-objectification 'fits very well with broader postfeminist discourses which present women as autonomous agents no longer constrained by any inequalities or power imbalances, who can somehow choose to "use beauty" to make themselves feel good'.[33] While Gill acknowledges that one way of understanding this situation is to see it as playful and ironic, as somehow both an assertion of liberation and a celebration of sexual power, her own reading is far more pessimistic in arguing that women's sexual subjectivity, rather than being liberatory, has 'turned out to be objectification in a new and even more pernicious guise'.[34] In terms of STUPID GIRLS, the video's own irony and playfulness is activated, not to reclaim sexualised femininity in the name of postfeminist equality, but rather to drive home its critique of women who now have choices but use those choices to turn themselves into sexual objects. In other words, on one reading the video can be seen as a broadside against a generation of young women who have clearly benefited from the message of second-wave feminism, indeed can be seen as the living evidence of its success, while simultaneously appearing to be completely oblivious to that message.

On this view, the video operates as a more or less straightforward second-wave feminist critique of postfeminism in so far as its attack on femininity chimes with the work of a number of prominent second-wave writers who sought to expose the insidious links between femininity and patriarchy. Three of the most vociferous of these critics are Shulamith Firestone, Germaine Greer and Susan Brownmiller, who all set out to expose the restrictive and damaging consequences bound up in the myth of femininity. For instance, in *The Dialectic of Sex*, Firestone equates femininity with what she calls 'the beauty ideal'. She argues that 'every society has promoted a certain ideal of beauty over all others. What that ideal is is unimportant, for any ideal leaves the majority out.' In other words, the political function of any given society's beauty ideal resides in its final unattainability. The result is that women are 'left scrambling', in the 'rush to squeeze into the glass slipper, forcing and mutilating their bodies with diets and beauty programmes, clothes and make-up'. For Firestone, women are only allowed to achieve individuality by looking good, where *good* is defined as the 'more or less successful approximation to an external standard', a standard defined by men.[35] Writing at the same time as Firestone, Germaine Greer takes up similar ideas in discussing 'the myth of the Eternal Feminine', what she herself terms 'the *Stereotype*'. She argues that the stereotype is 'the dominant image of femininity which rules our culture and to which all women aspire'. This image, however, is a manufactured one, an effect 'built up layer by layer' from the cultural trappings of femininity deployed to beautify women – clothes and jewellery, hair and make-up, behaviour and demeanour. The ultimate function of these 'servile fripperies' which define the feminine stereotype is to confirm the woman's primary function as sex object. The political problem with the stereotype is that it must work within stringent limits. As Greer argues, 'nothing must interfere with her function as sex object' and, in the end, the only thing that she can signify is 'the lineaments of satisfied impotence'.[36] And it is precisely this impotence, the necessary disavowal of sexual subjectivity, that underpins Greer's definition of the female eunuch. But perhaps the most sustained second-wave critique of the political workings of femininity is Susan Brownmiller's 1984 study, *Femininity*. For Brownmiller, femininity 'is a romantic sentiment, a nostalgic tradition of imposed limitations'. She suggests that, for the woman who works at femininity the world 'extends little courtesies and minor privilege'. However, these apparent cour-

tesies and privileges are in two senses illusory. Firstly, to work at one's femininity necessarily entails competition, a process that sets women against each other in their attempts to attain the 'feminine ideal'. The irony of this game is that even for women who are good at it 'femininity always demands more', can never be completed. The upshot is that femininity is a game with definite rules but no winners. Secondly, Brownmiller argues that women can only work at femininity in the first place 'by accepting restrictions, by limiting one's sights, by choosing an indirect route, by scattering concentration and not giving one's all'. Femininity, then, emerges as 'a grand collection of compromises' that every woman 'simply must make in order to render herself a successful woman'.[37] So for all these critics, femininity is a powerful force for preventing women's success in the world. They can only ever aim to be successfully feminine, successful at being a woman, and the project of successfully being a woman distracts from, interferes with, and ultimately prevents, their success in any other field.

It is not difficult to see how STUPID GIRLS' own attack on the 'servile fripperies' of contemporary hyperfemininity might be fitted into this frame. Its exquisitely groomed goddesses of consumer culture are damned as inauthentic, merely the cosmetically and surgically enhanced products of privileged spending power, mindlessly pursuing this season's fashion at the expense of all else. To use Greer's terms, not only does the feminine stereotype determine the definition of the female sex, but the idea that 'she is more body than soul, more soul than mind' is pushed to its limits.[38] For in STUPID GIRLS to be feminine is to be only a body. However, while on one level there appears to be a snug fit between this reading of the video and second-wave feminism's scepticism of femininity, on other levels the fit is much less comfortable. Most importantly, whereas Firestone, Greer and Brownmiller in various ways locate the feminine ideal as a product of complex historical and political forces which impose femininity onto women in order to control them, the video eschews any structural explanation for its characters' behaviour and instead blames the individual women for making the wrong choices, that is to say, for being stupid. While in some ways this is a subtle difference it is nevertheless a crucial one. Not only does it undercut many of the political precepts of second-wave feminism – notably systemic inequality, sisterhood and collective action – but by emphasising that it is the choice of individual women to be stupid, to want to dance 'in a video next to 50 cent' instead of aiming to become the 'next female president', STUPID GIRLS assumes that patriarchy is no longer a problem and that real choices can be freely made. By contrast, Greer contends that women's impotent femininity is a product of social and economic conditioning. She argues that while women do know what they are, they are prevented from knowing what they may be or might have been by 'the ineluctable result of law' and their specific role within a capitalist economy.[39] Brownmiller locates the origins of femininity partly in 'borrowed affectations of upper-class status', partly in its relationship to the 'seductive glamour' of the biologically female body, but also in the 'historic subjugation of women through sexual violence, religion and law, where certain myths about the nature of women were put forward as biological fact'.[40] Moreover, Firestone discusses precisely the 'severe feminine neurosis about personal appearance' that STUPID GIRLS takes as its subject. However, whereas the video places the blame for being stupid squarely on the shoulders of individual women, Firestone sees the definition of stupidity as part and parcel of structural sexed oppression. She argues that:

> When women begin to look more and more alike, distinguished only by the degree to which they differ from a paper ideal, they can be more easily stereotyped as a class: They look alike, they think alike, and even worse, they are so stupid that they believe they are not alike.[41]

The politics of the position outlined here, as well as by Greer and Brownmiller, is quite different to that found in the video. For Firestone, women's apparent stupidity is an effect of a more generalised process of stereotyped femininity which works to control and oppress women as a sexed class. By contrast, in individuating its women and making clear distinctions and value judgements between competing versions of ideal femininity, the video declasses women, replacing political narrative with personal drama as its explanation for its characters' stupidity.

It is right here, of course, that the entire dilemma concerning the relationship between second-wave feminism and postfeminism continues to replay itself, where definitions of the latter always take place within, and indeed require, the shadow cast by the former yet at the same time the very existence of the former term implies a desire, even a need, to wriggle free from the latter. In other words, of all the potential paradoxes associated with the idea of post-feminism perhaps the key one is that, in attempting to articulate the feminism of now, it seems to need to return to an earlier manifestation of itself in order to do so. This kind of paradox finds particularly interesting expression in STUPID GIRLS. While self-evidently being a product of a postfeminist histori-cal cultural moment, its narrative of female empowerment and its images of strong, positive role models really only cohere if located within the political context of second-wave feminism. However, the video's historical context inevitably interferes with its narrative, blaming individual women for choosing a lifestyle of docile femininity over a life of freedom and possibility, a choice which itself betrays the video's historical postfeminism. And yet, the video clearly does not celebrate postfeminism, attacking the superficiality of con-sumer culture, criticising the barbarism of cosmetic surgery, and vilifying as mindless and inauthentic the kind of women who construct themselves out of these things. Moreover, this critique of women who willingly engage in sexual self-objectification is quite different to the second-wave's critique of the institutional objectification of women's bodies and its demand for women's right to sexual subjectivity. The result of this is a cultural text which, on the one hand, is clearly energised by both feminist histories and discourses while, on the other hand, being confused about which particular history it draws from and which particular discourse if seeks to promote. Indeed, in this respect the video can be said to operate as a kind of anti-postfeminist, postfeminist feminism.

So, the video, like so much of the debate surrounding postfeminism, is characterised by paradox. But paradox can occasionally be productive. Or rather, our response to paradox can be productive inasmuch as paradox can point towards new questions, new ways of thinking, and, in certain cases, new answers to those questions. One response to the questions generated by the relationship of postfeminism to second-wave feminism has been to offer more and more definitions of what the prefix 'post' actually refers to and to sketch in ever finer detail exactly what it is that distinguishes one term from the other. While much of this work has proved invaluable in reinvigorating feminist theory, one way of understanding it is as an attempt to solve a paradox. In other words, it proceeds from the assumption that there is a proper, identifiable relationship between the two instead of a messy tangle of overlapping, complementary and competing ideas. A possible drawback of this response is that it can become simply a scholastic end in itself, confusing political objectives with theoretical ones and ending up as a self-perpetuating intellectual project. Better, perhaps, to accept that the situation is paradoxical and that a complete solution is not possible. Moreover, in the long run, it may bear more fruit if we direct attention towards some of the other, lower level, questions that emerge not only from the friction generated between second-wave and postfeminism but also from the analytical relationship between postfeminist theory and contemporary cultural products. In other words, a different response to the same paradox would be to start not by trying to erect a watertight postfeminist framework which one can use to interrogate forms of cultural representation but rather to start with those representations themselves. Indeed, it may well be that we discover as much about the complexities and the specificities of the postfeminist moment through our theoretical and analytical encounters with popular culture as from our internal disciplinary dialogues. Another way of putting this is to say that things can be overlooked if we don't remain alive to the texture of cultural representations, to their capacity to evade easy explanation. To simply see cultural representations as possible illustrations of theoretical ideas does a disservice to both the representations and the theory.

For instance, as we have done here, it is perfectly possible to use analysis of Pink's STUPID GIRLS to rehearse the controversy that attends the debate about the relationship between second-wave feminism and postfeminism. It is also possible for the critic to adjudicate on its putative feminist message, to celebrate its attempt to expose the damaging consequences of over-investing in shallow femininity or to lambast the vacuity of its self-refuting politics. This is more or less the route followed by Meredith A. Love and Brenda M. Helmbrecht who have their cake and eat it in their analysis of the video when they suggest that it presents to women ' "Pink" images that are both exploitative and commercial (and maybe even damaging) – yet this same image tells fans not to be so concerned with images'.[42] However, to leave it there begs a number of questions, questions that arise not simply out of the theoretical paradox of postfeminism but also out of the representational and narrative economies of the video itself. These questions are prompted by the video's underpinning binary logic which functions to frame the issues it seeks to address within a series of either/or options. For the struggle over the heart and mind of its young girl protagonist is played out around two potential narrative futures which are set in contra-distinction. The first, which is articulated by the devil on her right shoulder, sees the girl wanting to be like the image-obsessed pop princesses and air-headed celebrities whose only talent is knowing how to look good, whose only achievement is being able to excite the look of others. The second, foretold by the angel on her opposite shoulder, sees her following the footsteps of more positive female role models, determined to be as strong and powerful as any boy, and whose articulacy and intelligence make her a candidate for the White House. The main point here, of course, is that on this logic it is simply not possible to be one *and* the other, to be intelligent and girlie, to enjoy reading and shopping, to be taken seriously and be good-looking, and to be successful and feminine. And it is in this respect that the video reproduces the 'opposition between feminist and feminine identities' that Joanne Hollows argues was 'so decisively produced' across so much work from the second-wave period and which has been variously reworked, recast and reimagined in feminist scholarship ever since.[43] As with all binarisms, the problem with such an opposition, for both the video and feminist thinking, is that it turns on the idea that there is a 'proper' inside to feminism and, by extension, a corresponding outside too.

In terms of the video, this insider position is defined not simply by the rejection of femininity, but just as importantly, by practising pursuits traditionally defined as masculine – principally contact sports and power-dressed politics. Indeed, there is no narrative possibility of playing with dolls and then growing up to be president. In short, to be a successful woman is to be(come) masculine. The contrary also holds: to be outside feminism is to succumb to the pleasures of femininity – Barbie dolls, watching TV, shopping, cosmetics and fashion – pleasures which are not given any value whatsoever, indeed are definitive of the video's titular stupidity. The troublesome irony, here, is not only that in order to fulfil her full potential the girl must adopt a male position, but also that the feminist position articulated by the video is overdetermined by an untouched and uncriticised masculinity. An even more interesting irony, perhaps, is that this position is articulated in a video to promote a song by an attractive and successful woman called Pink, an observation which, at least in part, undercuts its call to reject either commodified femininity or the pleasures of the popular. This opens up one further way of reading the video – not to read it in isolation but to place it within the context of other representations, representations which themselves have a history and a context. That is to say, it is important that, just as the video is conscious of its own relationship to other cultural texts, as critics we should likewise be alive to how any one text's meanings are generated in the heat of its movement in the intertextual relay. So while the video does draw on discourses from second-wave feminism, and while these are complicated by its postfeminist context, they form only part of its discursive tapestry and are, in fact, mixed with and re-mixed by the discourses which constitute the star image of Pink. For in the end, it does matter that that the feminist utterances of STUPID GIRLS are enunciated by Pink. And it matters not only in the moment of consumption but also in the moment of criticism. To be more precise, it matters that she is seen as 'much smarter' than her contemporaries, that she makes 'music that's far riskier . . . than anything else in mainstream pop', that she is a 'sonic oxymoron' and a 'populist iconoclast' mixing rock rebellion with pop style.[44] In short, it matters greatly to how we read the video that on the one hand Pink, the singer, likes to 'stir things up, create dissent, create discussion' and on the other hand Pink, the woman, is 'intelligent, strong and beautiful', that she is 'rebellious and sexy'.[45] For the 'punky bad girl' role model offered up by Pink's star image does not straightforwardly square with the narrative thrust of the video and to a large extent is held in tension with it. In other words, while it is possible to read the video as anti-postfeminist inasmuch as it takes commodified hyperfemininity as its parodic target, such a reading becomes difficult to sustain as soon as it is located within an analysis of Pink's broader star persona. Indeed, it is the tension generated between what initially appear to be competing feminine ideals that allows Huff to argue that Pink 'rails against the idea that women have to choose between being smart and being sexy, as if the two are mutually exclusive'.[46] This, in turn, points up the imperative for us critics not to conduct our analyses of texts in isolation, as if they are ring-fenced entities, and, moreover, not necessarily to take them at their own word. For Huff's reading of STUPID GIRLS seems to be quite at odds with what actually happens in the story of the video. However, if the video is seen as one part of a much broader set of discourses articulated through and by Pink's public persona then it becomes clear that Huff is on to something. Indeed, the model of contemporary womanhood that tends to emerge from analysis of the Pink star image – from the songs and videos, from the reviews of those songs and videos, from the publicity material and press releases, from the official and unofficial websites, from her professional performances and public appearances – is one in which it is possible to be intelligent *and* good-looking, to be politically moti-vated *and* work within the popular, to be sexy *and* respected, to be successful *and* feminine. Seen in this context, STUPID GIRLS is a site not where femininity is simply rejected but one where it is renegotiated. Moreover, it is part of an increasing number of sites within popular culture which are engaged in one way or another in attempting to negotiate an acceptable and relevant form of postfeminist feminist identity, one which may imply, as Lotz has observed, 'confusion and contradiction', but nevertheless one which is not simply predi-cated on a binary opposition between femininity and feminism.[47]

This kind of analysis of Pink's STUPID GIRLS might also point us towards what a specifically postfeminist criticism might look like. Such an approach avoids the twin pitfalls involved in the transition to a postfeminist culture identified by Tasker and Negra: tokenism and anti-intellectualism.[48] In other words, it is part and parcel of the attempt to (re)open the questions that postfeminism appears to settle: questions to do with female agency and social power, questions to do with the value of women's culture and the attempts to trivialise it, and questions to do with gendered representation and how this variously enables or delimits the possibilities for being in the world. The way it seeks to address such questions is not to get hung up on the desire to define and redefine the concept of postfeminism with ever more precision so that it can then be theoretically mapped *ex post facto* on to the study of popular texts in order to take the temperature of contemporary gender politics. Such an approach replays the bad assumption that it is possible to identify a singular authentic feminism which can be used to both read the texts of popular culture and gauge our progress towards full emancipation. Rather, postfeminist cul-tural criticism can be seen as a version of what Ang and Hermes call a 'flexible and pragmatic form of criticism' which avoids 'predefined truths, feminist or otherwise'.[49] In other words, it accepts that there may be very real and impor-tant differences between postfeminist culture and (post)feminist politics, that the terms are not theoretically reducible to one another and that the latter cannot be simply distilled from the former, but is also aware that there is no one, unitary postfeminist political vantage point from which postfeminist culture can be observed. Moreover, in struggling to find a form of analysis that is simultaneously culturally relevant and politically energised, postfeminist criticism seeks to avoid the zero-sum game of binary thinking. That is to say, it sets out to complicate the relationship between things and terms that are often thought of as dichotomous – male and female, black and white, heterosexual and homosexual, second-wave feminism and postfeminism. Indeed, one of the key aims of this book is to deconstruct such dualisms by exploring the ways in which they are produced, naturalised, normalised and occasionally questioned through forms of representation. As Evelyn Fox Keller argues in a different context, the desire to move beyond the zero-sum game imposed by binary logic requires us 'to count past two, or in between one and two'. In fact, it is only by making this jump that 'we might discover what we never imagined possible'.[50] In the same spirit, it is possible to do things with representations other than merely read, read against, or interpret them. In short, one can think with them as well as about them. Taken together, these observations impel us towards a kind of postfeminist criticism in which popular culture, in this context, specifically music video, is seen to function not only as one of the sites on, through, and against which cultural identities are produced and understood but also as a site capable of reinvigorating our critical and political imagination.

This, then, is what we mean by the politics of representation. For representations are not simply a manifestation of what has already been said and thought, that is to say the product of an extant politics, but rather representations are political in so far as they allow us to think and say something new. In other words, for us, representations are first and foremost always a form of presentation. There are two interrelated aspects to this. Firstly, even though every instance of representation inevitably speaks through and to some extent rehearses previous representations, it is nevertheless a new articulation. Secondly, any individual instance of representation entails a specific combination of codes and conventions drawn from the full array of cultural discourses available at any one time. And, although they come from very different positions, both Dyer and Foucault remind us that it is this complex network of discourses which not only delimits and constricts what can be said but equally importantly makes saying anything possible in the first place. As Dyer argues,

> cultural forms set the wider terms of limitation and possibility for the (re) presentation of particularities and we have to understand how the latter are caught in the former in order to understand why such-and-such gets (re)presented in the way it does. Without understanding the way images function in terms of, say, narrative, genre or spectacle we don't really understand why they turn out the way they do.[51]

Specifically in terms of music video there are a number of important factors which bear on the 'way they turn out the way they do' and, moreover, how they make their meaning. Predominant amongst these are narrative and spectacle, as well as performative styles and the deployment of specific formal and aesthetic techniques. However, perhaps most important are the ways in which the notions of genre and authorship function in relation to music video, ways which intersect with, but also depart from, the ways they work in other cultural forms. It is to the former of these terms that we now turn.

NOTES

1. Sheri Kathleen Cole, 'I am the Eye, You are my Victim: The Pornographic Ideology of Music Video', *Enculturation*, vol. 2, no. 2 (1999), p. 1, http://enculturation. gmu.edu/2_2/cole/index.html; Imani Perry, 'Who(se) am I? The Identity and Image of Women in Hip-Hop', in Gail Dines and Jean M. Humez (eds), *Gender, Race and Class in the Media*, 2nd edn (London: Sage, 2003), p. 136; Julie L. Andsager and Kimberley Roe, 'Country Music Video in Country's Year of the Woman', *Journal of Communication*, vol. 49, no. 1 (1999), p. 80.
2. Lisa A. Lewis, *Gender Politics and MTV: Voicing the Difference* (Philadelphia: Temple University Press, 1990), pp. 110, 109.
3. E. Ann Kaplan, *Rocking Around the Clock: Music Television, Postmodernism, and Consumer Culture* (London: Methuen, 1987), p. 126; David Gauntlett, 'Madonna's Daughters: Girl Power and the Empowered Girl Pop Breakthrough', in Santiago Fouz-Hernández and Freya Jarmen-Ivens (eds), *Madonna's Drowned Worlds: New Approaches to her Cultural Transformations, 1983–2003* (Aldershot: Ashgate, 2004), p. 174.
4. Noel Carroll, *Theorizing the Moving Image* (Cambridge: Cambridge University Press, 1996), p. 268.
5. Sally Stockbridge, 'Music Video: Questions of Performance, Pleasure, and Address', *Continuum*, vol. 1, no. 2 (1987), http://wwwmcc.murdoch.edu.au/ ReadingRoom/1.2/Stockbridge.html (10/02/2010); Nicola Dibben, 'Representations of Femininity in Popular Music', *Popular Music*, vol. 18, no. 3 (1999), p. 348.
6. Charlotte Brunsdon, *Screen Tastes: Soap Opera to Satellite Dishes* (London: Routledge, 1997), p. 28.
7. Yvonne Tasker and Diane Negra, 'Introduction: Feminist Politics and Postfeminist Culture', in Yvonne Tasker and Diane Negra (eds), *Interrogating Postfeminism* (London: Duke University Press, 2007), p. 4.
8. See, for example: Jin Lee Hye and Wen Huike, 'Where the Girls Are in the Age of New Sexism: An Interview with Susan Douglas', *Journal of Communication Inquiry*, vol. 33, no. 2 (2009), p. 93; Misha Kavka, 'Feminism, Ethics, and History, or What Is the "Post" in Postfeminism?', *Tulsa Studies in Women's Literature*, vol. 21, no. 1 (2002), p. 29.
9. Sarah Projansky, *Watching Rape: Film and Television in Postfeminist Culture* (New York: New York University Press, 2001), p. 93.
10. Katie Roiphe, in Rachel Cooke, 'Katie Roiphe: The Interview', *Observer*, Review, 1 June 2008, p. 11.
11. Susan Faludi, *Backlash: The Undeclared War Against Women* (London: Chatto & Windus, 1991), p. 14.
12. Susan Faludi, 'I'm Not a Feminist but I Play One on TV', *Ms* (March/April 1995), p. 32.
13. Leslie G. Roman and Linda Eyre, *Dangerous Territories: Struggles for Difference and Equality in Education* (London: Routledge, 1997), p. 77.
14. Angela McRobbie, 'Postfeminism and Popular Culture', *Feminist Media Studies*, vol. 4, no. 3 (2004), p. 255.
15. McRobbie, 'Postfeminism and Popular Culture', p. 255.
16. McRobbie, 'Postfeminism and Popular Culture', p. 256.
17. McRobbie, 'Postfeminism and Popular Culture', p. 257.
18. Susan J. Douglas, 'Manufacturing Postfeminism', *In These Times*, 26 April 2002.
19. Imogen Tyler, '"Who put the 'Me' in feminism?": The Sexual Politics of Narcissism', *Feminist Theory*, vol. 6, no. 1 (2005), p. 37.
20. Kathleen Rowe Karlyn, '*Scream*, Popular Culture, and Feminism's Third Wave:

"I'm Not My Mother"', *Genders*, no. 38 (2003), http://www.genders.org/g38/g38_rowe_karlyn.html (04/07/2005).

21. Joanne Hollows and Rachel Moseley, 'Popularity Contests: The Meanings of Popular Feminism', in Joanne Hollows and Rachel Moseley (eds), *Feminism in Popular Culture* (Oxford: Berg, 2006), p. 2.

22. Michel Foucault, 'Technologies of the Self', in Luther H. Martin, Huck Gutman, and Patrick H. Hutton (eds), *Technologies of the Self: A Seminar with Michel Foucault* (Amherst, MA: University of Massachusetts Press, 1988), p. 16

23. Michel Foucault, *The History of Sexuality Volume Two: The Use of Pleasure*, trans. R. Hurley (Harmondsworth: Penguin, 1992), pp. 10–11.

24. Foucault, 'Technologies of the Self', p. 19.

25. Brunsdon, *Screen Tastes: Soap Opera to Satellite Dishes*, p. 84.

26. Rachel Moseley and Jacinda Read, ' "Having it *Ally*": Popular Television (Post-) Feminism', *Feminist Media Studies*, vol. 2, no. 2 (2002), p. 240.

27. Janet McCabe, cited in Alice Wignall, 'Can a Feminist Really Love Sex and the City?', *Guardian*, 16 April 2008; Lynne Segal, 'A Fond Farewell', *Guardian*, 29 January 2004; Noreena Hertz, 'A Fond Farewell', *Guardian*, 29 January 2004.

28. Richard Dyer, *The Matter of Images: Essays on Representations* (London: Routledge, 1993), pp. 1–4.

29. Dyer, *The Matter of Images*, p. 2.

30. Charlotte Brunsdon, 'The Feminist in the Kitchen: Martha, Martha and Nigella', in Hollows and Moseley (eds), *Feminism in Popular Culture*, p. 44.

31. P!nk, 'Stupid Girls' (LaFace Records, 2006).

32. Rosalind Gill, 'From Sexual Objectification to Sexual Subjectification: The Resexualisation of Women's Bodies in the Media', *Feminist Media Studies*, vol. 3, no. 1 (2003), p. 104.

33. Gill, 'From Sexual Objectification to Sexual Subjectification', p. 104.

34. Gill, 'From Sexual Objectification to Sexual Subjectification', p. 105.

35. Shulamith Firestone, *The Dialectic of Sex: The Case for Feminist Revolution* (New York: Bantam Books, 1970), pp. 151–2.

36. Germaine Greer, *The Female Eunuch* (London: Paladin, 1971), pp. 18, 364, 68, 69.

37. Susan Brownmiller, *Femininity* (London: Paladin, 1986), pp. 2, 3, 6, 3.

38. Greer, *The Female Eunuch*, p. 63.

39. Greer, *The Female Eunuch*, p. 17.

40. Brownmiller, *Femininity*, p. 5.

41. Firestone, *The Dialectic of Sex*, p. 152.

42. Meredith A. Love and Brenda M. Helmbrecht, 'Teaching the Conflicts: (Re) Engaging Students with Feminism in a Postfeminist World', *Feminist Teacher*, vol. 18, no. 1 (2007), p. 51.

43. Joanne Hollows, *Feminism, Femininity and Popular Culture* (Manchester: Manchester University Press, 2000), p. 17.

44. Robert Christgau, 'Dear Mr President', *Village Voice*, 18 April 2006; Stephen Thomas Erlewine, 'I'm not Dead: Review', *allmusic.com*, http://www.allmusic.com/cg/amg.dll?p=amg&sql=10:3pfyxqrdldke (24/08/2007); D. Spence, 'I'm not Dead: Review', *ign.com*, http://uk.music.ign.com/articles/700/700279p1.html (24/08/2007); Barry Walters, 'Music Reviews: Pink: I'm not Dead', *Rolling Stone*, 4 April 2006, http://www.rollingstone.com/artists/pink/albums/album/9558059/review/9580060/im_not_dead (24/08/2007).

45. P!nk's Page, http://www.pinkspage.com/uk/node/19515 (24/08/2007); S. Rock, 'P!nk Pink Posters Encourage Women To Be Smart and Sexy – Not Stupid

Girls', *EzineArticles.com*, 9 May 2006, http://ezinearticles.com/?P!nk-Pink-Posters-Encourage-Women-To-Be-Smart-and-Sexy---Not-Stupid-Girls&id=194099 (24/08/2007).

46. Quentin B. Huff, 'Far From Buried, But Don't Call it a Comeback', *Popmatters*, 17 May 2006, http://www.popmatters.com/pm/review/pink-im-not-dead (13/04/2008).

47. Amanda D. Lotz, 'Postfeminist Television Criticism: Rehabilitating Critical Terms and Identifying Postfeminist Attributes', *Feminist Media Studies*, vol. 1, no. 1 (2001), p. 105.

48. See Tasker and Negra, 'Introduction: Feminist Politics and Postfeminist Culture'.

49. Ien Ang and Joke Hermes, 'Gender and/in Media Consumption', in James Curran and Michael Gurevitch (eds), *Mass Media and Society*, 2nd edn (London: Arnold, 1996), p. 342.

50. Evelyn Fox Keller, 'How Gender Matters, or, Why it's so Hard for us to Count Past Two', in Gill Kirkup and Laurie Smith Keller (eds), *Inventing Women: Science, Technology and Gender* (Cambridge: Polity Press/The Open University, 1992), p. 56.

51. Dyer, *The Matter of Images*, p. 2.

2. GENRE AND MUSIC VIDEO:
CONFIGURATIONS AND FUNCTIONS

Genre, whatever else it might be, is first and foremost about categorisation, about sorting cultural products into discrete groupings based on similarities and common properties. Moreover, this act of categorisation is always purposeful. In other words, this process is done for a specific reason, whether that reason is socio-economic, cultural or academic. In the first place, from an industrial standpoint, genre performs specific economic functions in so far as it works to organise the financing, production and marketing of cultural products so as to ensure maximum return from investment. For consumers, genre is one of the principal ways of choosing which products to buy in the first place and also perhaps the key marker of taste – a means of expressing likes and dislikes and identifying and communicating with like-minded people. In academic discourse, the concept of genre is multi-functional. For not only are the socio-economic and cultural aspects of genre a focus of analysis across a number of disciplines, but the notion of genre is also mobilised as a way of rationalising the study of popular culture; defining the parameters of a form; as a model of textual explication; and as a way of theorising how those texts are understood in the process of consuming them. Indeed, it is precisely this multifunctionality that leads to the idea that genre is a kind of conceptual golden thread, seemingly capable of describing the whole process of creating, selling and consuming cultural products as well as providing a critical framework through which both this process and individual texts can be interpreted and explained. And it is precisely this standard view of genre that becomes de-stabilised when we consider music video, for its role as a secondary product means that there is no single generic thread that links production, promotion and consumption. Indeed, any particular music video's own generic properties are often subsumed under the genre of music that it is promoting.

In contradistinction to the study of genre in literature and film, where genre fiction/film is often seen as the antithesis of serious artistic endeavour, in the study of popular music generic structures are seen as a framework against which, and within which, creativity and originality take shape and are defined. This is not to say, however, that genres of popular music are straightforward to define. As Dave Harker points out, 'terms like "rock", "blues", "African music" or "the Liverpool Sound" are used rather differently in practice – by fans (including journalists), by musicians (including critics) and by academics (including reviewers)'.[1] For fans, musicians and academics may have very different reasons for discussing genre and thus may use very different criteria for deciding which genre a piece of music belongs to. When we add the needs of the music industry and music retailers into the mix we are confronted by a range of genres that vary from the very broadly defined to the very narrowly defined. So, for example, if we take the term 'hip hop' we find that for music retailer HMV it is a sub-category of 'urban/dance' music. By contrast, Henry Adaso's blog lists and describes ten sub-genres of hip hop while Wikipedia lists more than seventy sub-genres and music styles derived from hip hop.[2] Despite the fact that some artists claim to have an individual style that avoids such classification, Joshua Gunn suggests that genre is inevitable in any discussion of popular music as fans and artists negotiate, and renegotiate, the boundaries of subcultural identity.[3] Indeed, the music of any given artist can be described under a number of labels depending who is doing the labelling. In the context of popular music, genre is understood not only, or even primarily, as corpora of texts defined by shared musical properties, but also as sets of codes and conventions that govern the actions and behaviours not only of musicians but of fans, audiences and musical communities too – what William Tsitsos, in his discussion of 'the American alternative scene', calls 'rules of rebellion'.[4]

The view of genre that emerges from this account is variously untidy and volatile. Whereas, on the one hand, it seems to offer a relatively straightforward, even commonsensical, way of grouping together similar texts based on common properties, on the other hand its manifestation as a 'boundary phenomenon', a way of settling subcultural or analytical 'boundary disputes', means that it is always in some sense arbitrary and open to negotiation and revision.[5] In short, genre is a messy concept. Nevertheless, despite its messiness, genre remains a useful way of discussing cultural products and artefacts. Work such as this book, which addresses the politics of representation, that is, the ways in which different social groups are represented in and through forms of culture, can benefit from situating the scrutinised texts within their generic contexts. Simply put, it helps to know if the representation of raced identity or femininity, or whatever, in a given text is 'unique' or if it is a prevalent feature of similar texts.

Andrew Tudor suggests two models for working within genre study; on the one hand to work inward to the text in applying a set of pre-determined criteria in order to identify and sort generic groupings or, on the other, to work outwards from the text and produce categories on the basis of the formal, stylistic and aesthetic evidence it provides.[6] It is this latter approach that we pursue below to identify and discuss four principal generic configurations of the music video, categories we have termed: pseudo-documentary; art music video; narrative; and staged performance. However, while offering a way of managing, organising and interrogating a vast number of videos, we want to stress from the outset that both this process of categorisation and the categories themselves are not intended as reductive or finite entities. Quite the contrary, we argue that genre operates in complex ways in relation to music video. Defining and delineating genres of music is not a straightforward task in itself and, furthermore, individual genres of music video, those that grow out of formal, stylistic and aesthetic evidence, do not map onto music genres in a straightforward fashion. Indeed, since genres of music video cut across genres of music, attempts to discuss, say, the 'rap video' or the 'rock video' are at best reductive and at worst acutely flawed. Moreover, although some music genres may privilege a particular type of video, any given music video may have, and often does have, far more in common with a video which promotes a song from another music genre than with others of its own. It is the intention of what follows, therefore, not only to point out the limitations of work which falls into this trap, but more importantly to directly address the various generic formations that characterise music video and the complex ways in which they interact with genres of music.

Genre and Music Video

Very little work exists that has attempted to use genre as a way of understanding music video. This is both surprising and predictable. It is surprising in so far as generic analysis of other forms of popular culture has played a central role in understanding not only their formal and stylistic properties and economic functions, but also the pleasures they afford their audiences. The study of both film and television, not to mention literature, would be unthinkable without it. As such, one might have expected that music video would have been approached in the same way. The lack of genre-based work in music video is, however, entirely predictable for a number of reasons. Firstly, as discussed in the introduction, academic criticism of music video has often been subsumed within accounts of MTV, or, more precisely, accounts of MTV which stress its postmodern formal and aesthetic properties. For instance, John

Fiske argues that the 'rock video or MTV' is broadcast television's 'only original art form'.[7] Whatever else one may make of such a claim, it is, of course, the conjunctive 'or' which concerns us here in so far as it works to erase the distinctions between medium, form and content, between music videos and the TV channel(s) that broadcasts them. Simply put, the music video becomes conflated, and confused, with the context of its distribution. This critical slippage not only tends to mask differences between individual music videos and the different generic structures of video, but also diverts critical attention away from the form and content of music videos themselves and shifts it towards the formal analysis of MTV as a putatively distinctive postmodern televisual phenomenon. One further implication of such rhetorical manoeuvres is that the apparent postmodernism of MTV is often too easily simply mapped onto music video itself. Here, all music videos become classed as postmodern forms of visual culture on the basis of merely *appearing* on MTV. This universalising way of understanding music video not only seems at odds with the postmodernist analysis which produces it, but again works to divert attention away from analysis of the videos themselves rooting it instead in the fragmented structure of MTV and its self-reflexive, ironic and parodic textual strategies. Moreover, even when critics such as E. Ann Kaplan or Andrew Goodwin stress the difference between the music video and music television, in the end, they still only discuss music videos in the context of MTV.[8] At a general level this serves to situate the term 'music video' as a generic label in its own right. In other words, the distinctive formal properties of the music video – short films which feature the song they are designed to promote – are mobilised as generic markers to distinguish it from both other kinds of video and other kinds of film and television. But even at its most specific music video becomes classed as a genre of television – a genre typified by fragmentation, reflexivity, non-linearity and so forth. Either way, the result of this equation is a body of work which is predicated on the interdependence of music video and music television, a notion that perhaps described the situation at the time when most of this work was written but which certainly does not adequately account for the present moment.

Indeed, it is no longer necessary, nor useful, to equate music video with MTV. The situation in which a single music channel broadcast predetermined videos interspersed with advertisements to an undifferentiated audience has, since the mid-1980s, given way to much more diverse ways of distributing and accessing music video. The conditions governing access to music video and the way they are watched have fundamentally changed. The decision is no longer simply whether or not to watch MTV, but rather a choice has to be made of which video to access, when to watch it, and on what platform. And this choice is almost entirely organised generically, that is to say, the broadcasting, selling and streaming of music videos is very often based on their subdivision along music genre lines. So, not only is music television itself now almost entirely organised generically through forms of branded narrowcasting, but sites such as Apple's iTunes use generic groupings as one of the principal means of organising their content and offering search/browse facilities to their users. Given this, to continue to see the term 'music video' as a sufficient generic label, or to study music video merely as a specific form of television programming, is, at best, reductive and, at worst, out of step with the ways in which music videos are now distributed, accessed, 'owned' and watched.

This use of genre, however, points us towards the second main reason why there has been little work which uses the concept to theorise music video. This has to do with the relationship between genres of popular music – precisely those genres used to brand channels and organise web searches – and genres of music video. Unlike other forms of popular culture, the music video is first and foremost a promotional tool, that is to say, a way of marketing another product which itself already operates and is understood generically. For instance, Kaplan argues that 'selling the record is the base-line, that will control the "look" of the video being made for sale of the song and its record'.[9] Similarly, Carol Vernallis argues that:

> music videos derive from the song they set. The music comes first – the song is produced before the video is conceived – and the director normally designs images with the song as a guide. Moreover, the video must sell the song; it is therefore responsible to the song in the eyes of the artist and record company.[10]

As such, it is tempting to simply equate the genre of music video with the genre of music it is designed to promote. And, indeed, this is what many critics have done and continue to do. However, while this common-sense approach works well for choosing which video to watch, it tells us very little about the videos themselves. Simply transposing categories derived from elsewhere onto music video is neither the only way of identifying generic types nor the most instructive. For despite the integral relationship between music videos and the songs they promote, genres of music neither map onto genres of music video nor, *pace* Vernallis, necessarily govern the look of any given video. In other words, although genre works as a 'framework of signs in relation to which difference and variation can be both produced on the one hand and read and understood on the other', *music genres* do not provide such a framework for the production or consumption of music videos.[11] Quite the contrary. The videos which accompany the songs comprising any one musical genre can display striking formal and aesthetic variation. By the same token, videos for songs from quite different music genres often have far more in common with each other than with those from within the same music genre.

Imani Perry's essay on the image and identity of women in hip hop is a good example of the kind of work which slips from discussion of musical genres to genres of video as if the two sets of texts entertain specific and identifiable relations with each other determined by the same generic label. She argues that in hip hop videos of the late 1990s:

> every time you turned on BET or MTV there was a disturbing music video. Black men rapped surrounded by dozens of black and Latina women dressed in swimsuits, or scantily clad in some other fashion. Video after video was the same, each one more objectifying than the next. Some were in strip clubs, some at the pool, beach, hotel rooms, but the recurrent theme was dozens of half-naked women.[12]

While it is undoubtedly true that many videos which promote hip hop music do contain these elements either in isolation or combination, it nevertheless remains the case that many others do not. For instance, the videos for Kanye West's THROUGH THE WIRE (2003), Tupac Shakur's RUNNING (DYING TO LIVE) (2004) and Talib Kweli's I TRY (2004) feature neither half-naked women nor the locations Perry discusses.[13] Viewing the same question from the other end, Trace Adkins' HONKY TONK BADONKADONK (2005) and Travis Tritt's THE GIRL'S GONE WILD (2004) evince all of Perry's ingredients of the hip hop video – the club, the beach, a pool and plenty of scantily clad women – but they are, of course, videos designed to promote country songs. As such, while any given music video can mobilise the iconography of the musical genre of the song it promotes, it is not impelled to do so. Moreover, even if it does, this still does not define the generic configurations which structure music videos. And it is precisely to these generic structures that we now want to turn.

Four Genres of Music Video

Perhaps the most well-known work that looks at 'types of music video' is E. Ann Kaplan's *Rocking Around The Clock*. Kaplan identifies five basic types of video on MTV, all of which, she argues, deploy techniques more usually associated with the avant-garde, but which are distinguished on the basis of their 'ideological imaginary'.[14] So even while, for Kaplan, the technical and formal strategies of MTV videos are seen to generally embody postmodernism, she identifies differences in terms of the way certain common thematic structures are articulated across her five categories. The romantic type, for example, is defined by 'the overall nostalgic, sentimental and yearning quality' and 'plays out the pain of separation'.[15] For Kaplan, videos of this type 'idealize parent-child relationships, manifesting pre-Oedipal, bisexual yearnings in the urge to merge with the loved one and recapture infant mother-child closeness'.[16] By contrast, in what Kaplan terms nihilist videos,

> the love theme turns from a relatively mild narcissism and a focus on the pain of separation, to sadism, masochism, androgyny, and homoeroticism; while the anti-authority theme moves from mere unresolved Oedipal conflicts to explicit, hate, nihilism, anarchy, destruction.[17]

However, while Kaplan's psychoanalytically derived typology of music video does allow her to discuss the ways in which certain videos of the 1980s construct different social and political modes of address, her typology cannot be used to understand the generic configuration of those videos. In other words, while it continues to serve as a model for interpreting music videos, it cannot adequately categorise them in terms of common content, style and technique, that is to say, in terms of the kinds of criteria central to the process of genre-building.

While Kaplan's work is perhaps the most cited attempt to classify music video, the overwhelming majority of work that has tried to define and discuss genres of music video has, in one way or another, followed the Aristotelian model of identifying the essential categories of the form and then articulating both the qualities inherent to each category and the differences which mark them as distinct from other categories. Joan D. Lynch, for example, argues that 'three basic structures [of music video] can be identified. The most common one by far, with multiple variations, is centred on the performance itself. There are also narrative videos and videos which are strongly influenced by experimental film'.[18] Similarly, Steve Jones identifies three 'narrative forms' of music video: mimetic narrative (the representation of concert performance), analog narrative (non-concert performance of the song intercut with other material), and digital narrative (impossible performance or no performance whatsoever).[19]

It is Joe Gow's discussion of 'popular formulas and emerging genres', however, that sets out perhaps the most useful approach for thinking about the ways in which generic structures operate in music video.[20] Although he begins by distinguishing between the 'conceptual video' and the 'performance video', which he sees as 'the two most basic formal possibilities in music videos', thus replaying the same logic as Lynch and Jones, he nevertheless goes on to offer a much more fine-grained account of what he calls the distinct 'formulas' which exist within and in between his two principal forms.[21] Indeed, he identifies six central genres of music video all of which are defined in terms of their relationship to the display of performance: (1) the anti-performance piece – videos which do not contain performance of the song; (2) pseudo-reflexive performance – videos which display the process of video production; (3) the performance documentary – videos which contain *vérité* documentary footage of onstage performance and/or off-stage activity; (4) the special effects extravaganza – videos in which human performance is overshadowed by spectacular imagery; (5) the song and dance number – videos which focus on the physical abilities of the dancing performer(s) and the vocal presentation of the song, usually through lip-synching techniques; and (6) the enhanced performance – videos which blend performance elements with other visual elements, a blend justified through either associational, narrative or abstract forms of motivation.[22] The advantage of these categories is that they are derived inductively on the basis of historically contingent similarities and differences between numerous instances of the same form. In other words, even though performance is common to all of Gow's categories (even in its absence), it is precisely the different ways in which performance is represented that is deployed as a marker of generic difference. Moreover, Gow's framework resists the essentialism of other attempts to define genres of music video and, ironically, even his own notion of 'basic categories'.

While Gow's intervention certainly represents one of the most sophisticated attempts to map genres of music video, its over-dependence on performance as the modulating variable produces its own limitations. In the first place, it works to separate very similar videos into different generic groups. For instance, a song and dance number may be almost identical to an enhanced performance video and there may be little difference between a pseudo-reflexive performance video and a performance documentary. More importantly, however, the enhanced performance video, Gow's largest grouping, containing more than half of the videos studied, serves to elide the often significant differences between videos of this type. As such, we want to offer our own four genres of music video – *pseudo-documentary*, *art music video*, *narrative video*, and *staged performance* – not only as a way of rethinking Gow's work and hooking it up with that of Lynch and Jones, but also as a way of addressing the much neglected relationship between music video and discourses of authenticity. Indeed, this is not just an exercise in drawing lines in different places, nor is it simply about offering different criteria for the establishment and definition of generic categories. Nor, for that matter, is it only about 'finding' generic structures within music video. While the process necessarily entails aspects of all three, just as important, for us, are the ways in which genres of music video function to legitimate both performance and performer. And it is worth bearing in mind, as Simon Frith argues, that the key economic function of a music video is to promote not the individual song but rather the artist or band who perform it.[23] For perhaps what emerges most powerfully from this kind of analysis is the inextricable linkage between genres of music video and the range of ways any given artist or band's appeal to authenticity can be sanctioned. In other words, like all discussions of genre the categories of music video we set out below are *descriptive* in so far as they provide a cognitive map of what one might expect to see in any given video depending on the category to which it belongs. But these categories are also *analytic* precisely to the extent that those same generic structures also contain within them models of authentication, models which may be activated differently in relationship to different performers or genres of music but which are nevertheless *always* activated.

Pseudo-Documentary Music Video

This genre of music video deploys the aesthetics of documentary realism to portray the 'working life' of the band or artist and, as such, functions to legitimate them as skilled, professional, musicians. So, while videos in this category are not documentaries proper inasmuch as they are primarily advertisements, pseudo-documentary videos nevertheless do use the stylistic devices associated with forms of documentary film – especially, though not exclusively, those related to *cinéma-vérité* – to capture the artists in their 'natural' environment, in other words, the artists doing the job of being musicians, performers, stars and so forth. As such, what Trihn T. Mihn-ha calls documentary's 'set of persuasive techniques' – the sense of witnessing naked reality occurring despite, not because of, the presence of the camera; the inclusion of grainy, often black and white, film stock, and the use of a shaky hand-held camera communicating immediacy and authenticity – create a documentary effect.[24] What they all do, in one way or another, is utilise the now familiar aesthetics of documentary style to present an illusion of *privileged access* to the performers and their day-to-day working lives, that is to say, access to aspects of the performers' work and lives that are normally restricted, inaccessible or private.

This documenting of apparent privileged access is realised in a number of ways. Most obvious, perhaps, is the recording of the artist(s) performing live to an audience. So, for example, Toby Keith's GET DRUNK AND BE SOMEBODY (2006) simply shows Keith and his band performing the song live, on stage in a large auditorium, intercut with footage of the crowd dancing, drinking, cheering and singing along. The video opens with a crane shot which sweeps over the crowd and establishes the 'liveness' of the performance. Thereafter, the video is structured around shots of Keith singing and dancing, images of his band playing their instruments, long-shots of the stage show from the rear of the venue, and shots of the audience either *en masse* from above, from a roving hand-held camera, or from the vantage point of the performers. Although the video presents its events in real time in so far as it begins with the commencement of the song and ends with the applause which follows it, the performance is not experienced simply as if the spectator were a member of the audience. Quite the contrary in fact, for we are not only afforded multiple vantage points from the crowd – front- and back-row views which offer different perspectives on the same event – but also points of access not available to the live audience – flying over the crowd towards the stage or on-stage with the performers looking outwards. Taken together, what we get is a focus on the *fact* of the performance both in terms of the production of the music – the instruments and voices which produce the sounds, the microphones, wires and other equipment which amplify those sounds, and, of course, the style and skill of the musicians who play the instruments and use the equipment – and the context in which it is performed and experienced. In other words, GET DRUNK AND BE SOMEBODY not only depicts Keith and his band as able live performers but also demonstrates that their work is appreciated by a large and enthusiastic audience.

This sense of privileged access, however, can be established in a number of other ways, as indeed the work of being an artist is not solely confined to live performance. Other videos in this category take the audience into the recording and rehearsal studios, backstage, on the road, and into a range of other working and 'private' contexts. For instance, Metallica's NOTHING ELSE MATTERS (1992) documents the recording of the song in the studio. So where Keith's video represents the spectacle of large-scale live performance, NOTHING ELSE MATTERS represents the ordinary, day-to-day working life of Metallica. The opening shots of the video show the processes of preparing to record the song: equipment arrives at the studio and is unloaded; guitars are tuned; microphones are adjusted; and tape is fed onto the spools of the recorder. With the introduction of the first lyrics, the video shifts gear and presents the band in the process of recording the song intercut with footage of them relaxing between takes. What we get is not only a sense of 'a day in the recording studio' but also a focus on the technical and creative context of the production of the music. Time and again the conjunction of equipment and performer is emphasised in close-up: fingers move sliders on the mixing desk and form chords on guitar frets; hands strum guitar strings and adjust headphones; feet pound drum pedals; and mouths sing into microphones guarded by pop shields. This conjunction of the technology of music and human artistry serves to authenticate the band as skilled, professional musicians at work in one of their 'natural environments' – the recording studio.

Guns 'N' Roses's PARADISE CITY (1988) stands as an exemplar of the pseudo-documentary genre of music video in that it not only presents a number of 'natural environments' which the band inhabit but also employs a range of documentary techniques to do so. While the video is structured around the live performance of the song, it nevertheless features documentary footage of other aspects of the life of a working band. The video begins before the performance starts. A hand-held pan shows the empty stadium in grainy black and white. A short montage sequence follows, also shot in black and white and with a shaky *vérité* camera, which shows the crew setting up and the band members both rehearsing for the gig and relaxing before it. With the introduction of the song's lyrics the video cuts to colour footage of the performance proper. Images of the band on stage are cut together with shots of the audience. Indeed, the presence of the crowd is signalled in one hand-held whip-pan which takes us from a medium close-up of Axl Rose, the band's singer, to a long shot of the stadium now heaving with thousands of people. As the video continues, moreover, footage of the live performance is intercut with montage sequences comprised of images of the band at work, images which apparently capture the reality of 'life on the road'. As with Toby Keith's GET DRUNK AND BE SOMEBODY, the performance footage combines shots of the band performing on the stage with images of the crowd's response to that performance. However, unlike Keith's video, these sequences are, in fact, taken from two separate performances, the first in New Jersey's Meadowlands Stadium and the second at the Castle Donington race track in the UK. While the former is shot in colour and the latter in black and white, they are, nevertheless, held together by the montage sequences which narrativise the journey from one venue to the other. Even though this narrative is not, strictly speaking, linear inasmuch as the video cuts backwards and forwards between the two events, the story it tells is not simply about the fact of live performance but more complexly about the experience of being in a rock band. And the montage sequences play a crucial role in the construction of this narrative. For what they present is the offstage life of the band, the 'down-and-dirty' reality of hotel rooms, tour buses, bars and 'girls'. We follow the band backstage and offstage and get to see them half-asleep in bed, drinking, smoking, practising in hospitality tents, boarding a plane, meeting fans, walking down the street, signing autographs, and, in one case, even signing someone's denim jacket as he stands urinating. Given all this, PARADISE CITY emerges as a particularly interesting version of the pseudo-documentary music video in so far as it not only documents the fact of live performance and the skill and musicianship of the band, but also affords its audience apparently privileged access to the pleasures and pressures of the life of the rock star. Indeed, while this category of video in general is concerned with offering a sense of the putative realities of the working artist, whether on stage, in rehearsal, recording in the studio, or simply living the life of a popular musician, PARADISE CITY is exemplary both in terms of the way it mobilises a number of these contexts in a single video and in its exploitation of documentary aesthetics.

Art Music Video

If the pseudo-documentary video establishes its authenticity by apparently depicting the 'real life' of professional musicians, then the art video claims legitimacy by appealing to notions of art and aesthetics. In other words, while the videos in the pseudo-documentary genre are concerned with capturing the skill and creativity of the artist(s) producing, recording and performing music, in this category the video itself operates as a site of creative expression which variously works as an aesthetic complement to the song or vies with it for artistic consideration. This is not to say, however, that what we term here 'the art music video' can, or for that matter should, simply be equated with video art. Even though there is an identifiable relationship between the two forms in terms of textual strategies and aesthetic techniques, the very fact that the art music video is a *music video* inevitably sets them apart. While the work of video artists such as Robert Wilson, Douglas Gordon, Nam June Paik and Sam Taylor-Wood, for example, is motivated exclusively by artistic concerns and exhibited within, and for, the art world, music videos, whatever their motivation, are always produced and exhibited within a commercial context precisely because, in the last instance, they are designed to advertise and sell another product. By the same token, the value judgement that informs discussions of video art – the idea that a work has some kind of social, cultural or political significance that sets it apart from other artefacts which are not art – cannot necessarily be transposed into discussions of music video. Put simply, in naming a genre of music video 'art' we are not suggesting that the videos in this category are in some way better or more worthy than those in other genres but, rather, that they deploy formal and aesthetic techniques associated with artistic practices. Indeed, the art music video stands in relationship to video art just as pseudo-documentary video stands in relationship to documentary, inasmuch as while the latter assimilates the techniques of documentary to produce a documentary effect, the former adopts artistic techniques to produce an artistic effect. In short, as the increasing co-option of music video into the art world attests, the art music video may in some cases *also* be an art work but it nevertheless remains the case that it is first and foremost a promotional video. Indeed, it is important not to confuse the generic description of 'art music video' with discussions of the art *of* the music video. While generic analysis is concerned with mapping similar properties across large numbers of works, discussions of art usually focus on either individual texts or the body of work of an individual artist or specific movement. Given this distinction, it is not an individual video's artistic value that justifies its inclusion in this category, but rather its use of the techniques and practices of the art world.

One way of thinking about this distinction is to consider R.E.M'.s video, WHAT'S THE FREQUENCY, KENNETH? (1994). On one reading, the video seems to display the generic markers of the pseudo-documentary in that it depicts the band performing the song in a rehearsal room surrounded by microphones, amps, instruments and other tools of the musical trade. However, unlike with pseudo-documentary, the video does not work as a visual demonstration of the musicianship and artistry of the band, nor does it give us privileged access to their working and/or private life. Indeed, nor does it even gesture towards constructing a sense of the reality of the situation and performance. Despite its content, this is not a video *about* the band at all but rather about the visual experience of light, colour, movement and sound. The video's anti-realism is signalled from the opening shot which introduces its three principal aesthetic tactics – tactics which combine to force the spectator to notice its artifice. So, not only is this opening shot deliberately poorly framed and exposed, but there is a stark disjunction between the image track and the sound track. In other words, what one might expect to be an establishing shot is rendered immediately unreliable and ambiguous. The band's lead singer is positioned centrally behind a microphone but is framed only from the neck down resulting in the intentional obfuscation of both identity and personality. Verisimilitude is further undermined at the level of the image itself, an image which is not only bathed in blue light but, in oscillating between over- and underexposure, also constantly flickers and threatens to bleach out into total whiteness. As the video continues, moreover, images slip in and out of negative, primary colours flood the scene and saturate the image, and the illusion of reality is further denied through the use of canted angles, 'bad' framing, and out of focus photography. In addition, bursts of white light intermittently fill the screen serving to remind the viewer of both the flatness of the screen and the provisionality of the realistic image. One result of this is the decoupling of image and sound, or more precisely of the pretence of the performance of the song and the song itself. While this is initially signalled by the absence of the band and images of idle instruments, in later shots lip-synching is out of kilter with what we hear and sounds of guitars are accompanied by images of drums. Perhaps most importantly, however, the increasing abstraction of the video into formalism and colour-field experimentation serves to recast the *band's* performance as part of the video's overall *aesthetic* performance. This not only operates to deconstruct and expose the artificial processes through which authenticity is constructed in certain pseudo-documentary videos but also establishes its own artistic authenticity precisely on this basis. Indeed, many of the aesthetic techniques evidenced in the video can be directly associated with forms of experimental cinema and in particular with structuralist film. As David Bordwell and Kristin Thompson argue, structural film is about challenging form, especially the realist principles of dominant narrative cinema. They note that, 'structural films were often called "anti-illusionist" because they drew attention to the ways in which the medium transforms the object filmed' to the extent that 'the viewer becomes sharply aware of the act of viewing'.[25] In the case of WHAT'S THE FREQUENCY, KENNETH? the abstract use of iridescent colour and the misframing of the object progressively direct attention away from the act of performance towards the material properties of the video itself.

It is not only colour and framing, however, that can be used in this way.

Other videos interrogate the illusion of three-dimensional space and the construction of movement within and through that space. The White Stripes's SEVEN NATION ARMY (2003) not only explores the graphic potential of the shot through the use of a restricted colour palette and geometric patterning but also flaunts a single filmic technique – the tracking shot. In the end, what the video presents is an impossibly perpetual tracking shot through kaleidoscopic space, a space which is, of course, an illusion. The filmic illusion of movement is also explored in Sia's BREATHE ME (2005). The video opens with the image slowly emerging from the emulsion of a Polaroid photograph as it develops. Thereafter movement is realised through presentation of successive Polaroids which contain the next frame of the video. In this way the process by which the trick of seamless and smooth movement is created from still and discrete images is rendered visible and noticeable. Taken together these videos and others can be seen, at least in part, to be about the medium itself in so far as they force attention onto the qualities and properties of the film/video through which representation is realised.

It is, of course, not just the formalism and aesthetic techniques associated with structuralist film and experimental cinema that identify videos in this genre. Indeed, music videos draw upon a whole range of artistic movements and practices. For instance, both Nick Cave and Kylie Minogue's WHERE THE WILD ROSES GROW (1995) and Dido's DON'T LEAVE HOME (2004) mobilise the story of Ophelia and, in particular, the style of its representation in Pre-Raphaelite painting. Videos such as Peter Gabriel's SLEDGEHAMMER (1986), Melanie G's WORD UP (1999), The White Stripes's FELL IN LOVE WITH A GIRL (2002), Junior Senior's MOVE YOUR FEET (2004), Goldfrapp's STRICT MACHINE (2004), A Perfect Circle's COUNTING BODIES LIKE SHEEP TO THE RHYTHM OF THE WAR DRUMS (2005), and the entire video work of the Gorillaz utilise the distinctive graphic language of animation, a language which, as Paul Wells argues, can reveal or invent 'worlds which enact themselves and offer alternative models of perception and experience', to produce specific artistic effects.[26] Moreover, a whole host of videos take up the style, imagery and techniques of art movements in order to make, on the one hand, some kind of social, cultural or political statement, or, on the other, to comment on the big questions that have preoccupied the arts for centuries, questions relating to the human condition, death, beauty and so forth.

However, it is perhaps the imagery, techniques and style associated with forms of surrealist art which can most often be found in the art music video. Indeed, Joan D. Lynch argues that videos which 'borrow the techniques' of Dada and Surrealism are 'the most interesting'.[27] This borrowing can work in a number of ways. For instance, the incongruous imagery of Goldfrapp's NUMBER 1 (2005), which features the heads of dogs transplanted onto human bodies to make a point about the beauty industry, can be traced back to the work of Marcel Duchamp via the photography of William Wegman. The surrealist potential of incongruity is approached differently in the Scissor Sisters' TAKE YOUR MAMA OUT (2004) as the dreamscapes of Dali and Magritte are combined with the absurd juxtapositions and the bizarre mismatches of scale which characterise Terry Gilliam's title sequence for *Monty Python's Flying Circus* (1969). Dali's influence can also be traced in the video for the Prodigy's 'Breathe' (1996) which, like many of his paintings, attempts to depict the unconscious and represent dreamwork. Indeed, the video deploys a series of demonic metaphors and metonyms dragged from the subconscious in order to visualise the mechanics of dreamspace, or, more precisely, of a Freudian nightmare: hair grows out of walls; blood bubbles up through a sink; bugs, rats and crocodiles infest the scene; gravity is disengaged as people and objects float towards the ceiling; and throughout the video the band members violently lurch and convulse as if possessed.

The assimilation of surrealist techniques is, of course, only one way in which the 'art' of the art music video is instigated. Whether or not a video employs the anti-illusionist tactics of structural film, mimics the style of a particular art movement or art work, uses the artistic platform of music video to explore metaphysical questions, or simply operates as a unique aesthetic experience in its own right, the main point here is that videos in this genre invite one to engage with them as art works precisely in so far as they mobilise the now familiar forms, practices, strategies and tactics of the visual arts. Indeed, what defines this genre of video is, somewhat ironically, the desire for the uniqueness and individuality associated with works of art. Moreover, it is this desire, and the specific way it is evidenced in any given art video, that works to authenticate not only the aesthetic gestures of the video itself, but perhaps more crucially, the song and its performers. In short, as our culture constantly reminds us, art is a serious business performed by serious artists and discussed by serious people. In associating itself with the art world and co-opting its techniques, the art music video both claims legitimacy for popular music and seeks to install the performers of popular music as serious artists.

Narrative Music Video

As the name suggests, the narrative video is defined by the fact that it tells a story. It can do this in a number of ways, but ways which nevertheless activate forms of visual narration that, on the one hand, variously illustrate, complement or extend the lyrical content of the song, or, on the other hand, function independently of it. A useful example of this is Tupac Shakur's 'Brenda's got a Baby' (1991), the lyrics of which tell the story of a twelve-year-old girl's pregnancy, abandonment of her baby, slide into drug-dealing and prostitution, and eventual murder at the hands of a client. The video which accompanies the song is almost entirely motivated by the desire to illustrate the story of the song, a story which itself is narrated in a linear fashion with a clear beginning, middle and end. The video begins with a black screen containing the words, 'based on a true story', thus not only establishing the expectation of narrative but also claiming legitimacy for the pathos of the story which follows. As we fade into a shot of a young black girl, clutching a baby, walking down the street, the lyrics 'I hear Brenda's got a baby' cue us to associate this character with the Brenda of the song.[28] Thereafter, key moments in the lyrical development of Brenda's story are narrated visually in a way which illustrates the song more or less literally. So, as Shakur's vocals inform us that 'her dad was a junkie' we see a character fastening a tourniquet preparing to 'shoot up'. Similarly, we are shown images of Brenda during childbirth, alone in a squalid bathroom, while Shakur raps 'she had it solo, she had it on the bathroom floor', and later as he tells us that, unable to cope, Brenda 'threw him in the trash heap' we see a shot of her dumping the swaddled baby into a garbage can. After being thrown out of home, getting robbed during a crack deal, and turning to prostitution to pay the rent, Brenda's story ends with a shot of a newspaper bearing the headline 'Prostitute Found Slain', a denouement reinforced by the lyric, 'prostitute found slain, and Brenda's her name'. BRENDA'S GOT A BABY, then, simultaneously operates as a coherent visual narrative in its own right in so far as it contains a set of clearly defined characters existing in a plausible fictional diegesis and a set of events which bear upon those characters, and, in conjunction with the song, as a form of visual narration inasmuch as it illustrates the narrative arc of the lyrical story.

The intimate relationship between the narrative of the video and the lyrical content of the song that characterises BRENDA'S GOT A BABY is not an essential property of the narrative video genre however. Indeed, other videos in this category display a far looser connection between image track and song lyric, or even no connection at all. Both Limp Bizkit's RE-ARRANGED (1999) and Audioslave's SHOW ME HOW TO LIVE (2003), for example, articulate stories that bear no relationship to the lyrics of the songs whatsoever. In the case of the former, the video tells the story of the band's incarceration for inciting a riot and we are shown scenes of the court case, the prison, and their ultimate execution. Unlike, say, Johnny Cash's 'Folsom Prison Blues' (1968) and '25 Minutes to Go' (1968), or Bruce Springsteen's 'Dead Man Walkin'' (1995), the song's lyrics are not about imprisonment and being on death row at all, but rather seem to be an expression of anger and pain felt in the aftermath of a failed relationship. The latter video presents its narrative through a combination of reworked footage from Richard C. Sarafian's 1971 film *Vanishing Point* and newly shot footage of the band driving through a similar landscape in the now iconic white Challenger of the film. What in *Vanishing Point* was Kowalski's (Barry Newman) road trip from Colorado to California, a trip which ends in his eventual death, becomes retold in SHOW ME HOW TO LIVE as Audioslave's own nihilistic journey. Most importantly in this context, though, is that the song's lyrical appeal to God for guidance has little, if in fact any, relationship to this existential narrative.

Most videos in this genre, however, fall somewhere between the literal narrativising of the story of the song, as in the case of BRENDA'S GOT A BABY, and the complete disjuncture between video narrative and lyrical narrative characteristic of both SHOW ME HOW TO LIVE and RE-ARRANGED. Indeed, most videos in this category combine un-narrativised shots of the band performing the song, shots which literally emphasise and/or visualise aspects of the lyrical content of the song, and a fictional diegesis that often works as an amplification of the story of the song which exceeds the limits of the lyrical narrative. Sara Evans's SUDS IN THE BUCKET (2004), for example, cuts between either non-narrativised or only partly narrativised shots of the artist performing the song and narrative sequences which tell the story of a couple's dismay when, to the delight of the local gossips, their young daughter elopes one morning leaving 'the suds in the bucket and the washing hanging out on the line'.[29] While many of the images are directly motivated by the song in the sense that they can be seen as literal visualisations of the lyrics, this does not hold for all of the video's narrative. Indeed, the fictional diegesis of the video regularly exceeds the story of the song by providing plot details not present in the lyrics. For instance, during the song's instrumental break and third chorus the images do not proceed from the lyrics but rather amplify the narrative by showing us events from the young lovers' story – events which are not part of the song. Moreover, the end of the video seems to reinterpret the lyrics in suggesting not only that the young girl was Evans herself but also that, having married her 'prince' and started a family, the story repeats itself in the next generation in relation to their own daughter.[30]

If SUDS IN THE BUCKET is an exemplar of the narrative video which combines performance footage with narrative sequences then Britney Spears's EVERYTIME (2004) is a good example of a video which adopts a somewhat different approach. For this video eschews performance in favour of a more or less self-contained linear narrative. Indeed, the few shots in which Spears is seen lip-synching to the lyrics are not separated from the fictional diegesis but incorporated within it. Furthermore, the video's narrative does not simply illustrate the lyrics of the song, or necessarily even amplify them, but, more complexly, it recasts them through their visual narration and, in doing so, affects their meaning. In other words, it takes what are relatively ambiguous lyrics about apologising to a lover and asking for forgiveness and anchors them in a much more specific tale of jealousy, desperation and, ultimately, suicide.

Narrative music video, then, can tell a story in a range of different ways and draw upon a host of different techniques to do so. Some are more or less literal visualisations of the lyrics, some move between images of performance and the fictional world of the story, and others present a far more unitary and self-contained diegesis. Either way, however, the use of narrative in music video is overwhelmingly deployed to authenticate an image of the performer(s). In other words, the kinds of stories told, the locations in which they are set, the characters they contain, and the style in which they are shot, work to confer legitimacy not only on the sentiments of the individual song, but more importantly on the place of the performer within the genre of popular music in which they work. So, whether it is the ghetto wisdom of Tupac Shakur, the rock rebellion of Audioslave and Limp Bizkit, Sara Evans' small-town country sensibility, or Britney Spears' pop-pathos, the narrative of the video positions the performer(s) within the symbolic landscape associated with specific musical genres.

Staged Performance Music Video

Unlike the other genres of music video which tend, albeit in different ways, to efface the commercial imperatives of the form, the staged performance video both embraces its promotional function and turns it into a virtue. So these videos do not offer an image of apparently unfettered reality, neither do they claim aesthetic legitimacy by appealing to traditions of art making, nor do they seek to tell a story. Quite the contrary, the principal defining characteristic of videos in this category is that they exploit a performance that is explicitly staged for the production of the video, that is to say, the performance of the song they depict is designed for the video and only takes place at all in order that it can be filmed. The performance, therefore, is always rendered as artificial: performers address the camera directly, often lip-synching into its lens; troupes of dancers perform choreographed routines in incongruous locations; action is removed from the real world and transplanted to studios and sets; and even space and time become ambiguous as linearity and verisimilitude are eschewed in favour of the sheer spectacle of the performance. Moreover, the artificiality of its performance is not only clearly signalled to the audience by the video itself, but its pleasures are bound up precisely with the invitation to watch the artists perform for the camera, and, by extension, for us. Indeed, through the choreographed display of song and dance, the staged performance video is often, though not necessarily, a self-conscious attempt to enhance the enjoyment of the song by both showcasing the image and skills of the artist it promotes and, in revelling in the possibilities of its own artificiality, by offering the viewer pleasures which are specific to the form – that is, of course, the pleasures specific to music video.

One of the most obvious ways in which the staged performance video signals its artificiality is by locating the action in a studio, and more specifically,

against either a plain background or within a highly stylised, often architec-
tural, studio space. Despite coming from a range of musical genres, Destiny's
Child's BOOTYLICIOUS (2001), JXL's remix of Elvis Presley's A LITTLE LESS
CONVERSATION (2002), Jet's ARE YOU GONNA BE MY GIRL? (2003), Justin
Timberlake's ROCK YOUR BODY (2003), Shania Twain's UP (2003), Kelis's
TRICK ME (2004), The Strokes's REPTILIA (2004), Snoop Dogg and Pharrell
Williams's DROP IT LIKE IT'S HOT (2004), Kanye West's GOLD DIGGER (2005)
and Kylie Minogue's I BELIEVE IN YOU (2005) all stage their performance in a
more or less empty space abstracted from the real world and with few, if any,
props. Indeed, Snoop and Williams's DROP IT LIKE IT'S HOT exemplifies many
of the features of this kind of video. The overwhelming majority of the action
takes place in the empty space of a brilliant infinity cove or against the equally
abstract void created by a totally black background. Moreover, even the few
props that are used – for instance, a glass of iced water, an ashtray, a scooter,
a boat, a Rolls Royce – are also abstracted from the real world and re-staged
in the monochrome emptiness of the video's space. Indeed, the staged nature
of the video and the performance is reinforced by the impossible presence of
a boat out of water and the gravity-defying angle of a parked car. The hyper-
stylisation of the video's design strategy also characterises the performances
within it. The video is organised around shots of Snoop and Williams, either
individually or together, lip-synching to the words of the song, shots of them
dancing, often with other dancers, and close-ups of the props which are sometimes directly related to the lyrics, but sometimes, as in the case of the dice and
the scooter, are not. Indeed, it is in the orchestration of these three principal
components that the video both reveals and celebrates its artificiality. For the
video makes it clear that what we are watching is certainly not a recording of a
single performance of the song but, quite the contrary, a complex montage of
a number of performances and parts of performances. The transition between
shots is motivated less by the demands of linearity and continuity than by a
desire to put its performers, and an image of their lifestyle, on display. So, in
terms of costume, it is not simply the range of different outfits that Williams
and Snoop wear in the video that is notable, it is also the promiscuity of the
changes between outfits that signals both the fractured nature of the performance and the blatant promotion of the Snoop Dogg brand. And it is not just
the clothing that does this, for a significant number of the props are either
related to Snoop's biography, as in the case of the drugs and the Crips' 'flag',
or, as with the skateboard, the scooter and the sneakers, to official Snoop Dogg
or Pharrell Williams merchandising and product lines. Crucially, however,
the whole performance is delivered for, or more precisely to, the camera,
thus acknowledging not only that its purpose is to be filmed but also that
the viewing of the performance is necessarily deferred. In other words, in its
stylised presentation of song and dance, motifs of Snoop's gangsta image, and

references to Williams' association with skateboarding culture, the video, as well as its audience, is always acutely aware of both its own artifice and promotional function.

Staging the performance in the abstracted space of the studio is only one way in which the deliberate artifice associated with this genre of music video is made apparent. Other videos in this category locate their performances on what is clearly a set, that is to say, a plausible location designed and constructed solely for the purpose of shooting the video. Yet others use real locations – common ones are the beach, the street, mansions, garages, underground car parks, rooftops, and so on – to stage 'unreal' performances, performances that are out of kilter with the environment in which they are set. Either way, what these videos do is stage their action, which is usually geared around the presentation of choreographed song and dance, in a natural environment or an environment built to look like a natural environment but in which, in the normal course of things, one would not expect to encounter such events. In short, when on the beach, parking your car, or just walking down the street, it is not common to see troupes of professional dancers performing in unison while someone sings a song. So, in the first instance, artificiality is signalled by the dissonance between the location of the performance and the nature of the performance itself precisely in so far as, in the last instance, this conjunction is self-evidently illogical and implausible. Destiny's Child's LOSE MY BREATH (2004) is a particularly interesting example of the way this kind of music video explores the creative potential afforded by the embrace of the artificial and illogical not only through the disjunction of setting and performance but by the very impossibility of that performance as well. On one level the video can be seen as a version of what Gow calls the 'song and dance number' in that it showcases 'the dancing talents of singers and supporting casts' in presenting the group lip-synching to the lyrics 'while physically expressing the rhythmic qualities of music through energetic and patterned motions'.[31] However, this in itself tells us little about the complexity of the way in which elements of song and dance are staged. Set in deserted city streets at night, the video begins with a backward tracking shot of the three members of the group walking in exaggerated step directly towards the camera. This shot not only establishes the space and time in which the action will take place but also sets up an image of the 'authentic' Destiny's Child, one which clearly draws on the history of their own representation both in previous music videos and in other forms of media as well. This is important in the context of this video because the next two shots introduce two other trios of dancers who, albeit dressed and styled very differently, are also clearly played by the members of Destiny's Child. Indeed, the video proceeds to present its song and dance as a stand-off between these two ersatz groups as each attempts to out-dance the other. As such, it is not just the mismatch between the location and the action that signals the artifice of the scenario, but its impossibility is reinforced as both the performance and performers are doubled through a combination of cross-cutting techniques and visual effects. Tripled, in fact, for the video ends with the return of the authentic Destiny's Child in a demonstration of their superiority and confirmation that the other two groups could only ever be Destiny's Child *manqué*. In this way, then, by activating such an illogical conceit, the video not only affords the audience access to three different song and dance performances by the group but ultimately works to make clear that there is only one genuine Destiny's Child.

The staged performance video is thus just that – a performance explicitly staged for the purpose of producing a music video. Unlike the other genres discussed above it does not attempt to either pass itself off as something else or, partly or entirely, disguise its promotional and commercial functions. Nevertheless, in a similar, though distinct, manner it does perform a number of legitimating functions. Most obviously, it directs attention to and works to legitimate the multiple skills of the performers it promotes. Often these will be the skills of song and dance and the vocal and physical attributes this involves. However, they may also be less palpable skills such as the ability to look a certain way or embody certain ideals or beliefs. For these videos allow their performers the opportunity to play out, and play with, an image of themselves and are, in the end, really only about exploring the possibilities of that image in relation to the musical genre which frames it. Indeed, what all of these videos do is stage a performance which authenticates an image of the performer that pre-dates the video in the sense that it has already been constructed and circulated through a range of mediated channels, but which is, nevertheless, confirmed and extended through the video.

Hybridity and Authenticity

The four genres outlined above describe the formal and aesthetic features of a significant number of both historic and contemporary music videos. However, this is neither to say that they adequately describe every music video nor that the categories themselves, like any generic category, are not subject to change and revision. Nor, for that matter, do we wish to suggest that the boundaries between the various genres are always clearly defined. Indeed, genres of music video, and the edges between them, are every bit as contingent as those in film, literature and, of course, popular music itself. Moreover, many music videos can be described as generic hybrids, drawing from two or more categories in a more or less self-conscious way. For instance, the Prodigy's SMACK MY BITCH UP (1997) uses restricted narration, a subjective camera, and deliberately shocking images – aesthetic techniques appropriated from forms of art film and experimental cinema – to tell a disturbing story about one young woman's drunken night out and the culture of sex and violence of which she is part. Similarly, Coldplay's FIX YOU (2005) also combines, in approximately equal parts, features of more than one generic category: the staged performance and the pseudo-documentary. The first half of the video is set in the eerily deserted streets of London and depicts Chris Martin, the band's lead singer, lip-synching to the song's lyrics. As in many staged performance videos, the direct address to the camera both explicitly acknowledges that the pro-filmic performance is staged solely for the purpose of producing a video and implicitly acknowledges the gaze of the intended audience. At about its midpoint, however, the video shifts gear and changes genre. For the latter half of FIX YOU operates as a recording of a live stadium performance inasmuch as it presents shots of the band on stage, images of the audience, and, ultimately, a soundtrack that slips from the studio-recorded track, which we hear for the majority of the video, to Martin's live vocal and the sound of the audience applauding and singing along. Indeed, the combination of pseudo-documentary and narrative which characterises Kanye West's THROUGH THE WIRE (2003), the mixture of staged performance and narrative diegesis which structures so many videos that feature songs which form part of a movie soundtrack, as well as the political critique of Eminem's MOSH (2004), which not only integrates aspects of staged performance, pseudo-documentary and narrative but does so through a complex mix of 2D and 3D animation techniques, demonstrate that hybridity in music video can occur along multiple axes simultaneously. This kind of hybridity, however, does not undermine either the conceptual constitution or methodological efficacy of the four principal generic groupings: pseudo-documentary, art, narrative and staged performance. Quite the contrary, this generic schema not only enables one to categorise and analyse videos which emerge as exemplars of their genre in relation to others of the same group but, just as importantly, provides a conceptual map against which border disputes are thrown into relief and patterns of hybridity can be charted.

Moreover, whether or not any individual video is singular or hybrid in generic configuration, it nevertheless remains the case that it will always perform some function of legitimation and authentication even if each genre does it in a different way. In other words, pseudo-documentary videos tend to privilege the skills of the working musician, the art video confers artistic credibility on the performer, the narrative video situates the performer within the iconographic landscape of the musical genre, and the staged performance video reinforces the mediated image of the artist(s) it promotes. And even if, generically speaking, hybrid videos are more complex, in the end they too work to situate performers within appropriate discourses of authenticity. This is why genres of music video cannot, and should not, be either collapsed into, or confused with, genres of music. For any one artist working in any one musical genre can produce videos across a number of music video genres all of which can, in their different ways, consolidate and extend the range of ways in which that artist can be represented and legitimated. One only has to think of the generic scope of the videos by artists such as Madonna, Michael Jackson, Eminem, Christina Aguilera and Robbie Williams not to mention a host of others, to realise that discourses of authenticity are no more tied to singular musical genres than they are to any given genre of music video. Indeed, the manufacture of authenticity in relationship to popular music is now far too complex to be reduced to either consideration alone. One final example will serve to illustrate this.

Arctic Monkeys are a British indie-rock band who achieved both commercial success and considerable critical acclaim following the release of their first single, 'I Bet You Look Good on the Dancefloor' in October 2005. Since that time they have been hailed in America by *Rolling Stone* as 'U.K. Rock Kings' and by *NME* in Britain as 'our generation's most important band', as well as winning a host of awards.[32] One of the most notable aspects of the story which attends Arctic Monkeys's rapid ascent is the way in which the band apparently bypassed the usual channels of public relations, marketing and promotion in achieving their success, favouring instead word of mouth, internet communication and the promotional activities of their fan base. Notwithstanding the exaggerated nature of some of the reporting of these bottom-up activities, what remains interesting is the ways in which discourses of rock authenticity accrued around, and became anchored to, the band from below, that is to say, not directly imposed by record companies and PR agencies. Given that the band refused many of the routine means of promoting themselves, in particular appearances on mainstream television shows, the videos which accompanied the release of their first two singles became a crucial means of both confirming and consolidating their claims to authenticity. These videos are generically and stylistically very different but nevertheless both work to sanction Arctic Monkeys's appeal to musical and political credibility by demonstrating that they have not 'sold out'. The first of these, I BET YOU LOOK GOOD ON THE DANCEFLOOR (2005), works squarely within the pseudo-documentary genre to establish the band's musical credentials. The video is seemingly shot during the recording of a performance of the song for transmission on a television show. It not only deploys many of the conventions of this genre in cutting between close-ups which emphasise the musicianship of the band and wider shots which situate this performance in a suitably low-key studio space but also uses the live soundtrack instead of the engineered version released as a single. As such, the putative realism of the pseudo-documentary video is mobilised to produce an image of Arctic Monkeys as an authentic live act who have no need for lip-synching, make-up and other artificial devices in order to be taken seriously. By contrast, their second video, WHEN THE SUN GOES DOWN (2006), establishes its legitimacy in relationship to the narrative video. Indeed, apart from one brief incidental appearance, this video does not feature any of the band members at all, but rather offers itself up to be read as a serious piece of social critique. It depicts the story of the experience of a young prostitute at the mercy of her pimp. We are shown the squalor and privation which characterise her life and the pain and suffering which she feels. Clearly, WHEN THE SUN GOES DOWN is making a quite different claim to the authentic than I BET YOU LOOK GOOD ON THE DANCEFLOOR, one which uses conventions of social-realist narrative to essay a political critique about the realities of contemporary urban life.

Taken together, then, both of these videos confer legitimacy on Arctic Monkeys as a serious indie-rock band, the former through the documentation of the realities of their working life and their musical skills, the latter through the association with a geographically specific musical scene, the band's home town, and a story about what it is like to live there. The main point here, however, is that two very different genres of music video perform an equally legitimating function for the same band in the musical genre in which they work. And it is this relationship between genre and the process of legitimating certain images as authentic which shifts the study of generic configurations of music video from being simply a taxonomic exercise into a much more complex intellectual question with potentially serious political implications. Indeed, this political dimension of genre is crucial in understanding music video's specific regimes of representation precisely in so far as the genres sketched here provide one of the key frameworks within which, and against which, formations of cultural identity take shape, become normalised, and, in some cases, are challenged.

NOTES

1. Dave Harker, 'Taking Fun Seriously', *Popular Music*, vol. 15, no. 1 (1996), p. 117.
2. Henry Adaso, 'A Guide to Hip-Hop Genres and Styles', *Henry's Rap / Hip-Hop Blog* (no date), http://rap.about.com/od/genresstyles/tp/HipHopGenreGuide.htm (22/06/2009).
3. Joshua Gunn, 'Gothic Music and the Inevitability of Genre', *Popular Music and Society*, vol. 23, no. 1 (1999).
4. See William Tsitsos, 'Rules of Rebellion: Slamdancing, Moshing and the American Alternative Scene', *Popular Music*, vol. 18, no. 3 (1999).
5. Christine Gledhill, 'Rethinking Genre', in Christine Gledhill and Linda Williams (eds), *Reinventing Film Studies* (London: Arnold, 2000), pp. 221–2.
6. Andrew Tudor, *Theories of Film* (London: Secker and Warburg, 1973), pp. 138–9.
7. John Fiske, 'MTV: Post-Structural Post-Modern', *Journal of Communication Inquiry*, vol. 10, no. 1 (1986), p. 74.
8. See E. Ann Kaplan, *Rocking Around the Clock: Music Television, Postmodernism, and Consumer Culture* (New York: Methuen, 1987); and Andrew Goodwin, *Dancing in the Distraction Factory: Music Television and Popular Culture* (London: Routledge, 1993).
9. Kaplan, *Rocking Around the Clock*, p. 58.

10. Carol Vernallis, *Experiencing Music Video: Aesthetics and Cultural Context* (New York: Columbia University Press, 2004), p. x.
11. Stephen Neale, *Genre* (London: BFI, 1980), p. 50.
12. Imani Perry, 'Who(se) Am I?: The Identity and Image of Women in Hip-Hop', in Gail Dines and Jean M. Humez, *Gender, Race, and Class in the Media*, 2nd edn (London: Sage, 2003), p. 137.
13. Moreover, as we discuss in the second part of the book, videos which promote hip hop songs which do feature the elements Perry sets out do not necessarily do so in the same ways or have the same political implications.
14. Kaplan, *Rocking Around the Clock*, p. 58.
15. Kaplan, *Rocking Around the Clock*, pp. 58, 59.
16. Kaplan, *Rocking Around the Clock*, p. 59.
17. Kaplan, *Rocking Around the Clock*, p. 61.
18. Joan D. Lynch, 'Music Videos: From Performance to Dada-Surrealism', *Journal of Popular Culture*, vol. 18, no. 1 (1984), p. 54.
19. Steve Jones, 'Cohesive But Not Coherent: Music Videos, Narrative and Culture', *Popular Music and Society*, vol. 12, no. 4 (1988), p. 19.
20. Joe Gow, 'Music Video as Communication: Popular Formulas and Emerging Genres', *Journal of Popular Culture*, vol. 26, no. 2 (1992), pp. 50–62.
21. Gow, 'Music Video as Communication'.
22. Gow, 'Music Video as Communication'.
23. See 'Afterword', in Simon Frith, *Music For Pleasure* (Cambridge: Polity Press, 1988).
24. Trinh T. Minh-ha, 'The Totalizing Quest of Meaning', in Michael Renov (ed.), *Theorizing Documentary* (London: Routledge, 1993), p. 99.
25. David Bordwell and Kristin Thompson, *Film History* (London: McGraw-Hill, 1994), p. 677.
26. Paul Wells, ' "Animation is the Most Important Art Form of the Twentieth Century" Discuss', in Paul Wells (ed.), *Art and Animation* (London: Academy Group, 1998), p. 3.
27. Lynch, 'Music Videos: From Performance to Dada-Surrealism', pp. 55–6.
28. Tupac Shakur, 'Brenda's Got a Baby' (Interscope, 1991).
29. Sara Evans, 'Suds in the Bucket' (RCA Records, 2004).
30. This strategy of cutting between performance footage and narrative footage in order to tell a story is a common feature of what Gary Burns calls 'movie-based music videos', videos which incorporate 'actual movie footage and become part of the promotional campaign for the film'. Examples of these types of videos include Bryan Adams' (EVERYTHING I DO) I DO IT FOR YOU (1991), Guns 'N' Roses' YOU COULD BE MINE (1991), Whitney Houston's I WILL ALWAYS LOVE YOU (1992), Wet Wet Wet's LOVE IS ALL AROUND (1994), Limp Bizkit's TAKE A LOOK AROUND (2000), Eminem's LOSE YOURSELF (2002) and Nickelback's HERO (2002). See Gary Burns, 'Formula and Distinctiveness in Movie-Based Music Videos', *Popular Music and Society*, vol. 18, no. 4 (1994).
31. Gow, 'Music Video as Communication', p. 59.
32. Mark Binelli, 'U.K. Rock Kings Arctic Monkeys', *Rolling Stone*, 10 March 2006, http://www.rollingstone.com/news/newfaces/story/9447897/uk_rock_kings_arctic_monkeys (08/04/2006); Tim Jonze, 'Arctic Monkeys: Whatever People Say I am, That's What I'm Not', *NME* (no date), http://www.nme.com/reviews/arctic-monkeys/7837 (08/04/2006).

3. MAKING IT REAL: AUTHORSHIP AND AUTHENTICITY

The question of authorship in music video, if asked at all, has tended to be posed either around the figure of the director as the controlling creative hand who stands behind the work or else around the figure of the performer as the artistic centre within the work. The first of these strategies for attributing authorship can be seen as an attempt to simply transplant the figure of the film auteur, which is itself really only a reworked version of the romantic definition of the artist, into the field of music video. In other words, following the dominant model of auteurism sketched out in Film Studies, certain directors are identified as highly individual artists who infuse their work with their own unique thematic concerns, personal vision and stylistic traits. Moreover, in arguing for the director-as-auteur one is also arguing for a fundamentally evaluative critical approach to the study of music video, an approach which not only distinguishes between those videos deemed as art and those dismissed as not art or non-art, but also one which seeks to discuss and adjudicate on the relative artistic merits of both the video and its director. The benefit of this strategy is, of course, that it redeploys familiar arguments about art and artistic worth to claim legitimacy and cultural value for what is generally taken to be a crude commercial form of popular culture.

This method of attributing authorship, a method which indexes the artistic worth of music video to the putative creative talents of the auteur, has been used to discuss and celebrate the work of a number of directors. Indeed, Heidi Peeters refers to 'the cult around music video directors such as Michel Gondry, Spike Jonze and Chris Cunningham' which she sees as a marker that music video is 'transcending the stigma of dull commerciality, entering the realm of culture, if not art'.[1] Such a claim is made possible, of course, precisely in so far as the auteurist method it is predicated on treats the director as an artist by linking their work to traditions of artistic practice – Suzie Hanna, for example, sees Gondry's videos as '"optical poetry" in the tradition of Oskar Fischinger'[2] – or else simply lauding them for their artistic skill and mastery of the medium. So, Steven Shaviro extols Cunningham's 'synaesthetic manipulation of sound and picture' in which 'sounds and images continually relay one another, respond to one another, and metamorphose into each other' and Scott Repass praises Spike Jonze's 'ability to blend several layers of intertextuality seamlessly' in creating his distinctive postmodern aesthetic.[3] And indeed it is perfectly possible to find both artistic creativity and thematic consistency across the oeuvre of both of these directors. Chris Cunningham's work, for example, is consistently marked by the use of digital imaging technologies to question the definition and limits of the human body. In contorting, distorting, shattering and violating the body, videos such as COME TO DADDY (1997), FROZEN (1998), AFRIKA SHOX (1999), WINDOWLICKER (1999) and SHEENA IS A PARASITE (2006) create a hauntingly surreal, often horrific, aesthetic of monstrous humanity. Whereas Cunningham's style emerges from a series of postproduction processes which digitally manipulate the photo/graphic image, Michel Gondry's distinctive surreal aesthetic, by contrast, is linked to the profilmic creation of fairytale dreamscapes in front of the camera often in real time. Indeed, the distortions in scale, the confusion between consciousness and subconsciousness, the anachronistically low-tech design of the production, not to mention the dream-logic narrative structure which characterise the videos for Radiohead's 'Knives Out' (2001), Björk's 'Bachelorette' (1997) and 'Human Behaviour' (1993), and Beck's 'Deadweight' (1997) and 'Cellphone's Dead' (2006), can all be understood as components of Gondry's auteurist footprint. Indeed, it is possible to trace both a thematic concern with the nature of reality and its link to consciousness and a stylistic technique which privileges the profilmic event and in-camera processes over postproduction visual effects across his work in music video as well as through a range of other feature films, shorts and advertisements. Similarly, Roger Beebe has employed this auteurist method to discuss the work of Hype Williams and Spike Jonze. In terms of the former, he claims that Williams's distinctive style came to define almost singlehandedly 'the aesthetic of hip hop video in the late 1990s'.[4] Moreover, despite evincing 'no unified style from video to video', Beebe goes on to understand Jonze's own auteurism as a specific form of 'metageneric' pastiche which draws not only on music video's past, but on the history of popular culture more generally.[5]

However, while turning to long-standing discourses of the art world and installing the figure of the auteur is certainly one way of claiming artistic legitimacy for both music video and criticism of it, it is not the only, or perhaps even the best, way of doing so. Indeed, there are a number of problems which arise from simply grafting the dominant model for understanding the art of cinema onto the study of music video. Firstly, the ability to unearth thematic and stylistic consistencies across numerous instances of any one director's output is incredibly rare. In fact, while the autuerist method of ferreting out such consistencies does yield results for directors such as Cunningham, Gondry, Williams and Jonze, on the whole the specificities of music video as a commercial form inevitably militate against this. This is not to say that there is not any number of creative directors working in the field, nor that they cannot or should not be thought of as artists. Rather, it is to make the more obvious point that the formal, generic and commercial imperatives of music video make it much less likely that a director will have the desire, or more precisely the opportunity, to develop a distinctive visual signature. Put crudely, directors who specialise in working in music video will not only produce many more films than a director working in cinema, but perhaps more importantly they will work with many different performers, often from a wide range of music genres, and by commercial necessity will prioritise the need to effectively promote the song over any desire to emboss the finished product with their artistic imprimatur. The result for many well-regarded and successful directors of music video is a long list of individual works which, even if they contain markers of creativity, will not cohere as an oeuvre marked by stylistic and/or thematic consistency. The second main problem really concerns the use of the auteurist approach in the first place. This is not simply to do with the fact that it tends to reduce music video to a sub-genre of film and its study to a sub-discipline of Film Studies, nor even to do with the knot of theoretical problems associated with defining singular authorship in audio-visual forms of popular culture.[6] Rather, the emphasis it places on the person deemed responsible for organising the look and feel of the images (the director) serves to marginalise or ignore both the people responsible for making the music and the people who perform in the video itself.

The second main approach to conceptualising authorship in music video starts from the other end, so to speak, in so far as it privileges analysis of the performer of the music, or more precisely their performance of the song in the music video, over the director of the visual action. Shaviro claims that 'In Western culture . . . the voice is generally taken to be a sign of interiority, authority, and authenticity.'[7] Indeed, Lisa Lewis argues that the soundtrack, and in particular the vocal track, often operates 'like a narrator's omnipotent voiceover' which guides the visual action. As such, it is not just the sheer presence of the performer, the fact that we can see them, but rather that we get to see them articulate the words and sentiments of the song that, for Lewis, encourages us to see them as the video's author.[8] The equation of performance in the video with authorship of it has been most notably and most extensively played out in relation to Madonna. For despite her working with a number of renowned music video auteurs – directors such as David Fincher, Jonas Åkerlund and, indeed, Chris Cunningham – the scholarship dedicated to understanding the 'Madonna phenomenon' almost uniformly presupposes that she is the author of the work in which she appears. In this respect it matters little whether she is being celebrated as the postfeminist icon who 'made it possible to articulate feminist ideas in an accessible (or indeed sexually provocative) style' or damned as being merely a 'material girl', a proponent of 'slut feminism' who has 'has marketing savvy in spades'.[9] For both responses are two sides of the same coin inasmuch as both are simply different readings of the same videos, videos which are themselves usually taken to be the product of Madonna's intentional creative ambitions. Indeed, it would be impossible to come to either conclusion without the presumption that Madonna was the guiding creative force behind the videos. On this view, music video can be seen as a key site through which the star image of certain performers is established and circulated. And while it is true to say that the overwhelming majority of work of this kind has been focused on Madonna, precisely the same model of authorship can be used to understand the videos of, say, Michael Jackson, Christina Aguilera, Björk, Eminem, Robbie Williams, Rihanna and Lady Gaga.

While in many ways this latter approach seems more attuned to the specificities of music video, it, too, comes with its own set of limitations. Firstly, the model of authorship evoked by this mode of criticism is no more theoretically rigorous or conceptually coherent than the traditional director-as-auteur model. Indeed, one way of describing this kind of work is as a form of star-as-auteur criticism. However, the relationship between stardom and authorship is more often than not presumed rather than established on the basis of theoretical or empirical analysis. In other words, the sheer presence of Madonna in a video, for example, is usually taken to be sufficient evidence of her authorship of it. Secondly, and relatedly, this form of inquiry demands the presence of the/a star in the first place in order for any analysis to be undertaken. And although this is an obvious claim it is no less important for being so. For not only is it predicated on an already established and relatively stable star image within which the performance in any one video can be interpreted, but in the second instance it requires the presence of a star as performer in the video. In other words, it is the a priori *fact* of their stardom that allows the critic to presume that they have control over the content of the video. The result of this is, once again, a critical strategy geared up to account for the exception rather than the rule. Put simply, the overwhelming majority of music videos fall outside of this critical purview in so far as they are neither made by stars nor feature a star. In this way, then, both director-as-auteur and star-as-auteur models of accounting for authorship in music video are not only rooted in the disciplinary vocabulary of Film Studies but also erect a critical strategy for explaining popular culture based on exclusivity. Ironically, therefore, they end up recasting a ubiquitous, everyday, popular product as a minority phenomenon. Or, more precisely, pursuing either of these strategies results in the attribution of cultural value to a limited number of videos that can be retro-fitted to these readymade models and leaves us with no method for thinking about the vast majority of videos that cannot. In many ways this is not at all surprising given that, like the more immediate model of auteurism it is derived from, the Romantic underpinnings of this concept of creativity are rooted in the traditions and operations of the art world which historically set the terms for distinguishing art from non-art. As such, to replay this critical strategy in relation to music video is just another instance of serving the same dish with a different sauce.

AUTHORSHIP AND AUTHENTICITY

One of the reasons why both of these approaches can only ever yield limited accounts of authorship in music video is because neither really ever attempt to deal with the music part of music video. In other words, by drawing on the critical vocabulary of Film Studies and the art world they overlook or ignore some of the key concerns of both the academics studying popular music and the audiences who enjoy it. And a major one of these concerns is the issue of authenticity – what it is, how it varies from genre to genre, how it is used by fans and critics alike as a key criterion for selecting, assessing and attributing significance to the music they listen to. These are, however, not straightforward concerns to address, for authenticity is not something that inheres in the music itself, a tangible property that can be easily discovered and measured. Rather, the impalpability of authenticity means that it is perhaps better conceived as an economy, or as Keir Keightley suggests, 'a value, a quality we ascribe to perceived relationships between music, socio-industrial practices and listeners or audiences'.[10] Neither the director-as-auteur nor the star-as-auteur model of thinking about music video, with their focus on the creativity of the artist, is able to deal adequately with the complexity of the question of authenticity. Indeed, Alan Moore argues that 'academic consideration of authenticity should . . . shift from consideration of the intention of various originators towards the activities of various perceivers'.[11] On this view, questions of intentionality, creativity and authorship become subsumed into the much more complex and important issue of authenticity precisely in so far as the presence of an auteur – director, star, or otherwise – does not in itself guarantee authenticity. This is not to say that they play no part in the creation of an authentic product, but rather that in both popular music and music video authorship and authenticity are constructed along multiple axes. In other words, authenticity does not inhere solely in the creative credentials of performers or directors but is, on the contrary, always 'ascribed to, rather than inscribed in, a perform-ance'.[12] Moreover, following the logic of this line of thinking, the attribution of authorship can only ever follow from, or be one possible by-product of, an already established authentic position. Put simply, within the field of popular music it is not possible to be an inauthentic auteur.

So while the discourse of authorship is important, it is trumped in the last instance by the process of ascribing authenticity. For, as Roy Shuker argues, it is authenticity that is the 'central evaluative criterion' in the appreciation of popular music, and authorship is a key means, but in no way the only means, of establishing that authenticity.[13] Indeed Shuker goes on to suggest that 'in its common-sense usage, authenticity assumes that the producers of music texts undertook the "creative" work themselves; that there is an element of originality or creativity present'.[14] As such, while it is impossible to be an auteur without being authentic it is difficult to be authentic without demon-strating the creativity of an auteur. And of course, there are a set of culturally and institutionally recognised procedures for displaying originality, creativity and individuality. As we have seen in the previous chapter, for example, dif-ferent genres of music videos can be used to situate an artist as, variously, an authentic member of a particular culture, a creative and artistic individual, or a skilled and talented performer. In this way videos can play a significant role in constructing and establishing an artist as authentic.

Michael Coyle and Jon Dolan argue that Kurt Cobain's authenticity as an alternative rock musician is based not on any innate personal or musical criteria but on his ability to respond to, and perform within, a certain set of discursive expectations.[15] In terms of the traditions of rock music within which Cobain worked, this involved establishing and maintaining an image of anti-commercial rebelliousness despite achieving significant commercial success. For, of course, 'real rock is always a rebellion, always a disrespect to the hier-archy, a blow to the empire'.[16] To be taken seriously, the rock musician has to display not only musical skill and creativity but also musical integrity and 'dis-respect to the hierarchy'. And they must display that musical integrity, moreo-ver, by simultaneously acknowledging their musical heritage and marking their distinctiveness from that heritage. Straw has argued that alternative rock is canonical, aware of its heritage, and dependent on it: to be part of alternative rock culture the musician must exhibit 'specific forms of connoisseurship' and knowledge of the genre's history, as well as making his or her own contribu-tion to that history.[17] However, it is not only knowledge that must be put on display. As Auslander points out, 'the concept of rock authenticity is linked with the romantic bent of rock culture, whose adherents want to imagine rock music as truly expressive of the artists' souls and psyches, and as consistently politically and culturally oppositional'.[18] To be authentic, therefore, the rock musician must demonstrably 'live' his rebellion.

It is in this context that music video, somewhat ironically, is now one of the key sites through which a rock musician puts both musicianship and rebellion on display. Analysis of Nirvana's IN BLOOM (1992) is instructive here, not only because of the way it achieves these ends but also because of its particular position in the band's career trajectory. Released to promote the fourth single from their breakthrough album, *Nevermind* (1991), the video attempts to reconcile Nirvana's by now considerable commercial success with the demand to disavow that success. The three previous videos which accompanied the earlier releases from the album, and indeed the original video for 'In Bloom' which was made before the album was released, all work to situate the band, and Cobain in particular, in the authentic 'down and dirty' milieu of Seattle's grunge culture. By contrast, IN BLOOM acknowledges the band's rapidly acquired status as a mediated brand, one which increasingly came to stand (in) for grunge itself. Operating principally as a pastiche of the popular US TV variety programme, *The Ed Sullivan Show*, the video opens with the host introducing the band as 'three fine young men from Seattle' who are 'thoroughly alright and decent fellows'. Shot in grainy, low definition black and white, the band is presented as a pastiche image of the kind of wholesome pop group that regularly appeared as musical guests on the show during the 1950s and '60s. With neatly combed hair, wearing matching suits, and presenting similar fixed grins, they strum their way through the song to the screams of the girls in the audience. The cross-cutting between shots of the clean-cut performers and images of the near hysterical audience continues until about the video's midpoint at which time an alternative narrative diegesis enters the mix and is intercut with the one already established. This second performance, however, does not feature the 'thoroughly alright and decent' Nirvana but the rough and ready, anti-establishment Nirvana. With long unkempt hair, and wearing frilly summer dresses and heavy para-boots, this version of the band sets about the proper work of the rock rebel – the systematic smashing up of the set and their instruments in angry protest. Both the video's premise and its action, therefore, work on multiple levels simultaneously. Firstly, and perhaps most obviously, the mobilisation of the wholesome image of Nirvana which begins the video, an image which functions as a synecdoche for the institutional machinery which seeks to transform the band into a marketable product, is really only there to demonstrate that Nirvana have not been co-opted into this model of capitalist business practice. In other words, despite the massive commercial success of *Nevermind*, IN BLOOM invites us to believe that the band have not sold out, are still in touch with their grunge roots, and are able to continue working as autonomous artists. Secondly, the video's underlying conceit itself demonstrates to the serious rock fan that Nirvana are aware not only of rock's musical heritage but also of the history of representing the genre which accompanies that heritage. For in its pastiche of *The Ed Sullivan Show*,

IN BLOOM is not simply critiquing the link between the mediation of rock and its commodification, but, more complexly, situating the band squarely within a tradition of performers who have appeared on the actual television show and achieved notoriety by not toeing the institutional line. Whether it was not removing the drug-taking reference from their lyric, as was the case with The Doors in 1967, not performing the prescribed song, as Bo Diddley did in 1955, or simply walking out in a manner akin to Bob Dylan's 1963 protest, a number of renowned rock rebels had used the buttoned-down conservatism of Sullivan's show to throw into relief their own anti-establishment image. Seen in this context, therefore, the video allows Nirvana not only to demonstrate that they are knowledgeable about rock's history of rebelliousness but also to present themselves as part of that history. Moreover, the acquisition of musical skill and knowledge of music traditions, not to mention a commitment to rebellion, are not frivolous undertakings but, on the contrary, require work and dedication. In other words, they are serious activities and, as such, impel us to take them seriously. This is no accident; as Keightley argues: 'serious-ness is the defining feature of rock, which must always be seen to be engaging with something "more" than just pleasure or fun. Rebellion, in this sense, is simply the most spectacular "something more." '[19] The video, then, despite its humour, is a serious attempt to ensure that the band are taken seriously as rock rebels and not dismissed as 'corporate shit'.[20]

Many of these discursive expectations which conspire to produce the authen-tic rock persona are, of course, generically specific. This is not to say, however, that appeals to authenticity are any less common, or any less important, in other genres of popular music. With the notable exception of mainstream pop, all genres of popular music have their own highly developed discourses of authenticity.[21] Whether the genre is defined by a relationship to a specific technology, such as the distinctive acid house sound of the Roland synthesiser; by identification with a specific location, such as the Manchester sound of the early 1990s or the Liverpool scene of the early 1960s; by anti-establishment attitude, such as gangsta rap or alternative rock, there is always something that marks the authentic and distinguishes it from the inauthentic. Indeed, Simon Frith argues that ' "inauthentic" . . . is a term that can be applied evalu-atively even within genres which are, in production terms, "inauthentic" by definition'.[22] It is possible, and in some cases even desirable, therefore, to be authentically inauthentic. The main point here, though, is that any discussion of authorship in music video simply must take account of the complex work-ings of authorship in popular music and its inextricable links to the notion of authenticity. For whatever other functions it may perform, the discourse of authenticity is the primary means of marking a product's difference from that deemed crudely commercial. Quite how that authenticity is secured, however, and who can claim in it in the first place, are not only complex questions but ones which point towards the political dimensions of authorship in/of music video.

In the discourses of popular music, cultural value and critical acclaim are rooted in what Laurie Schulze et al. refer to as a 'high popular culture / low popular culture antagonism'.[23] In other words, the same distinctions that have historically been used to differentiate 'high art' from 'mass culture' are replicated within the field of the popular to similarly separate out the valued from the not valued, the worthy from the worthless. Whether this takes the form of crediting new bands or genres with avant-garde ambitions or utilising Romantic notions of the 'artist-as-hero' to give licence to the integrity and sincerity of their musical expression, the result is the same. In any genre, music critics and fans adjudicate between the artistic and the commercial, the original and the formulaic, the authentic and the inauthentic. And these distinctions, although their precise implementation may vary between country music and rock music, hip hop and dance, are not simply specific to the genre or to popular music itself but rather are made along time-honoured lines. It is in this sense that Motti Regev argues that:

> Cultural forms gain artistic recognition when their producers of meaning 'prove' that they (a) contain 'serious' meanings and aesthetic genuineness; (b) they are produced by a definable creative entity and (c) the creative entity is autonomous, producing its works for their own sake.[24]

In terms of popular music the latter two are by far the most important. Within most, if not all, genres of popular music, bands or artists who are seen as authentic and credible musicians must not only play and perform their music but should also write it. By the same token, re-mixes and cover versions of songs must be distinctive enough to show the creative impress of the performers who rework them. Even in genres, such as dance or hip hop, where sampling – what Shusterman calls the 'proud art of appropriation' – forms a key part of musical production, there will invariably be a known and named 'creative entity' responsible for the finished track.[25] The converse of this scenario also holds inasmuch as, generally speaking, those musicians who rely on the services of professional songwriters are disdained. Song writing as a profession still has resonances of Tin Pan Alley and the factory-style production of music that that phrase has come to encapsulate. Indeed, to perform a song written by someone else is often taken to be a key marker of inauthenticity and lack of artistic originality and integrity. As we have already seen in relation to Kurt Cobain and Nirvana, performers of popular music, if they are to be taken seriously as artists, must go to great lengths to demonstrate that their music is not made with commercial intent even, and especially, when they have significant commercial success.

The political point of all this, however, is that the distinction between high culture/art and low culture/popular which underpins the discursive construction of authenticity and inauthenticity is not simply a mechanism for sorting good culture from bad. Andreas Huyssen argues that the distinctions drawn between 'high' and 'mass' culture have a long history in Western thought and that such distinctions have always been gendered. Within this binarism the masculine position has historically been associated with serious authentic art while the feminine has been located as the opposite – trite, frivolous and inauthentic.[26] It is the masculine side of these couplets which is given value while the feminine side is defined as worthless, or worse, ignored altogether. This way of thinking, a way which not only holds the feminine in contradistinction to the masculine but also values the masculine over the feminine, resonates within the field of popular music where those genres defined as masculine and dominated by men are the ones that are usually afforded value and credibility and the type of music performed by, and, importantly, enjoyed by girls and women is often denigrated. As Miranda Sawyer describes it:

> If large groups of women like an artist, that artist automatically slips down the credibility chart. It doesn't matter if it's Robbie Williams, Abba, Usher, Faithless – if loads of women like it, the unspoken logic goes, it's rubbish. If you're a band like, say, Blur, you have to shed your female fans in order to become respected.[27]

Moreover, despite some notable exceptions, women have been restricted to a limited number of genres of music and roles within them. There are now, and have been historically, more successful women artists in R&B than in hip hop, in pop than in rock. And, of course, R&B and pop songs are more likely than hip hop or rock songs to be written by professional songwriters and merely performed by the artist whose name is on the record. What is more, women have been singers more often than they have been drummers or guitarists; they have been dancers more often than they have been DJs. In other words, women often work in the roles and genres that are least likely to attract critical acclaim or artistic credibility and are, therefore, the least likely to be deemed authentic. If anyone is considered to be the creative entity behind this sort of music it is the songwriter, the producer, even the performer's manager rather than the performer themselves. The R&B or pop singer's lack of credibility stands in stark contrast to the position of the rock band members who write their own songs or the hip hop artists who perform their own rap. Given this, there remain really only two routes by which female performers are able to lay claim to some level of authenticity. The first of these was paved by singer-songwriters such as Joni Mitchell, Carly Simon and Suzanne Vega and is defined by the degree to which they able to retain control of the production, performance and (very often personal, emotional) content of their songs. More recently, this route has been taken not only by singer-songwriters such as Sheryl Crow, Aimee Mann, Dido, KT Tunstall, Lily Allen, Duffy, Lisa Hannigan, Laura Marling and Ellie Goulding, but also the women artists who write and perform under the pseudonyms of, respectively, Florence and the Machine, Little Boots, Bat for Lashes, and Marina and the Diamonds. The second pathway (which is not necessarily always distinct from the first) involves the cultivation of a star image and attendant public persona based on artistic eccentricity. If Nico, Patti Smith, Grace Jones, Kate Bush, Sinéad O'Connor, Björk, Tori Amos and PJ Harvey can be seen as staking-out the possibilities for this route, then Fiona Apple, La Roux, Amy Winehouse, Charlotte Gainsbourg, Paloma Faith, Jessie J and Lady Gaga have followed in their wake. At this point it will be fruitful to examine the work of two putatively similar groups to consider the ways in which this gendered difference is constructed around and through discourses of art and commerce, authentic and inauthentic, masculine and feminine.

In many ways the video ME AND MY GIRLS (2006) is unexceptional. Operating squarely within the conventions of the staged performance genre, it is set entirely in a studio and features four female performers lip-synching to the lyrics of the song and performing a range of choreographed dance moves. Formally, the video moves between both static and mobile establishing shots which situate the performers within the highly stylised space of the studio and in relation to each other, and a combination of medium shots and close-ups which take us nearer to each of the four members of the group. By focusing on a particular detail of the dance routine or accentuating moments of the vocal performance, these latter shots serve not only to individuate the performers but also to reinforce the hierarchy between them in so far as the performance of the lead singer, Yasmin, is privileged over that of Jade and Cloe, and to a lesser extent Sasha, who raps the song's bridge section. This tension between collectivity and individuality is also played out in the styling of the group. For the most part, the three principal performers all wear the same patterned black jeans and heeled boots. In these segments of the video, the girls' individuality is signalled by the variation in their vest tops and nuances in make-up and hairstyle. The introduction of Sasha not only marks a musical change but also a change in costume and performance style. With henna-patterned arms and bejewelled foreheads, wearing flowing silk skirts, ornamental belts and cropped tops which frame their bellies, the group perform a choreographed routine reminiscent of certain kinds of Middle Eastern dance. The final shot of the video, a close-up of Yasmin gazing provocatively out towards the audience as the image fades to black, both brings the action to a close and re-confirms her privileged place within the band and within the visual economy of the video.

In these ways then, ME AND MY GIRLS is not only an exemplar of the staged performance genre of music video, but also typical of a multitude of contemporary videos by either female vocal groups or individual women pop stars. Indeed, both formally and aesthetically, the above account could equally serve as a description of videos by The Pussycat Dolls, Girls Aloud, Destiny's Child, Rihanna, Christina Aguilera or Britney Spears, not to mention a host of others. But if, stylistically speaking, ME AND MY GIRLS is thoroughly unexceptional then in other ways, and especially in relation to the way it calls into question the very definition of the form it so comfortably imitates, it is quite remarkable. For Yasmin, Sasha, Cloe and Jade are not real flesh-and-blood pop stars but, in fact, children's toys: members of the Bratz™ range of dolls manufactured by MGA Entertainment. More precisely, the video features four animated versions of the 'passion for fashion™' dolls which, besides being a globally successful toy (more than 125 million Bratz™ dolls have been sold worldwide since their launch in June 2001), star in their own TV show, make movies and records, have their own magazine and computer games, and design a range of couture children's clothing, as well as licensing a whole host of related branded products and accessories which, taken together, have generated in excess of $2 billion in sales figures.[28]

However, despite five successful albums, a number of chart singles and a recent 'world tour', Bratz™ have never achieved critical acclaim. Indeed, the fact that they are animated characters with no human voice of their own would seem to militate against them being taken seriously as performers, as anything other than children's toys. They cannot write their own songs, they need human stand-ins for their live performances, they have no existence prior to or outside of their promotional and commercial role. Yet, although these factors would seem to self-evidently deny a band any claim to authenticity they do not always mean a band cannot be taken seriously.

Gorillaz, another animated band with their own range of merchandise (including clothes, books, computer games, dolls[29] and novelty items) were short-listed for the prestigious Mercury Music Prize in 2001 and have their work regularly reviewed in both the music and mainstream press. In many ways the different fortunes of the two bands exemplify the issues that surround the notions of credibility and authenticity in popular music and the way in which it is structured along both generic and gendered lines. So while Bratz™ and Gorillaz have in common their virtual existence, their commercial success and their plethora of associated merchandise, they nevertheless differ significantly in the way their existence is discussed and understood. For where Bratz™, the band, are seen as merely another product of a major manufacturing company, part of the Bratz™ brand, Gorillaz are the creation of an already established and critically acclaimed rock musician, Damon Albarn, and his collaborator Jamie Hewlett, a comic book artist with a cult following. Gorillaz, therefore, have a readily identified author for their music and their videos, a 'creative entity' with a voice to explain and defend their existence, while Bratz™ call upon the services of professional songwriters, people who also write for a number of pop acts such as Britney Spears, Kelly Clarkson and Jessica Simpson. Furthermore, the combination of the authenticity of Albarn's voice and the music that is produced in Gorillaz's name serves to situate them on the confluence of a number of critically acclaimed, 'high popular culture' genres – hip hop, house, indie rock, and world – while Bratz™ sit comfortably on the R&B/pop borderline. Moreover, Gorillaz conforms to a standard rock band line-up: one that is predominantly male and consists of a keyboard player, bassist, lead guitarist and drummer. As such, their virtual existence does not disbar them from critical acclaim but rather serves to enhance Albarn's status as an original and creative artist. As such, they provide an outlet both for his musical inventiveness and their anime-influenced art music videos serve to showcase the work of Jamie Hewlett. Bratz™, by contrast, are not only a clearly commercial product but one that is modelled on another commercial product – the girl group. Girl groups have played a significant yet half-buried role in the history of popular music. Their music has been a regular feature of the singles chart and their influence has been felt by bands from the Beatles onwards. They have, however, rarely been awarded critical acclaim to match their commercial success.[30] Indeed, the women in these groups are often depicted as nothing more than puppets manipulated by the men they work with/ for. So, just as Gorillaz are seen not as a 'creative entity' in themselves but as an outlet for Damon Albarn and Jamie Hewlett's creativity, the Ronettes' hits are often depicted simply as examples of producer Phil Spector's creativity and the Spice Girls as examples of Simon Fuller's managerial prowess. Moreover, not only do Bratz™ follow a typical girl group line-up with four singers/dancers one of whom takes the lead vocal, but the music produced under the name of Bratz™ is typical girl group music – chart music which appeals to a largely female audience. And their videos are typical girl group, chart music, videos with choreographed dance routines, fashionable outfits, and brightly coloured sets. Bratz™, therefore, are not merely computer graphics with no authorial voice of their own – they are a pastiche of other *real* women who are packaged as products and deprived of an authorial voice of their own.

AUTHOR ERASURE

This process of de-authorisation and de-authentication is important precisely because the question of who can be seen as the authoritative, authentic voice of a video impacts in crucial ways on how that video can be read. It is perhaps an obvious point, but one which is nonetheless worth stressing, that women who feature in videos as performers of their own song overwhelmingly tend to be afforded agency and identity, precisely a voice, in a way denied to other, usually anonymous, female performers, characters or extras. The women who we see dancing in the underground fetish club scenario of Christina Aguilera's DIRRTY (2002), for instance, are not permitted the same authorial influence or performative centrality as Aguilera herself and thus are figured very differently within the video's visual economy. A useful way of considering this point and its political significance is through an analysis of the two very different videos used to promote Khia's 'My Neck, My Back (Lick It)'. The song was first released in America in 2002 and emerged out of the genre of popular music variously known as Southern Rap and Dirty South Hip Hop: a genre renowned for overtly sexually lyrics and videos. Indeed, 'My Neck, My Back (Lick It)' can be understood as a 'sexual instruction' song in which the female singer outlines explicitly what she wants her male partner to do to her in order to give her sexual pleasure and, as such, fits neatly into the lyrical conventions of a genre in which sex, drugs and partying are the key lyrical themes. It is also a lyric that situates Khia as part of a long tradition of black women singers who have expressed sexual desires and demands in their songs – a tradition that stretches from blues songs such as Bessie Smith's 'I Need a Little Sugar in My Bowl' (1931) and Ida Cox's 'One Hour Mama' (1939) to the more contemporary 'Rock the Boat' (2001) by Aaliyah or 'Georgia Peach' (2006) by Rasheeda. And it is a tradition that is politically important. Gwendolyn D. Pough argues that 'by singing so freely about their sexual urges and desires the blues women worked against the policing of Black women's bodies and the politics of dissemblance'.[31] Similarly, Beverley Skeggs argues that by rapping about sexual desires 'female rappers turn themselves from sexual objects into sexual subjects. In doing so they challenge the basis of the social order which seeks to contain them.'[32] So it is possible, in this light, to see Khia's 'My Neck, My Back (Lick It)' as working within a number of discourses of authenticity: it situates Khia as a member of a genre community; it demonstrates knowledge of Dirty South's musical heritage; and it is political precisely inasmuch as it transgresses normative ideas of appropriate female behaviour.

The video that was used to promote the single on its original release in America in 2002 serves to reinforce this reading of the song by similarly situating Khia in the hip hop community and, more importantly, by making it clear that Khia is the author of the song's sentiments. The video is a staged performance based around a single scenario – a house party at which guests are seen to variously relax in the garden and outdoor pool, eat food from the barbecue, and, later in the evening, dance inside the house. This scenario is crucial in so far as it establishes a plausible, mundane context in which sexual activity could both take place and be discussed. The normalcy of the setting is reinforced by the way the partygoers are dressed and the way they behave. They wear everyday clothes – swimsuits by the pool, and jeans or shorts with t-shirts, vest tops, or bikini tops elsewhere. They swim, roll on the grass, cook on the barbecue, and dance – both individually and with one another. Within this setting Khia is squarely located as the author of the song's sexual demands. Not only is she the main focus for the gaze of the camera but at every turn her performance acknowledges that gaze and, by implication, the audience's own gaze. Quite literally, in fact, as even when she has her back to the camera she turns her head to meet us face to face. Throughout the video we see Khia lip-synching the words of the song. The sexual demands of the lyrics become Khia's own demands, embodied in her authorial voice and performance of in-control sexuality. For, in consistently returning our look and taking ownership of the lyrics, not only does Khia claim authorship of the song's graphic sexual narrative but also positions that narrative as part of a discourse of female sexual empowerment.

The second video released to promote the song in the UK and Europe, and the one that is perhaps now most readily associated with it, tells a very different story and has very different political implications in doing so. Indeed, in this video not only is Khia's authorship erased but a narrative of postfeminist sexual empowerment becomes very difficult, if not impossible, to sustain. For the video features neither Khia herself nor the house party scenario but is instead based around the performance of three stiletto-heeled, bikini-clad young women washing a bright yellow H2 Hummer. The first image that we see – a close-up tracking shot of the buttocks of the women as they walk towards the car – sets the scene for the video: these women are bodies to be looked at and are rarely afforded the opportunity to return the camera's/ our gaze. There are close-ups, in turn, of the rim of the steering wheel, the nipple-like button of an air-vent, and the polished surface of a wing mirror being slowly licked. One of the women polishes the car's phallic armrest in a manner redolent of masturbation and, with a knowing look, wipes a dipstick in a similar fashion. Another is shown in the back seat of the car rubbing the pipe of a vacuum cleaner seductively over her neck and cleavage. Any notion of active female sexuality is belied as the women themselves are shown to be the ones responding to the command to 'lick it', giving pleasure rather than receiving it. Moreover, in contrast to the original video where Khia is never caught unawares by the camera, we are constantly given access to isolated and objectified parts of these women's bodies. Indeed, for much of the video we are presented with a concatenation of disconnected body parts where the buttocks of one woman are replaced by the lips of another, and images of hands wielding wet sponges are followed by close-ups of thighs in an unidentifiable confusion of female flesh. All markers of the women's individual personality are effectively removed, literally washed away, so that all that is left are differently clothed, but similar, bodies. Difference, when it is marked at all, is marked by their colour-coded costumes and distinctive jewellery, serving, rather as it does in the Bratz™ video for 'Me and My Girls', as the key mechanism through which identity, or, perhaps more accurately here, non-identity, is signalled.

In order to make the video acceptable for broadcasting, both versions clean up the sexually explicit and crudely expressed lyrics by replacing offensive words with more socially acceptable ones. In particular, the words 'my pussy and my crack' are replaced with a breathy sigh and the words 'just like that' so that the chorus becomes 'Lick my aaah just like that'. It is interesting to see how this plays out in the different videos: how it works to reinforce a reading of Khia as a strong sexually assertive woman in the US video but serves to emphasise the passivity of the anonymous women in the UK version. As Khia is shown to sing the words – to her dancing partner, to the man painting her toenails as she lounges by the pool, to the men who surround her as she sings at the barbecue – the assertiveness of the original lyrics is not diminished. We see a woman making demands, telling her lover, or potential lover, what he must do to give her pleasure. The breathy sigh suggests that *she* is receiving pleasure, that she is confident that her demands will be met. And, throughout the video, the response to Khia and the demands she makes is positive: the men in the video respond with smiles and admiring glances. In the other video, however, no one woman is shown to sing the words of the chorus. The three women are only ever shown lip-synching to the discrete phrases of it. More precisely, one woman is shown mouthing the words 'my neck' while washing the door of the car, another mouths 'my back' while sponging the car's fender, yet another sighs breathily while leaning against the car and being sprayed with water. The men in the video, a group of middle-aged firemen who appear only towards its conclusion, respond very differently to those in the US version. They leer at the women as they wash the car, discuss them with each other and, ultimately, spray them with water from a phallic hose held between their legs at crotch level. With the money shot in the can, so to speak, the video ends as the hose is switched off and a trickle of water leaks from the tip of the nozzle. The disconnected words that the individual women are seen to mouth, and the sigh they are shown to make, therefore, become simply vocalised sexual responses rather than words with meaning. Instead of being a sign of pleasure anticipated or received, the sigh comes to indicate *re*action: no longer part of a demand for something to be done but rather a response by the women to something that has been done to them. The sexual assertiveness of the lyrics, where a woman is confidently and explicitly instructing her partner in ways to give her sexual pleasure, is, thus, wholly nullified.

So, on the one hand we have a clearly authored video where Khia is represented as an authentic voice of a music genre and the community associated with it, and as someone who has something to say about both the pleasures and politics of heterosexual relationships. On the other hand, however, we have a video where authorship is obfuscated, authenticity is elided, and the voice with something to say is silenced. The lyrics are divorced from any naturalistic setting and removed to a soft-core fantasy world where women's bodies are put on display, where commonplace actions are sexualised, and women themselves, as active agents, are effectively hidden in images of body parts and metaphors for male sexual gratification. And there are any number of other videos where the women who are featured are merely body parts to be looked at with no suggestion that they might have a voice or an identity outside of the video. In videos such as N.E.R.D.'s LAPDANCE (2001), Nelly's TIP DRILL (2002), Rocco DeLuca's COLORFUL (2006), or The Fratellis's FLATHEAD (2007), among countless others, the women who appear are clearly in supporting roles. They are objectified, in the sense that the focus is on their bodies and their sexualised performance, they have no voice, and they serve merely to enhance the authority of the male artists. Indeed, these videos make it quite clear where the authentic voice of the video lies – with the male performer(s) – whether this is achieved by Nelly's knowing glances at the camera that invite us to be complicit with his actions as he strokes, prods or showers money onto naked flesh, or Rocco DeLuca's constant presence as his image clothes the nude figure of a nameless woman and protects her from the camera's gaze. However, videos such as Benny Benassi's SATISFACTION (2002) or WHO'S YOUR DADDY? (2005), DJ Peran's WE WANT TO BE FREE (2003), Eric Prydz's CALL ON ME (2004), Junior Jack's STUPIDISCO (2004), Alex Gaudino's DESTINATION CALABRIA (2006), MSTRKRFT's EASY LOVE (2006), Michael Mind's BLINDED BY THE LIGHT (2007) and De Souza's GUILTY (2007), and many more, work in a way that is similar to the UK version of MY NECK MY BACK (LICK IT) in that there is no identifiable authorial presence in the video, simply an array of women's bodies and body parts. Any men who appear in such videos are, at best, peripheral to the action: they are there primarily to look at the women, and just as importantly, to be seen to be able do so with impunity. They have as little claim to the authentic authorial voice as the women they are there to ogle. By default, then, the authentic voice of the video comes from the men who made the music. They are the ones who are recognised as skilled within their genre. The music gives them the credibility to be the voice of the video.

What is important when we consider authorship in music video, therefore, is not simply who directed any given video or even who is seen to perform in the video but rather who can produce the authentic voice of the video. And who can have that voice is not fixed or stable – it may be the artist who made the record the video promotes, it may be the person who can be seen to lip-synch to the words of the song, it may be the director of the video. Who it is in any single instance, though, fundamentally bears on the meanings we can make from the video and the pleasures we can get from it. In the following section of the book we will examine how both genre and authorship interact with other discourses to produce ways of understanding the representation of gender, race and ethnicity in a range of music videos.

NOTES

1. Heidi Peeters, 'The Semiotics of Music Videos: It Must be Written in the Stars', *Image [&] Narrative*, no. 8 (2004), http://www.imageandnarrative.be/issue08/heidipeeters.htm (25/06/2005).
2. Suzie Hanna, 'Composers and Animators: The Creation of Interpretative and Collaborative Vocabularies', *Journal of Media Practice*, vol. 9, no. 1 (2008), p. 34.
3. Steven Shaviro, 'The Erotic Life of Machines', *Parallax*, vol. 8, no. 4 (2002), pp. 22–3; Scott Repass, 'Review', *Film Quarterly*, vol. 56, no. 1 (2002), p. 29.
4. Roger Beebe, 'Paradoxes of Pastiche: Spike Jonze, Hype Williams, and the Race of the Postmodern Auteur', in Roger Beebe and Jason Middleton (eds), *Medium Cool: Music Videos From Soundies to Cellphones* (Durham, NC: Duke University Press, 2007), p. 316.
5. Beebe, 'Paradoxes of Pastiche', p. 319.
6. For a discussion of the theoretical problems that attend singular conceptions of film authorship, see Berys Gaut, 'Film Authorship and Collaboration', in Richard Allen and Murray Smith (eds), *Film Theory and Philosophy* (Oxford: Oxford University Press, 1997), pp. 149–72.
7. Shaviro, 'The Erotic Life of Machines', p. 26.
8. Lisa A. Lewis, 'Being Discovered: The Emergence of Female Address on MTV', in Simon Frith, Andrew Goodwin and Lawrence Grossberg (eds), *Sound and Vision: The Music Video Reader* (London: Routledge, 1993), p. 131.
9. David Gauntlett, 'Madonna's Daughters: Girl Power and the Empowered Girl-Pop Breakthrough', in Santiago Fouz-Hernández and Freya Jarman-Ivens (eds), *Madonna's Drowned Worlds: New Approaches to her Cultural Transformations 1983–2003* (Aldershot: Ashgate, 2004), p. 174; Stephen Brown, 'Material Girl or Managerial Girl? Charting Madonna's Brand Ambition', *Business Horizons*, vol. 46, no. 4 (2003), pp. 8, 4.
10. Keir Keightley, 'Reconsidering Rock', in Simon Frith, Will Straw and John Street (eds), *The Cambridge Companion to Pop and Rock* (Cambridge: Cambridge University Press, 2001), p. 131.
11. Allan Moore, 'Authenticity as Authentication', *Popular Music*, vol. 21, no. 2 (2002), p. 221.
12. Moore, 'Authenticity as Authentication', p. 220.
13. Roy Shuker, *Key Concepts in Popular Music* (London: Routledge, 1998), p. 20.
14. Shuker, *Key Concepts in Popular Music*, p. 20.
15. Michael Coyle and Jon Dolan, 'Modelling Authenticity, Authenticating Commercial Models', in Kevin J. H. Dettmar and William Richey (eds), *Reading Rock and Roll: Authenticity, Appropriation, Aesthetics* (New York: Columbia University Press, 1999), pp. 17–35.
16. Coyle and Dolan, 'Modelling Authenticity, Authenticating Commercial Models', p. 25.
17. Will Straw, 'Systems of Articulation, Logics of Change: Communities and Scenes in Popular Music', *Cultural Studies*, vol. 5, no. 3 (1991), p. 377.
18. Paul Auslander, 'Seeing is Believing: Live Performance and the Discourse of Authenticity in Rock Culture', *Literature and Psychology*, vol. 44, no. 4 (1998), p. 5.

19. Keightley, 'Reconsidering Rock', p. 129.
20. Kurt Cobain, cited in Coyle and Dolan, 'Modelling Authenticity, Authenticating Commercial Models', p. 21.
21. See, for example, Sara Cohen, *Rock Culture in Liverpool: Popular Music in the Making* (Oxford: Clarendon Press, 1991); Richard A. Peterson, *Creating Country Music: Fabricating Authenticity* (Chicago: University of Chicago Press, 1997); and Tricia Rose, *Black Noise: Rap Music and Black Culture in Contemporary America* (Hanover: Wesleyan Press, 1994).
22. Simon Frith, *Performing Rites: Evaluating Popular Music* (Oxford: Oxford University Press, 1996), p. 71.
23. Laurie Schulze, Anne Barton White and Jane D Brown, ' "A Sacred Monster in her Prime": Audience Construction of Madonna as Low-Other', in Cathy Schwichtenberg (ed.), *The Madonna Connection* (Boulder: Westview Press 1993), p. 17.
24. Motti Regev, 'Producing Artistic Value: The Case of Rock Music', *Sociological Quarterly*, vol. 35, no. 1 (1994), p. 85.
25. Richard Shusterman, 'The Fine Art of Rap', *New Literary History*, vol. 22, no. 3 (1991), p. 617.
26. Andreas Huyssen, *After The Great Divide: Modernism, Mass Culture, Postmodernism* (Indiana: Indiana University Press, 1986), p. 52.
27. Miranda Sawyer, 'Why It's A Man's World', *Observer*, Observer Music Monthly, 20 June 2004, http://observer.guardian.co.uk/omm/story/0,,1240294,00.html (02/04/2007).
28. See Margaret Talbot, 'Spoilt Bratz', *The Daily Telegraph*, 28 January 2007, http://www.telegraph.co.uk/fashion/stellamagazine/3358500/Spoilt-Bratz.html (02/04/2007); Margaret Talbot, 'Little Hotties', *The New Yorker*, 5 December 2006.
29. Gorillaz 'vinyl figures' have been produced in a number of limited (albeit not small) editions and their packaging proudly proclaims that they are 'a work of art, not a toy'.
30. See, for example, Charlotte Greig, *Will You Still Love Me Tomorrow? Girl Groups from the 50s on* (London: Virago, 1989).
31. Gwendolyn D. Pough, *Check It While I Wreck It: Black Womanhood, Hip-Hop Culture, and the Public Sphere* (Boston: Northeastern University Press, 2004), p. 58.
32. Beverley Skeggs, 'Two Minute Brother: Contestation Through Gender, "Race" and Sexuality', *Innovations*, vol. 6, no. 3 (1993), p. 299.

PART II

SEXED, RACED AND GENDERED IDENTITY IN MUSIC VIDEO

4. MUSIC VIDEO IN BLACK AND WHITE: RACE AND FEMININITY

So far in this book we have been concerned, first, with exploring the current position of music video in both cultural and critical discourse, a story in which its sheer visibility in the former context finds curious reflection through its near invisibility in the latter. Second, we have sketched a broadly feminist and broadly poststructuralist conceptual framework for pursuing the analysis of music video, one that is attentive to its formal and aesthetic characteristics on the one hand, but also sensitive to its specific function and place within the sphere of popular culture on the other. This is the dilemma that emerges from the reading of music video which locates it as being exemplary of postmodern and postfeminist culture but as irreducible to either postmodern or postfeminist politics. Then, third, in offering a blueprint for a critical vocabulary capable of addressing this dilemma we have indicated some of the ways in which notions of genre and authorship work very differently in relation to music video compared to other forms of culture, and how, in turn, these ideas bear in important ways on how we can understand the pleasures and politics of music videos. We have not yet, however, been directly concerned with the ways in which music video, or rather individual music videos, seek to construct specific cultural identities more or less precisely and more or less coherently. In other words, while we have opened up the question of what Stuart Hall calls 'the "machineries" and regimes of representation' in terms of the aesthetic language of music video and the critical language of (post)feminism, what we want to pursue now is the ways in which such regimes and machineries might occupy 'a formative, not merely expressive' place in the constitution of social subjectivities.[1] In what follows, therefore, we consider the relationship between music video and cultural identity not simply as a straight unbroken line – as a litany of imposed subjectivities – but rather as a dialogic encounter between different identity positions which may variously be regressive or transformative, reactionary or progressive, nostalgic or yearning, and, of course, accepted or rejected.

It is in this sense that the present chapter takes up the question of the representation of raced sexual identity in music video. We argue that patterns of raced imagery that emerged from, and were consolidated in, Victorian discourses of colonialism and imperialism and which functioned historically to uphold and legitimate white privilege, continue to inform the very different ways in which black people and white people are represented in contemporary popular culture generally and music videos in particular. While the former are figured as essentially hypersexual and inscribed in the *fact* of the black body itself, precisely the whiteness of the latter serves to license a more fluid relationship to the presentation of the sexualised body. More generally, it is our contention that the specific generic codes of music videos render them particularly fertile sites for the exploration of the interdependent construction of race, sex and gender. For race is not only deployed within music videos to delimit or sanction sexual behaviour; sex and gender also signify race in ways which in some situations, perhaps even in most, tends to reproduce and shore up existing hierarchical power relations, yet in others can be activated in such a way as to call those relations into question.

WOMEN'S BODIES AND THE INSCRIPTION OF RACE

There is a moment during the video for Christina Aguilera's 'Can't Hold Us Down' (2003) in which she appears alongside rapper Lil' Kim. The scene is notable for a number of reasons which foreground a range of issues concerning the representation of gender and race, and their relationship to sexual behaviour. Situated within a clearly codified black urban space, the women are depicted taunting a group of predominantly black men alongside, and on behalf of, a group of predominantly black women. Their behaviour is both assertive and overtly sexual, and the video links both of these to a narrative of collective female action. The lyrics of the song they perform deal explicitly with the gender politics of sexual behaviour. For instance, Aguilera comments on the 'common double standard of society' whereby 'the guy gets all the glory the more he can score / while the girl can do the same and yet you call her a whore', a sentiment immediately reinforced by Kim who questions the hypocrisy which sees men able to 'give her some head or sex her raw / but if the girl do the same then she's a whore'.[2] However, it is not simply that Aguilera and Kim articulate lyrics which can be read as overtly feminist that makes the scene interesting, nor even the obvious display of 'sisterly' solidarity. Rather, the interest lies in the complex and contradictory ways in which raced identity is represented both lyrically and visually. For on the one hand the lyrics refer to a universal female experience (the consistent appeal to 'all my girls around the world'), while on the other hand blackness and whiteness are clearly inscribed on and through the bodies of Aguilera and Kim. Indeed, it is the precise nature of that inscription, a process in which Aguilera simultaneously performs whiteness and non-whiteness while Kim is seen to embody 'essential blackness', that not only problematises any straightforward 'message' of the video, but more generally serves to highlight the very limited range of ways in which female heterosexuality continues to be represented in popular culture and the way these representations are inevitably raced.[3]

In the context of CAN'T HOLD US DOWN, this process of racing the female body is further complicated by the way that authorship is established in the video. In the first place, the song *is* a Christina Aguilera song in the sense that she is credited with writing it, it appears on her album, and it is marketed as a 'Christina Aguilera product'. Kim's authorial role, therefore, both literally and figuratively operates in parentheses. She 'features' on the track but does so under the aegis of Aguilera – one could say that she performs to Aguilera's tune. This is important because, in the second place, it is Aguilera's authorship that is seamlessly imputed to the video and, more specifically, to her performance of non-white femininity. For not only is the video set in non-white space, what appears to be a neighbourhood of Manhattan's Lower East Side, but Aguilera's body is styled very precisely to signal a raced/ethnic identity that is at once indeterminate but determinately non-white. Her hair is dyed jet black, loosely permed and, for most of the video, held beneath a mauve baseball cap embroidered with the legend 'Lady C'. She is wearing pink velour jogging shorts that are split to the waist, a pink boob tube that exposes her navel, a cropped, sleeveless lilac sports jacket, and white knee-length sports socks with mauve high-heeled mules. Her eyes are thickly kohled, her nose is pierced with a gold stud, her neck displays multiple gold chains, and her ears flaunt heavy, nameplate golden hoops. The important point here is that Aguilera co-opts these markers of 'otherness' – the ghetto, the jewellery, the make-up, the clothing – in order to license a performance of femininity not easily accommodated within traditional definitions of whiteness. It is in this sense that tropes of ethnicity and race function, as bell hooks argues, as the 'spice' or 'seasoning that can liven up the dull dish that is mainstream white culture'.[4]

It is at this point that Kim's role in the video can be understood as a particular version of this co-option, what hooks refers to as 'eating the other'. On the one hand, Kim is able to author her own performance of black feminine agency enacted through sexual spectacle. Kim is first seen as she forces her way through the crowd of women wearing an exotically patterned bikini, a sheer black lace blouse worn completely open, an elaborately buckled leather belt fastened tightly around her naked waist, and gold-coloured stiletto heeled shoes buckled around her ankles. Her hair is long and wild, and her neck vaunts heavy gold chains. As Kim starts rapping the bridge section of the song we are offered close-ups of her body and thereafter her performance style repeatedly emphasises the fact that her body is on display to be looked at and admired/desired. On the other hand, however, this act of self-inscription is doubly bounded: constrained by the history of representations of blackness and subsumed into Aguilera's authorship of her own non-whiteness. At stake here, then, is what hooks refers to as 'culture's desire (expressed by whites and blacks) to inscribe blackness as a "primitive" sign, as wildness, and with it the suggestion that black people have secret access to intense pleasure, particularly pleasures of the body'.[5] The result of this is that Aguilera is afforded vicarious access to the bodily pleasures and vitality signalled by Kim's presence. However, to say that this desire is expressed by both blacks and whites is not the same as saying that the implications of expressing it are the same for blacks and whites in so far as its expression is framed by asymmetrical power relations. In other words, while there may well be benefits for both blacks and whites in exploiting the relationship between blackness and the primitive, it nevertheless remains the case that there are a greater number of benefits available to whites. In the case of CAN'T HOLD US DOWN, while Kim is able to author her own image as sexual predator, Aguilera is able to exploit Kim's parenthetical inscription of otherness to re-author her own identity as (non)-white. To put it another way, Kim's possibilities for self-determination are circumscribed by discourses of blackness (whether, that is, to simply adopt them, to embrace them, or to challenge them). The discursive resources open to Aguilera, by contrast, are various and fluid in the possibilities they offer for self-inscription.

It is worth pausing for a moment to remember that, as Patricia Hill Collins reminds us, 'contemporary ideas about race, gender, and sexuality did not drop from the sky'.[6] Indeed, the discourses activated in this video have a long tradition in histories of representation and it is only by attending to those histories and tracing those traditions that we are able to grasp the complex ways in which music video instigates patterns of raced and sexed femininity. In other words, black heterosexual womanhood has been historically constructed very differently to its white counterpart. For example, Anne McClintock suggests that there is a long tradition in European culture of equating Africa, and Africans, with the sexual that dates back at least to the second century AD. Moreover, 'by the nineteenth century, popular lore had firmly established Africa as the quintessential zone of sexual aberration and anomaly'.[7] More importantly, McClintock argues that 'women figured as the epitome of sexual aberration and excess. Folklore saw them, even more than the men, as given to a lascivious venery so promiscuous as to border on the bestial.'[8] Similarly, in his study of the iconography of female sexuality in nineteenth-century art, literature and medicine, Sander Gilman argues that black female bodies were figured as 'more primitive, and therefore more sexually intensive' than those of white women, and, more specifically, black women's primary and second-ary sexual characteristics, the genitalia and buttocks, were seen as primitive, as 'animal-like', a physical sign of an uncontrolled and, indeed uncontrol-lable, animalistic sexuality.[9] The exemplar of black womanhood, and indeed of blackness, was the Hottentot woman, a number of whom – most notably Saartje Baartman, an indentured servant brought to Europe from colonised Africa – were both 'displayed' in public exhibitions and balls and represented in advertising posters, medical literature and erotica throughout the nine-teenth century. Gilman suggests that contemporaneous scientific discourses, reinforced by patterns of cultural iconography and notions of the pleasurable, rendered black women's bodies inherently 'different', and indeed antithetical to those of white women. He writes that:

> The black female looks different. Her physiognomy, her skin colour, the form of her genitalia mark her as inherently different. The nineteenth century perceived the black female as possessing not only a 'primitive' sexual appetite, but also the external signs of this temperament, 'primi-tive' genitalia.[10]

These anatomical differences were initially reported by European travellers, but, according to Gilman, what was crucial to their legitimation as reliable markers of difference was the development of a putatively scientific, objective medical model which sought to discover and explain polygenetic differences between the races. Gilman cites the work of J. J. Virey, the author of *Histoire Naturelle du Genre Humain*, the then standard study of race, as significant in establishing 'innate difference' by recourse to apparently observable differ-ences of physiology and physiognomy. In referring to Virey's work, Gilman writes that 'their [black women's] "voluptuousness" is "developed to a degree of lascivity unknown in our climate for their sexual organs are much more developed than those of whites" ... His central proof is a discussion of the Hottentot female's sexual parts.'[11] As such, observable physical traits, or more precisely physical differences, were mobilised to construct black women not only as antithetical to 'European sexual mores and beauty' but also as 'the lowest exemplum of mankind [*sic*] on the great chain of being'.[12]

If the genitalia were a way by which hypersexed black womanhood was explained in medical discourse, it was the buttocks of black women that often provided a focal point in the display of black physical difference for the pleas-ure of the white Victorian onlooker. Indeed, the buttocks of the black female were interesting/fascinating simply because they were observable evidence of the putative difference between black and white women. However, the main point here is that the buttocks of the black woman 'function as the semantic signs of "primitive" sexual appetite and activity' and, in relation to the Hottentot 'as a somewhat comic sign of the black female's primitive, grotesque nature'.[13] Indeed:

> The presence of exaggerated buttocks points to the other, hidden sexual signs, both physical and temperamental, of the black female. This association is a powerful one. Indeed, Freud, in *Three Essays on Sexuality* (1905), echoes the view that female genitalia are more primitive than those of the male for female sexuality is more anal than that of the male. Female sexuality is linked to the image of the buttocks, and the quintessential buttocks are those of the Hottentot.[14]

In other words, Victorian discourses of evolution, of medicine, of colonisation and exploration, and of the nature of sexual desire combined and focused on the materiality of the buttocks of black women in a way that rendered those women sexual, dangerous and Other. Black women's bodies were made available to be looked at, exhibited in their nakedness at a time when white women's bodies were corseted, covered and hidden. In mapping *availability* on to black women's bodies and *unavailability* on to the bodies of white women, it was black women that were presented as fascinating curiosities for the entertainment of a white audience.

While nineteenth-century discourses were constructing black women as animalistically hypersexed bodies, accessible for scrutiny and pleasure, those same discourses were simultaneously constructing white women as, on the one hand, civilised and restrained, and on the other hand as fragile bodies in need of protection from the sexual.[15] Indeed, Rose Weitz argues that the notion of white women's bodies as fragile went hand-in-hand with an emphasis on the importance of romantic love for women, thus regulating and delimiting (white) female sexual desire and behaviour.[16] Crucial here is the production of white women as asexual, that is to say as precisely above and beyond the base needs and desires of the 'primitive' body. Indeed, as Dyer suggests, 'the model for white women is the Virgin Mary, a pure vessel for reproduction who is unsullied by the dark drives that reproduction entails', a notion that, when stretched to its extreme, implies that even thinking about white women and sexual activity becomes 'scandalous and virtually sacrilegious'.[17] White women are, therefore, positioned as responsible for the restriction of sexual behaviour, the control of male sexual drives and impulses. White women's bodies not only function symbolically as 'the unattainable' but also, in practice, are only ever attainable through the protocols of courtship, romantic love and marriage. In other words, access to the purity of the white female body is something that can be achieved if, and only if, the institutionalised barriers that protect it are successfully overcome. The achievement of the pure, white, female body not only renders it the property of the deserving (white) man but also locates that purity at the centre of racialised power hierarchies. Indeed, the white female was placed at the centre of a number of prominent nineteenth-century discourses of power. Just as the purity of white women undergirded the institution of marriage, it was also integral to narratives of empire and imperialism in so far as the white woman was located as 'the locus of true whiteness' while the white man struggled in dark continents, 'yearning for home and whiteness, facing the dangers and allures of darkness'. As such, 'male imperialism is presented as done for white women as . . . the literal and socialising reproducers of the race'.[18]

However, it was not only white men who faced the 'dangers of darkness'. White women, throughout the nineteenth century, were a significant presence in colonised lands. Their role as the guardians of sexual morals and cultural refinement, sustained by the presumed asexuality of their bodies and their embodiment of virtue, positioned them not only as the civilised but also as the civilisers, that is to say, the principal agents through which the process of 'civilising primitive peoples' was enacted. At least in part, this 'civilising of primitive peoples' was enacted through the introduction of Victorian domesticity into colonised lands. As McClintock argues, 'In the colonies . . . the mission station became a threshold institution for transforming domesticity rooted in European gender and class roles into domesticity as controlling a colonised people.'[19] Indeed, the rituals of domesticity were defined around the presence of the bodies of white women as the wives, daughters, sisters and so on, of white men. And it was precisely through such rituals of European domesticity that the colonies were to be cleansed of 'savagery', 'ignorance' and 'primitive' ways. Such cleansing was not only a metaphor for the process of colonisation generally, but the colonies, by reverse implication, were symbolically located, themselves, as sites of dirt, filth and contamination that were in need of cleaning. Cleanliness and imperialism thus became mutually reinforcing discourses, an idea illustrated in much of the advertising for soap and other cleaning products of the time. As McClintock herself suggests, soap was figured as 'a technology of social purification, inextricably entwined with the semiotics of imperial racism'.[20] Indeed, 'soap and cleaning rituals became central to the demarcation of body boundaries and the policing of social hierarchies'.[21]

If in such advertisements black people signified simultaneously dirtiness and savagery then, by contrast, white people, and especially white women, epitomised cleanliness, purity, even civilisation itself. One advertisement for Sunlight Soap, for example, depicts two white Victorian ladies, immaculately dressed in elegant gowns, standing on either side of a pitcher and bowl, washing dishes in a spotlessly clean kitchen. The skin of their neck and shoulders is surpassed in its whiteness only by the brilliance of their dresses. Indeed, the leg-of-mutton sleeves and full skirts of those dresses irradiate the scene with a whiteness which is reflected in the sheen of the polished floor, the lustre of the porcelain crockery, and the mirror of the water. This one incongruous image of Victorian domesticity, to a large extent, exemplifies what McClintock calls the 'four beloved fetishes' of civilisation – soap, the mirror, light and white clothing.[22]

Of course, this process of physically and symbolically deploying the white woman as the domesticator and civiliser was not without risk: placing the pure, white, female body in such unknown and hazardous contexts redoubles its fragility. For empire was not only acquired by white men for white women, but the putative frangibility of the white female body underpinned imperial practices and policies. The sanctity of the body was always vulnerable and in need of protection, for any violation of it was also an attack on civilisation itself. As Vron Ware suggests:

> One of the recurring themes in the history of colonial repression is the way in which the threat of real or imagined violence towards white women became a symbol of the most dangerous form of insubordination . . . Protecting the virtue of white women was the pretext for instituting draconian measures against indigenous populations in several parts of the Empire . . . White women provided a symbol of the most valuable property known to white man and it was to be protected from the ever-encroaching and disrespectful black man at all costs.[23]

As such, the defence of white women's bodies was intimately bound up not only with the establishment and protection of civilisation itself, but also the control and repression of black people.

These imperial discourses are only one branch of a long tradition of cultural representation which produces white and black womanhood as very different. Much of this difference turns upon a series of binary oppositions, oppositions which both disguise the complexities of lived experience and structure thinking in ways which tend to both mask and shore up hierarchies of power. Simply stated, within this tradition of representation, white women are defined by sexual sublimity in direct contrast to the presumed hypersexuality of black women. On the one hand, black women's 'hypersexuality' is seen to derive from a series of apparently natural traits that link them to the animal, the primitive and the 'dirty'. In defining the black woman first and foremost through a series of physical characteristics, her body is not only made available to both white and black men but the buttocks of that body are figured as emblematic of black womanhood generally and the icon of black female sexuality more precisely. White women's sublimity, on the other hand, is seen precisely as a product of civilisation, a process by which the natural is regulated, ordered and thus mastered. This process produces white womanhood itself around a policed and policing body, a body which is typified by qualities of restraint, virtue and cleanliness. If black female sexuality is literally embodied in voluptuous black buttocks, then, by contrast, white female sexuality is, strictly speaking, not embodied in frangible corporeality at all, but is rather displaced, and ideally replaced, by a fascination with the purity of 'clean white bodies and clean white clothing'.[24]

None of this is to suggest that these patterns of raced representation began in the nineteenth century, nor that they have simply re-emerged with the inception of the music video. On the contrary, it is possible to trace the genealogy of these definitions of blackness and whiteness from the Victorian era to the present day through various forms of popular culture. For example, both lyrically and in terms of performance, the collocation of black female sexuality, the animal and the feral has been a continuing, albeit not always dominant, feature of black music during the twentieth century – not only the music produced by black men but also that produced by black women artists as well. Such a continuation can be mapped through analysis of artists such as Josephine Baker, Eartha Kitt, Tina Turner, Grace Jones and Mel B (Scary Spice), who make explicit use of animals/animal skins in the presentation of themselves as sexual women, and finds its contemporary expression in performers such as Ashanti, Mary J. Blige, Destiny's Child, Rihanna, Alicia Keys, Kelis and, perhaps most strikingly, as we discuss below, the solo work of Beyoncé Knowles. By the same token, the representation of white female sexuality as controlled, 'civilised', and/or fragile, although often more difficult to *see*, is nevertheless visible in the 'appearance' of vulnerability found in artists such as Twinkle and Marianne Faithfull from the 1960s and the 'inaccessibility' of the glamorous and sophisticated women singers of the 1940s and 1950s such as Peggy Lee or Jo Stafford. Think, for example, of the 'untouchability' of singer Julie London in the 1956 film *The Girl Can't Help It*, where she appears only as a vision haunting the male lead. It is this sense of the unobtainability of white women that finds its contemporary manifestation in artists such as Lady Gaga, Sophie Ellis-Bextor, Duffy, La Roux, Little Boots and, most notably, Kylie Minogue.

The main point here, however, is that many of the iconographical markings of whiteness and blackness which characterised nineteenth-century scientific, artistic and commercial modes of representation, and which have been replayed in every generation of the twentieth century, continue, albeit in modified form, to structure much contemporary cultural production. Indeed, given the number of social and political changes that have impacted on women's lived experiences since the Victorian era, there is a surprising, and potentially worrying, continuity in the way in which women's raced identity is represented. We now want to discuss some of the ways in which these patterns of raced representation are reproduced in music videos. More specifically we will discuss videos by two contemporary pop stars, Beyoncé Knowles and Kylie Minogue.

The videos we shall discuss are Knowles's BABY BOY (2003) and Minogue's CAN'T GET YOU OUT OF MY HEAD (2001). The comparison between the visual representation of the singers is particularly revealing given that, on the one the hand, they have a number of striking lyrical and generic similarities which, on the other hand, only serve to highlight the very different ways in which they instigate raced femininity. In the first instance, the sentiments of the songs are practically identical in so far as the lyrics of both deal with sexual obsession and fantasy. (Minogue's 'I can't get you out of my head / boy your loving is all I think about' is matched by Knowles's 'I think about you all the time / I see you in my dreams'.) In the second place, and perhaps more importantly, both are staged performance videos, a generic mode that not only legitimates the skills of the singers but also authenticates their respective star images. In other words, these videos stage specific performances of Knowles's and Minogue's personae which mobilise images of and ideas about the performers that pre-date the videos themselves. What is being authenticated through the same process, therefore, is two very different versions of contemporary heterosexual femininity. Indeed, it is precisely the different positions that Knowles and Minogue occupy on the spectrum of raced representation that permits us to use these videos as 'ideal types', an analytical move which then allows a series of further comparisons to be mapped. 'Ideal type' is used here in a Weberian sense, not to imply a model of perfection, something that can or should be attained, but rather as a conceptual or abstract model that is used for analytical purposes to reveal aspects of the world that might otherwise remain obfuscated. Indeed, Weber stresses that 'in its conceptual purity, this mental construct cannot be found empirically anywhere in reality'.[25] Nevertheless, as a heuristic device for describing and explaining the world, ideal types allow us to make interesting comparisons between the 'type' and the 'real'. It is in this sense that BABY BOY and CAN'T GET YOU OUT OF MY HEAD function as ideal types. For not only do they rehearse corresponding sides of the binarism which serves to codify representations of black and white as internally cohesive categories, but comparative analysis makes visible the different ways in which blackness and whiteness are constructed through forms of cultural representation.

THE FERINE AND THE FIGURINE

bell hooks suggests that popular music is one of the primary cultural locations for representations of black female sexuality. She argues that, 'although contemporary thinking about black female bodies does not attempt to read the body as a sign of "natural" racial inferiority, the fascination with black "butts" continues [in so far as] . . . the protruding butt is seen as an indication of a heightened sexuality'.[26] Take, for instance, the lyrical observation in Mos Def's 'Ms Fat Booty' which celebrates an 'ass so fat you can see it from the front', the titular instructions of songs such as Marques Houston's 'Pop that Booty' and Kesha's 'Booty Call', or the exaltation of the 'black butt' in Destiny's Child's 'Bootylicious', Bubba Sparxxx's 'Ms New Booty' and Notorious B.I.G.'s 'Big Booty Hoes'.[27] Moreover, while lyrics of this kind very often motivate a visual corollary in their related videos, music videos nevertheless do not always require such motivation in order to display black women's bodies and, in particular, their 'butts'. Wayne Wonder's NO LETTING GO (2003), Beenie Man's KING OF THE DANCEHALL (2004), Timbaland and Justin Timberlake's CARRY OUT (2009) and Nelly's AIR FORCE ONES (2002) feature different lyrical concerns (respectively, an apology for infidelity, a sexual braggadocio, a flirtatious seduction and a paean to Nike sneakers) but all contain images of black women 'booty dancing'. One particularly good example of the way that black women's butts function as a synecdoche of their putative hypersexuality is the way the lyrics for Ludacris's 'P-Poppin'' are 'cleaned up' and how this translates to their articulation in music video. The song is about a particular kind of sexual transaction called 'pussy poppin''. It features two male performers (Ludacris and Lil' Fate) who rap about paying women to 'pop their pussy', a kind of sexual performance focusing around the display of the vagina for the pleasure of the male customer, and one female performer (Shawnna) who raps about the economic gains to be made by women engaging in the transaction. In terms of the 'clean up', the only substantive adjustment made to what are crudely sexual lyrics is that the word 'pussy' is replaced by 'booty'. Ironically, therefore, this act, seemingly done in the interests of censorship, ends up reconfirming the 'butt' as the key marker of black women's heightened sexuality. Moreover, analysis of either of the associated music videos reinforces this reading. For it matters little if one studies the censored or uncensored version – the principal difference, apart from the lyrical substitution, is that there are greater levels of absolute nudity in the latter – precisely inasmuch as the main focus of both is images, often in close-up, of near-naked black butts shaking for the pleasure of the male rappers and, by extension, of the male audience. In this sense, then, hooks's account of black female sexuality and, in particular, its equation with the butt remains intact, undiluted and unambiguous.

However, while the 'protruding black butt' undoubtedly remains an important lyrical and visual feature of music videos a number of other tropes also link these contemporary representations of blackness back to Victorian modes of raced representation. Indeed, through regular and explicit references to the natural and the animal, the black female body and black sexuality continue to be figured as primal, wild and uncontrollable. To some extent these images appeal to a culture which is, as hooks suggests, 'eager to reinscribe the image of black woman as sexual primitive'.[28]

The video for Knowles's 'Baby Boy' (2004) can be seen as an exemplar of this mode of representing black female sexuality. There are a number of inter-related aspects to this. Most obviously, the locations used in the video either imply 'nature' or they are set directly in nature. For the most part, the video is shot out of doors *in* nature – the jungle, the beach and the ocean. Where the action takes place indoors there is always the threat that the outside will encroach: boundaries between indoor and outdoor are blurred by the use of 'natural' materials in the architecture (wood, leather, fur), and, moreover, the use of louvered walls confuses any clear demarcation between inside and outside. In fact, so flimsy is this physical boundary that the elements regularly breech it and find their way inside. Not only is the wind seen to blow the hair of the dancers, but also, in one remarkable shot, the ocean floods the dance-floor and washes over the feet of the women as they dance. Furthermore, the action in the video takes place either at twilight or, predominantly, at night and is lit in such a way that the body of Knowles, and the other performers, is often partially obfuscated by the darkness rendering any distinction between the body and its environment uncertain. Indeed, the darkness often envelopes the frame entirely, acting as a moment of transition between different (parts of) bodies and locations.

However, although the 'naturalness' of the locations is important in itself, it is the way that locations act to define the body, interact with the body, and situate the performing body that is interesting here. Indeed, Knowles's feet sink into the sand, her skin sweats from the heat, her hair is blown by the wind and soaked by the water, and, at one point, her whole body is seen half-submerged in the ocean. This interaction between the body and the environment not only functions to equate the black woman with/as nature but also works to establish the possibilities of and limits to performance. The untamed landscape is matched by the 'untamed' and 'uncontrolled' body of Knowles. Most notably, this uncontrollability is focused around her buttocks and her hair. Whether turned towards the camera, repeatedly and rapidly shaken during dance routines, or simply protruding from beneath her clothes, her buttocks are constantly moving and on display. Her hair, too, is in constant motion. Whether straightened or curly, loose or tied, wet or dry, and regardless of whether her body is moving or not, her hair moves or is moved: it swings as she walks, it is shaken as she dances, it is blown by the wind and fans, and it is brushed across, or away from, her face and mouth. Indeed, as hooks argues, the cascading hair of black female singers is designated as a key marker of their sexualised personae and, in fact, along with the buttocks, signifies 'animalistic sexuality'.[29]

Moreover, the many outfits that Knowles wears in the video reveal her flesh, or more precisely the very *fleshiness* of her flesh. For example, she wears a number of different skirts that are short, sit low on the hips and are split from top to bottom on both sides. As she moves the skirts move to reveal the buttocks and emphasise the voluptuousness of her thighs. By the same token, the array of tops that she wears always allows access to both the movement of her breasts and to the flesh of the stomach and her navel. As such, it is not just Knowles's body that writhes, ripples, shakes and bounces but her flesh too. The costumes are designed so that we always have access to the fleshiness of the naked black body; an unruly body, that like the hair, is in constant, involuntary motion.

The final scene of the video, in which Knowles performs a dance routine on the beach at night, is a heady distillation of the ways in which the conventions of the music video continue to represent black female sexuality as feral and animalistic. This scene is especially interesting inasmuch as the performance is not motivated by the demand to add an image track to the published music track – the standard conception of the music video. In other words, the music which accompanies this sequence is, in fact, a coda, operating in excess of the audio track as it is released on CD, its presence merely licensing the availability of Knowles to the desires of the spectator. As such, in uncoupling the performance in the video from the performance on the audio track, the video, and especially this final self-contained scene, can be seen as a privileged site where the conventions of representing black female sexuality *visually*, through the display of Knowles's body, are literally put on display.

Wearing only a bikini, and lit by flaming torches – fire being the only element that hitherto has not explicitly been visually depicted in the video – she is shown crawling, catlike, through the sand, and, later, rolling and writhing in it orgasmically. She is sweating and dirty with the sand that sticks to her, further breaching the boundary between her body and nature itself. Moreover, her movements become increasingly frenetic and frenzied as the sequence progresses, her 'out-of-control-ness' climaxing when she grabs a handful of sand and flings it towards the spectator. What this sequence, along with the rest of the video, enacts is a reinscription of black female sexuality as first and foremost hypersexuality – primitive, feral, uncontrolled and uncontrollable. Moreover, its very uncontrollability reinscribes the black female body as available, literally to the look of the spectator and symbolically to the desires and fantasies of both black and white men.

While crude, the contrast between the video for Knowles's 'Baby Boy' and the video for Minogue's 'Can't Get You Out of My Head' is nevertheless instructive. For if the former produces black female (hyper)sexuality as wild, savage and animalistic, then the latter is no less proficient in producing white female sexuality as pure, restrained and controlled. Indeed, if on the one hand both women perform seduction and sexual attractiveness, on the other hand the nature of that performance is very different vis-à-vis their putative sexual availability: Knowles represents a universal availability, while Minogue's availability is always provisional, restricted and contingent. In the end, the conception of white female sexuality inscribed in and through Minogue's body differs little from the one which emerged out of Victorian and colonial discourses.

The video opens with Minogue, sitting at the wheel of a car, driving into a futuristic metropolis typified by both the clinical environment of the city and the clean lines of its skyline. Indeed, both the evident architectonic space and the sheer brilliance of the image per se that characterise this opening sequence typify the form and content of the video generally. Not only is the video episodic – that is, structured around self-contained, discrete segments – but the architectonic itself frames, informs and limits the potentialities of Minogue's performance of white female sexuality. Most obviously, all of the locations featured in the video are architectural in the sense that they are artificial, manufactured, built environments. In other words, even when the location is rendered abstract or uncertain, it is nevertheless always and unambiguously not a *natural* environment. In fact, with the exception of human bodies – which, as we argue below, is not really an exception at all – no organic matter features in the video and, indeed, such matter has no place in the world it constructs.

Moreover, the way that the action, the performers and the environment are lit emphasises the clinical artificiality of both the body and the space that frames the body. Put simply, the luminescence of the image never allows shadow, tone, and certainly not darkness, to intrude into the frame. Even in the final scene, apparently set at night on a rooftop, the action is bathed in light with Minogue herself seeming to both emit and reflect that light. Indeed, during this scene, and throughout the video, light itself is turned into a prominent aesthetic presence as the lights in the skyscrapers 'dance' in time to Minogue, and stylised flares, either from the sun or some other undefined light source, regularly hit the camera, blinding the spectator. One effect of this type of lighting, of course, is that the boundaries between the white body, other bodies and the space they inhabit are always clearly defined, and more often than not, clearly visible.

The body in the video, and especially Minogue's body, is not only sculpted and flattened by light, but its movement is mechanised and controlled, and it is hyperstylised by its clothing and costume. For example, while on the one hand dance routines are strictly and complexly choreographed, physical performance itself, on the other hand, is often reduced to minimalistic, simple body movements. In one instance the dancers remain static, individually posed within an overall tableau, but for the repeated flexing of the fingers. Here, dance is reduced to the mechanised movements of the robotic body. Indeed, the controlled body, and the control of the body, defines both the choreography and the performance. Even when bodies are complexly intertwined they do not touch, connecting only through the relation of one body to the next within the totality of the overall design. Moreover, the choreography individuates the bodies of the dancers in so far as each performs a different range of movements at different times yet, at the same time, it also subordinates those bodies to the demands of the overall routine in the first instance, and, more importantly, to Minogue's performance in the final instance. For Minogue's body is the one which is privileged, always distinct and distinguished, aestheticised and exhibited for the appreciation of the spectator. She is differentiated within the totality of the choreography, positioned figuratively, and often literally, apart from the other dancers. By the same token, her movements, while limited and restricted, are not only foregrounded by the choreography but also by the salient techniques of the production process itself. Most obviously, she is the principal preoccupation of the camera: she features in almost every shot, often in close-up, and the video is structured around the demands of displaying her body. More interestingly, however, the frequent and regular use of slow motion and super-slow motion both reinforces her distinction by exempting her from the constraints of 'normal' time and serves to further regulate and control the movements of her body and hair precisely by slowing down her image. Indeed, while her hair is controlled by a number of physical devices and materials – it is variously tied, sprayed, fixed or entirely covered – at moments where unruly movement is threatened, especially during dance routines, the use of slow-motion photography arrests, contains and restrains this threat. In short, the fixity of her hair mirrors the stasis of her body, an idea most evident in the significant number of shots which feature Minogue's body, posed and presented, not moving at all.

Moreover, in moments when Minogue's body does move it is notable that her flesh does not. This is both made apparent and made possible, in part, by the design of her costumes. On the one hand, her outfits variously constrain the flesh, cover the flesh, or reveal evidence of the armature beneath the flesh. For instance, the final outfit she is seen wearing reveals the shoulders and the knees but covers and obscures the breasts, the stomach and the hips. In other words, it directs attention towards precisely those areas of the body that are not fleshy and away from those that are. In an earlier scene the body is almost entirely covered and hidden by a white, loose-fitting track suit. In fact, the only bits that are revealed are the sternum, the neck, and occasionally the armpits. Indeed, these outfits display, strictly speaking, not the exterior body, the flesh of the body, but rather its interior, the architecture of the body. On the other hand, however, where the flesh is revealed, what is revealed is precisely its lack of movement, the clean lines and firm edges of its sculpture. In perhaps the most striking scene of the video, Minogue is seen wearing a brilliant white, hooded jumpsuit, split from ankle to waist on both sides, with a deep cowl neckline which plunges to below the navel. The design of the dress both conceals and reveals Minogue's body, and, as she moves, the fabric falls open to reveal that the flesh of her breasts, stomach and thighs remains firm, taut and static: the sight of her flesh set against the fluidity of the dress merely confirms the flesh's rigidity.

Indeed, more generally, this sequence presents a potent image of white female sexuality as controlled, restrained and unavailable. The most striking aspect of this scene is precisely its thoroughgoing whiteness. Not only is Minogue dressed in white, exposing porcelain-white flesh, and performing in a totally white environment, but she is further whitened by the cleansing glare of the light. The only colour in the scene, the red of the dancers' outfits and, most notably, Minogue's lips, serves only to throw into stark relief the non-colour of everything else. The purity of the frame and the sanctity of Minogue's body are never allowed to be sullied, disturbed or threatened by the disruption and disorder of the natural. The dancers, for instance, are de-humanised; the few movements they make are roboticised and functional, and their faces are obscured by dark, perspex visors, altering the contour of their heads and restricting their gaze. They cannot look at or touch Minogue's body, and are rarely even in the same frame, further setting the uniqueness of Minogue apart from the uniformity of the dancers. And, of course, uniqueness is a key marker of provenance and providence: things which are unique are both valuable and vulnerable, difficult to come by in the first place and, once acquired, in need of protection and preservation.

The uniqueness of Minogue is established not only by her differentiation from the mechanised choreography of the dancers but also through the de-naturalisation of her own body. More specifically, if the humanity of the dancers is reduced to the machinic, then the representation of Minogue's body implies that it has transcended the human, the organic. In other words, the flawlessness of her white skin, the stillness of her hair, and the way the flesh of her body seems to resist the pull of gravity situates Minogue somewhere beyond the human and outside of the natural. Here, then, the slippage from whiteness signalling purity, cleanliness and frangibility to whiteness as defining an 'ideal' and idealised female sexuality coalesces around the figurine image of Minogue's pale skin. Ironically, the very (hyper)visibility of the body which renders it available to the look simultaneously protects it from the contaminating touch, thus securing its physical unattainability.

What the video for 'Can't Get You Out Of My Head' presents us with, then, is an image of female sexuality which stands in stark contrast to the one produced by Knowles's 'Baby Boy'. While both produce images of the sexually attractive, seductive, heterosexual woman, these representations of sexuality and seduction are very different, and, in the end, are constituted through, and overdetermined by, the limits of the raced imaginary. While on the one hand black female sexuality continues to be constructed as hypersexuality, as animalistic, primitive and instinctive, on the other hand white female sexuality is defined principally in terms of its sexual sublimity, that is to say, in terms of the rejection/colonisation of instinctive behaviour through/by culture and civilisation. The ferine sexuality of the black woman renders her always and already sexually available while, by contrast, the providence of the white female body secures both the white woman's unattainability and, by extension, her desirability. If the former is depicted as an essentially natural sexuality, rooted precisely in the filth, dirt and mess of the natural world, then the latter emerges as a denaturalised sexuality, abstracted from the world, purified and cleansed of its messiness. By the same token, one implication of the 'naturalness' of black sexuality is that it is inevitably embodied, anchored to, and enacted through, the flesh of the body itself. The denaturalisation of white sexuality, by distinction, means that it is relatively disconnected from the corporeality of the body, residing instead in the image/vision of the body, indeed the presentation and representation of it. One of the more interesting consequences of uncoupling white female sexuality from corporeality and relocating it in the *presentation* of the body is that, unlike black sexuality, it becomes, in the final instance, mutable. Which is to say, while black female sexuality is always embodied and fixed in the flesh – precisely in the fleshiest parts of the body – white sexuality, in displacing the organics of the body, is open to redefinition. Indeed, the *re*presentation of black female sexuality implies and invokes an essential sexuality that is already in and of the world while the presentation of white female sexuality always offers the potential for reinvention. Besides, even where reinvention does not take place in any given instance, such a transformative possibility, a possibility historically denied to black women, nevertheless remains. And, of course, this capacity to define and redefine privileges white in the imaginary and, moreover, that symbolic privilege is one of the key ways in which power is negotiated, performed and ultimately secured.

INHABITING THE OTHER

This is not to say, however, that images of hypersexual black femininity found in music video, and in contemporary popular culture more generally, are simply transpositions from earlier historical periods, nor that they necessarily always imply a racist political agenda. Indeed, one strand of recent black feminist theory and artistic practice has directed itself towards exploring the possibilities of recuperating, appropriating and recasting this history of representation. For example, Rana A. Emerson argues that 'Black women may use the sphere of culture to reclaim and revise the controlling images, specifically "the Jezebel", to express sexual subjectivity.'[30] And, as Lorraine O'Grady observes, in order to 'reclaim black female subjectivity so as to "de-haunt" historic scripts and establish worldly agency' and thus effect a transition from an object into a subject of history, black women must be able to repossess colonised images of the black female body. It is in this sense that 'the black female's body needs less to be rescued from the masculine "gaze" than to be sprung from a historical script', a script which serves to position her at 'the outermost regions of "otherness"'.[31] On this view, then, the reclamation of past scripts is not simply about raising them to the surface in order to win them back and/or deconstruct them but is, in fact, a precondition, or at least a first stage, of being able to say anything new in the present.

This is important in so far as it impels us to think about instances where the range of discourses available to black women might be expanded not only through the practices of artists, poets and intellectuals but also, perhaps more crucially, through a more quotidian engagement with the products of popular culture. In terms of music video such instances may well be exceptional, especially in comparison to examples which are recuperative or simply exploitative of their racist antecedents. This is not surprising given the historical asymmetrical power relations that frame contemporary discourses of race. Indeed, to return to the issue with which we began – the *fact* of Lil' Kim's blackness set against the *possibility* and *performance* of Christina Aguilera's non-whiteness – the only way of comprehending the complexities of raced subjectivity offered by the video is to address the differing discursive positions occupied by Aguilera and Kim. For while Kim literally embodies black hypersexuality, her sexuality produced and defined by the site/sight of her black body, Aguilera is able to produce her sexuality through the selective and playful presentation of tropes of raced identity. Put simply, while Kim struggles to, at best, recuperate what hooks has called a 'pornographic fantasy of the black female as wild sexual savage', Aguilera is allowed a far more fluid and creative engagement with both raced and sexual identity.[32] It is precisely this fluidity, of course, that is a dividend of Aguilera's privileged position in relation to power.

Instances where the discursive limits of black femininity are expanded in or through popular representation may well be exceptional, perhaps even improbable, but they are not impossible. Indeed, analysis of Beyoncé Knowles's videos since BEAUTIFUL LIAR (2007) reveals a complex, perhaps even paradoxical, combination of nostalgic, appropriative and originative black female subjectivities. BEAUTIFUL LIAR itself deliberately sets out to confuse the body's relationship to raced and ethnic identity. From its opening shot, in which its two principal performers, Knowles and Shakira, are opaquely seen through shifting smoke, the video employs a number of self-conscious deceptions which work to obfuscate and problematise individual identity rooted in notions of raced or ethnic specificity. Indeed, despite their different raced/ethnic positions (respectively, African American and white-hispanic Colombian), on a number of occasions, the two women appear not only to be identical, but also able switch position in order to inhabit the other's body. These deceptions, realised through a combination of styling, performance and technique, gesture towards the possibility of transmuting, perhaps even transcending, biological conceptions of identity which have historically served as a key means of subordinating non-white people. This idea is replayed and reworked in both GREEN LIGHT (2007) and VIDEO PHONE (2009) through a more thoroughgoing exploration of the tropes of whiteness. Not only are both staged-performance videos set in the surgically clean, abstract and seemingly infinite space of the studio, but, in a manner reminiscent of I CAN'T GET YOU OUT OF MY HEAD, they deploy a range of tactics that forestall the linkage between the female body and discourses of nature and the natural. Most obviously, the array of outfits Knowles is seen wearing are not only constructed from a range of synthetic materials (especially plastic), but they also frame and restrain her body in ways that are quite different to BABY BOY. Moreover, the vivid brilliance of their colours and their graphic, sometimes geometric, design is underlined by editing techniques which emphasise the artificiality of the performance, in other words that it is a *staged* performance. It is here that the notion of ideal types can be cashed. For, despite featuring Knowles, GREEN LIGHT and VIDEO PHONE can be mapped more easily against the co-ordinates of whiteness than blackness. The result of this is an uncoupling of the black/primitive dyad or, at the very least, a break in the logic that associates black femininity with a feral hypersexual body. Perhaps the most startling example of this process is to be found in the closing moments of SINGLE LADIES (PUT A RING ON IT) (2008). The video, shot in black and white, features Knowles as the lead of three dancers performing inside the bright white space of an infinity cove. But the brilliance of this space merely serves to intensify Knowles's performance of embodied black femininity in so far as the rhythm of the dance and the ease of her movements seem to emanate from the fact of her blackness. However, what appears to be an anomaly, a metal glove on her left hand, finds its function at the video's end when, after the song is over, Knowles raises her open hand to the side of her face, smiles at the camera, and closes her fist. What is heard at this point, the sound of mechanical gears operating her movements, works to subvert the reading of what has gone before. Indeed, one way of understanding this might be to suggest that the video is critiquing the long-standing association of blackness and the natural, or, more precisely, it is demonstrating that this association is far from natural, rather that it is a product of representation. Taken together, then, while these videos are all still clearly concerned with the construction of black female sexuality, it is a sexuality of the present, cognisant of modernity and a subject of its own enunciation.

The implications of this analysis are threefold. Firstly, it underscores the point made earlier in the book about the importance of film style and technique in the construction of sexed and raced identity and thus the need to pay close attention to their operation. Secondly, what BEAUTIFUL LIAR, GREEN

LIGHT, VIDEO PHONE and SINGLE LADIES reveal is that, in certain instances, a broader range of possibilities and resources are currently available for representing black femininity in popular culture than have hitherto existed. Of course, one of the reasons why Knowles perhaps has greater scope to explore different subjectivities is her now considerable star power and the attendant authorial freedoms it brings. However, it nevertheless remains the case that these videos do stand as evidence of the potential for expanding the discursive field in ways which might benefit black women. Thirdly, whiteness itself is opened up for critique. Put simply, if it can be inhabited, mimicked and parodied so proficiently by a non-white performer then it too is revealed to be an historical contingency, a set of technologies of the self through which people both *see* others and *live* themselves. Expanding the meanings of blackness and questioning the normality of whiteness can thus be seen as two sides of the same analytical coin which understands cultural representation as a key site of power and a key means through which it can be challenged.

NOTES

1. Stuart Hall, 'New Ethnicities', in James Donald and Ali Rattansi (eds), *'Race', Culture and Difference* (London: Sage, 1992), pp. 253–4.
2. Christina Aguilera (Featuring Lil' Kim), 'Can't Hold Us Down' (RCA, 2002).
3. It is worth stressing at this point that this discussion is about the ways in which women are variously figured in and through forms of visual culture. As such, while on the one hand we do not wish to ignore the complexities of cultural identity and identification (for example, as we discuss in the next chapter, Aguilera is of Irish and Ecuadorian descent and publicly identifies herself as Latina), on the other hand what we discuss here are the cultural tropes of raced identity (the ways in which distinct categories of white and black structure ways of being human and ways of being a woman) that are constructed and contrasted through forms of representation.
4. bell hooks, *Black Looks: Race and Representation* (Boston: South End Press, 1992), p. 21.
5. hooks, *Black Looks*, p. 34.
6. Patricia Hill Collins, *Black Sexual Politics: African Americans, Gender, and the New Racism* (London: Routledge, 2004), p. 85.
7. Anne McClintock, *Imperial Leather: Race, Gender and Sexuality in the Colonial Contest* (London: Routledge, 1995), p. 22.
8. McClintock, *Imperial Leather*, p. 22.
9. Sander L. Gilman, 'Black Bodies, White Bodies: Toward an Iconography of Female Sexuality in Late Nineteenth-Century Art, Medicine, and Literature', *Critical Inquiry*, vol. 12, no. 1 (1985), p. 212.
10. Sander L. Gilman, *Difference and Pathology: Stereotypes of Sexuality, Race, and Madness* (Ithaca, NY: Cornell University Press, 1985), p. 85.
11. Gilman, *Difference and Pathology*, p. 85.
12. Gilman, *Difference and Pathology*, p. 83.
13. Gilman, *Difference and Pathology*, p. 90.
14. Gilman, 'Black Bodies, White Bodies', p. 212.
15. The white women we discuss here, of course, are middle-class women. Indeed,

representations of white working-class women differ significantly from those of middle-class women. For discussion of representations of working-class white women, see McClintock, *Imperial Leather*; and Rose Weitz, 'A History of Women's Bodies', in Rose Weitz (ed.), *The Politics of Women's Bodies: Sexuality, Appearance and Behaviour*, 2nd edn (Oxford: Oxford University Press, 2003).

16. Weitz, 'A History of Women's Bodies', p. 6.
17. Richard Dyer, *White* (London: Routledge 1997), p. 29.
18. Dyer, *White*, p. 36.
19. McClintock, *Imperial Leather*, p. 35.
20. McClintock, *Imperial Leather*, p. 212.
21. McClintock, *Imperial Leather*, p. 33.
22. McClintock, *Imperial Leather*, p. 32.
23. Vron Ware, *Beyond the Pale: White Women, Racism, and History* (London: Verso, 1992), p. 38.
24. McClintock, *Imperial Leather*, p. 211.
25. Max Weber, 'Objectivity in Social Science and Social Policy', *The Methodology of the Social Sciences*, ed. Edward Shils and Henry H. Finch (New York: Free Press, 1949), p. 90.
26. hooks, *Black Looks*, p. 63.
27. Mos Def, 'Ms Fat Booty' (Rawkus Records, 1999).
28. hooks, *Black Looks*, p. 73.
29. hooks, *Black Looks*, p. 70.
30. Rana A. Emerson, ' "Where My Girls At?": Negotiating Black Womanhood in Music Videos', *Gender and Society*, vol. 16, no. 1 (2002), p. 133.
31. Lorraine O'Grady, 'Olympia's Maid: Reclaiming Black Female Subjectivity', in Amelia Jones (ed.), *The Feminism and Visual Culture Reader* (London: Routledge, 2003), pp. 179, 175.
32. hooks, *Black Looks*, p. 67.

5. THAT LATIN(A) LOOK: PERFORMING ETHNICITY

In the previous chapter we argued that race is not simply the result of bio-cultural heritage but is rather the product of particular discursive formations which become inscribed upon the body through processes of representation. This, at least in part, explains the confusions in identity set in motion by BEAUTIFUL LIAR (2007) inasmuch as its two performers, Beyoncé Knowles and Shakira, appear to both exchange identities and inhabit isomorphic bodies. Even if race cannot be reduced entirely to a set of free-floating signifiers, what this nevertheless does indicate is its arbitrary and contingent relationship to the raced body. This is most apparent in the way that the whiteness of Shakira's body and her Latina identity are disavowed in the production of a 'black Shakira' and the blackness of Beyoncé's body and her African American identity are elided in her performance of 'Latina Beyoncé'. And to a significant extent, this display of malleable raced identity points us towards the political rub in so far as the identities being swapped in BEAUTIFUL LIAR, if not straightforwardly black, *are* decidedly non-white. On one level this can be explained by the different locations black and white occupy in discourse and the concomitant differences in the ways they are constructed through representation. As Dyer notes, 'in the realm of categories, black is always marked as a colour . . . and is always particularising'. White, on the other hand, is 'not anything really, not an identity, not a particularising quality', because it seems to be, and usually aspires to be, 'everything and nothing' at the same time.[1] In terms of BEAUTIFUL LIAR, it is the particularising markers of the raced/ethnic female body, a set of symbolic codes made familiar through constant cultural iteration, that are able to be interchanged precisely because of their specificity.

It is perhaps worth pausing for a moment to remember that the categorical specificity of blackness is no more an index of a 'true' or 'real' raced identity than the putative non-specificity of whiteness is evidence of its non-raced universality and authority. Both are positions within discourse and power, and, moreover, the nothingness of whiteness requires the somethingness of blackness for its 'non-existence'. Ethnicity, too, is caught up in this game of absence/presence, instigated as another set of particulars which efface the structures and properties of whiteness. One way of unpicking this idea is to explore another video featuring Shakira, HIPS DON'T LIE (2006), in terms of the way it co-opts specific tropes of a range of ethnicities to produce a generalised, non-white, exotic 'other'. For this time, it is not markers of blackness that frame the performance of Shakira's sexed identity but rather a hotchpotch of Caribbean, Latin American and Arabic pan-ethnic signifiers. Most obviously the action takes place amidst a carnival, quite possibly coded as the Colombian Carnaval de Barranquilla, a reference to Shakira's birthplace. This not only works to establish the setting as a non-white space, but, more complexly, the physicality and collectivity that characterise the carnivalesque in the Bakhtinian sense give licence to the video's parade of sounds, images, behaviours, costumes and languages that signal particular ethnic identities. Indeed, it is only within this array of identity positions that Shakira's own performance of ethnicity can take shape, or, in other words, it is this array that provides her with the resources with which to author and enact her own exotic otherness. This observation helps describe not only her outfits – an eclectic mix of tasselled tops, low-slung jeans, hip scarves, ruffled skirts, bejewelled dresses that reference a number of different cultural traditions – but also bears on how we can understand the style of dance employed in the video. For in one sense the constant focus on the movement of Shakira's hips and stomach clearly invoke forms of belly dancing but do so at one remove from the specificities of Arabic traditions. Indeed, forms of Latin dance provide an equally influential frame of reference for the staging and choreography of the performance. The main point here is less that this is a hybrid ethnicity than that it is a generalised 'other' ethnicity produced as a pick-and-mix from the representational markers that so often function as a metonym for a specific ethnicity.

One way of theorising this situation is to view it through the conceptual prism provided by Edward Said's notion of Orientalism.[2] Said argues that the notion of the Orient is a historically contingent 'way of thought', a 'semi-mythical construct', produced by the 'West' and projected onto the 'East'. Orientalism, as a discursive practice through which the world is known and understood, serves to render heterogeneity homogeneous, reducing complex cultural practices to a more or less uniform exotic 'other'. For Said this is not an act of misrepresentation since 'neither the term *Orient* nor the concept of the West has any ontological stability' precisely to the extent that 'no stable reality exists as a natural fact'[3]. This is important in so far as the notion of Orientalism is descriptive not simply of a set of attitudes and sentiments by which the West knows the East, but, more complexly, of a mirroring process in which the West knows itself by what it is not. As Said argues:

> the development and maintenance of every culture require the existence of another, different and competing alter ego. The construction of identity . . . involves the construction of opposites and 'others' whose actuality is always subject to the continuous interpretation and reinterpretation of their differences from 'us'.[4]

It is this idea, then, that enables us to locate HIPS DON'T LIE as a specific form of Orientalist text. For, despite not just assimilating signifiers of the East it nevertheless does produce a precise image of a generalised 'other'. Indeed, the exotic position occupied by Shakira is constructed from a long list of femininities marked in representation as ethnically specific that congeal in this video into a particularised yet amorphous non-whiteness. This way of representing ethnicity in music video, a mirroring process in which the production of ethnicity as exotic 'other' goes hand in hand with the production of whiteness as an unthought norm, is both common and complex, involving not only the text of the video itself but also a range of intertexts which are brought to bear on its comprehension.

THE ETHNIC ROUTES OF CHRISTINA AGUILERA

In order to untangle some of this complexity what follows focuses on one particularly interesting example of the way in which the notion of Latina identity is inscribed according to this expanded concept of Orientalism. More specifically, we explore the ways in which an image of 'Latinaness' is constructed around the figure of Christina Aguilera. Indeed, it is possible to chart a movement in her star image constructed through her music, music videos and promotional material between the 'white pop princess' that began to take shape on Disney's *Mickey Mouse Club* to the 'majestically filthy' exhibitionist that emerged in the 'suggestively sexy' video for 'Dirrty' (2002).[5] However, to merely map these two moments is an act of oversimplification in so far as it ignores the much broader web of textuality which serves to construct Aguilera's identity as simultaneously multivocal and specific, but certainly never ambiguous. Indeed, this notion of Aguilera's ethnic simultaneity attended the construction and circulation of her star image from the earliest stages of her pop career. For example, while in the wake of the release of her first album *Christina Aguilera* (1999) the mainstream media were keen to construct her as 'the teen dream',[6] 'following in the footsteps of Disney alum Britney Spears'[7], both 'teenage, female, innocent and blonde'[8], an article in *Latina* magazine was stressing that she was a 'singer of Ecuadorian descent' who 'young Latin girls can look up to'.[9] This task of ethnic co-creation is neither easy nor politically unproblematic. In the first instance, popular representation has, as Myra Mendible argues, long constructed these ethnic positions in contradistinction to each other.[10] In part this clearly hooks up with Said's account of the operations of Orientalism in providing a discursive mechanism for cultures to define themselves as distinct and unique. However, one implication of this is that it ought to make it difficult for someone, in this case Aguilera, to occupy simultaneous ethnic positions, or at least to do it in a way that appears authentic. Put crudely, a position of simultaneity appears, at least initially, to be at odds with the model of identity formation that underpins Said's work, a model based on opposition and difference. However, Said stresses that, despite the long-standing attachment to a 'naive belief in the certain positivity and unchanging historicity of a culture, a self, a national identity', ethnicity is 'not natural and stable' but rather 'constructed and occasionally even invented outright'.[11] It is the tension between these competing conceptions of ethnicity – one that sees it as a thoroughly discursive and contingent *practice* and the other which locates it as a socio-historical *truth* – which perhaps explains why, in the second place, the fact that Aguilera lays claim to an authentic Latina identity in addition to an already established white identity is controversial.

Controversy, of course, is never far away from discussions of ethnicity precisely because such discussions necessarily imply notions of authenticity and boundaries. Indeed, ethnicity is never simply a neutral term descriptive of 'real' social groupings. Quite the contrary, it is a political term that is used to demarcate insider from outsider, 'us' from 'them', 'we' from 'you'. As such, it is always a boundary phenomenon, a way of creating borders that delimit who belongs to any ethnic group and who does not. Ethnicity, therefore, always seems to imply a simultaneous sense of constancy and contingency. Ethnic identity is always predicated on some sense of collectivity, similarity and solidarity: a collective name based upon narratives of common ancestry, a sense of shared memory and destiny, and experience of a common culture. These are, in turn, often linked to a symbolic relationship to a geographical location. Therefore, while ethnic identity implies a sense of durability and fixity, ethnicities are, in the end, always contested and contestable, and thus primarily political processes which construct 'the collectivity and "its interests"'.[12] This idea not only frames the specific controversy that attends Aguilera's image but also a much broader set of disputes about the meaning and ownership of ethnic identities.

Latinidad is a case in point. Seen by some as a positive and progressive concept, the promotion of which is a way of 'undermining the appropriation of "America" by Anglo imperialism and ethnocentrism', it is decried by others for creating a myth of authentic pan-ethnic identity and flattening out the differences between the range of national and regional cultures the term seeks to encompass.[13] A brief analysis of Jennifer Lopez's star persona provides a useful example of this dilemma. On the one hand it can be thought of as a constant reminder of the Latina presence in America, her performance of 'embodied and butted Latinidad' a challenge to Anglo definitions of feminine beauty, her professional success a rebuttal of stereotypes of Latina failure.[14] On the other hand, is the fact that the Nuyorican Lopez can play the role of a Tejana singer (*Selena*, 1997), a Mexican mother (*Mi Familia*, 1995), a Cuban nanny (*Blood and Wine*, 1996) and a Southern-California Mexican-American (*Anaconda*, 1997) symptomatic of a culture that has a 'tendency to view Latinos as if they all looked the same' and reduces Latinidad to 'an undifferentiated and homogeneous group of peoples and cultural traditions'?[15] Either way, the questions that are provoked remain the same and relate to what Wilfred Sellars calls 'we intentions': who can and should be inside the boundary, and how wide should the circle of 'we' be drawn?[16]

It is in the context of this kind of dispute over language and representation, and, more generally, over what Alberto Sandoval-Sánchez refers to as the 'Latino renaissance that has taken over the Anglo entertainment industry', that the representation of Christina Aguilera's ethnicity, or ethnicities, becomes both interesting and apprehendable.[17] For it is not simply the fact that Aguilera has, from the very start, been deliberately promoted to both a mainstream/ Anglo market and a Latina/o one by using different representational strategies (most obviously the production of a number of Spanish language singles and albums) that is at stake here. Rather, what matters is that both identity positions are equally authentic, authored and inhabited. In other words, it is not that one position is the 'real' identity and the other is the invented or phony one. This would replay the naive belief in eternal conceptions of ethnicity that Said warns against. Indeed, what emerges from this kind of situation is a conception of cultural identity that is, in the final instance, irreducible to either the fact of the biological body or the experiential knowledge of a lived culture. Identities become mutable, negotiable and divorced from any notion of an essential self. On this view, identity can be performed, worn and inhabited; precisely, that is to say, presented and represented. One implication of this is that Aguilera's relationship to Latina identity is neither authentic nor inauthentic. Rather, it is always first and foremost a *presentation* of an authentic Latina identity which is itself, of course, complex, unstable and in a constant state of negotiation and renegotiation.

One way of thinking about the idea of performing authentic ethnicity is to consider the work of Jennifer L. Willis. In her study of Latino Night in a bar in a small town in Northwest Ohio, she argues that there are four key 'screens' through which patrons have to pass in order to participate in the event and be accepted as part of the Latino Night community: music – an appreciation of Tejana/o and/or Latina/o music; language – an understanding/acceptance of Spanish as the predominant language; dancing – a familiarity with, or a willingness to learn, Tejana/o and Latina/o dances; and ethnicity – in this context, being comfortable within a more or less self-defined Latina/o space.[18] In other words, these 'screens' not only function to identify a specific ethnic collectivity within a particular space and time, and to regulate access to, and membership of, that collectivity, but also to establish the markers of belonging to that community. The crucial point, here, is that the Latina/o-ness of the Latina/o community is being defined, not by biological descent, but rather by a range of symbols, rituals and practices, that is to say, a set of cultural signifiers derived from and (re)articulated within forms of representation and discourse. And, of course, these screens are only one part of, or a complement to, a reservoir of cultural signifiers of Latina/o-ness such as specific language competences, food, clothing, hairstyles, jewellery and other body embellishments, and, indeed, the raced and sexed body itself. It is through the way aspects of this reservoir of signifiers are deployed, combined and privileged, or conversely suppressed, hidden and relegated, that particular configurations of identity become manifest and acquire meaning. It is also through this process of selection and rejection that what Cofer calls 'the myth of the Latin woman' takes shape. For Cofer, this myth is a 'one-dimensional view' of 'the Hispanic woman' which defines her as 'the "hot tamale" or sexual firebrand'. She argues that in the media's 'special vocabulary, advertisers have designated "sizzling" and "smouldering" as the adjectives of choice for describing not only the foods but also the women of Latin America'.[19] This analogy chimes not only with Maria Elena Cepeda's observation that Latin(o) music is described in terms of its ' "heat", "intoxication", and "spice" ', but also with the conflation of the 'waist' of the Americas and the waistline of the Latina described by Shari Roberts.[20] Referred to as the 'torrid zone', this geographical-corporeal space is 'hotter than the rest of the planet' and its inhabitants are 'wilder, sexier, and more naked than other people'.[21]

It is within this context that analysis of Aguilera's videos is revealing inasmuch as they self-consciously work within and deploy two sets of codes in the production of two distinct images of femininity, one constructed as a specific Latina identity within the generalised category of the exotic 'other', and one that is another iteration of normative de-particularised whiteness. In order to explore this idea, it is worth examining four videos, GENIE IN A BOTTLE (1999) and COME ON OVER BABY (ALL I WANT IS YOU) (2000), and their Spanish language counterparts GENIO ATRAPADO and VEN CONMIGO (SOLAMENTE TÚ). These make interesting viewing inasmuch as subtle differences in the shooting and editing serve to present Aguilera, in each pair of videos, not only to both

Anglo and Latina/o audiences but also as, alternately, a 'wholesome "all-American gal"' and a sensual Latin woman. While on a cursory glance these pairs of videos seem practically identical but for the change of language, it is nevertheless the case that the few differences that are apparent are both interesting and significant in terms of the representation of ethnicity. For in both cases, what we get is the production of two quite distinct videos to promote the different versions of each song. These distinctions are instigated within, and rendered visible through, the text despite the fact that, in each instance, they are promoting the same song and are constructed from the same shoot.

In terms of the GENIE IN A BOTTLE / GENIO ATRAPADO dyad, both videos are staged in and around a beachfront house and deploy three key scenarios which are intercut: the doorway of the house and its wooden veranda; Aguilera lying on the beach at twilight, singing to camera; and a choreographed dance sequence involving Aguilera and a group of dancers staged on a decked area on the beach. However, even if these three elements are common to both, the way in which the action is shot and subsequently edited marks each video as distinctive in the way it situates Aguilera's ethnicity. There are two key aspects to this. Firstly, the energetic dance routine, which features Aguilera dressed in a vest top, loose-fitting orange trousers and a pair of trainers leading a group of similarly styled performers, is afforded far greater prominence in the English language version of the video. This not only acts as an image of familiarity and continuity in so far as it reconnects Aguilera's nascent pop persona to her earlier persona developed as a Disney 'Mouseketeer', but also as an image of transition in that it (re)positions that pop persona generically as a 'new teen star'.[22] In the Spanish language version, by contrast, this sequence plays a much reduced role and is largely replaced by a performance segment wherein Aguilera, standing alone on the veranda of the house, sings directly to camera. In this sequence she is wearing a tasselled halter-neck top cropped to the midriff, a short black denim jacket, and low-slung, fitted black capri pants. In stark contrast to the dance routine, therefore, not only does the cut and style of Aguilera's clothing frame her naked stomach, but the physical restraint and sensuality of her performance directly solicits the spectator in a way that the dance routines do not. Moreover, this heightened sensuality also informs the second key difference to the extent that the physical proximity between Aguilera and the audience appears to be far less in GENIE IN A BOTTLE than in GENIO ATRAPADO. In other words, we are permitted far greater closeness in the latter compared to the former. This is, perhaps, most apparent in the sequence featuring Aguilera lying in the sand. Again, there are two key differences here. First, and most obvious, there is simply more use of this sequence in the Spanish language version of the video. Second, whereas in both videos she is shown lying on her stomach singing to the camera, in GENIO ATRAPADO her head, face and hands are framed much more tightly within the composition of the shot. Indeed, the camera literally appears to be physically closer to Aguilera, a closeness that, by extension, the spectator is invited to occupy. The implications of this increased closeness are twofold: indelible evidence that Aguilera is actually singing in Spanish; and the construction of Aguilera as both knowingly sexual and sensual. Taken together, these differences work to produce two different Aguileras. On the one hand, the young 'all-American' pop princess still too innocent to understand what she is singing about, and, on the other, the self-consciously sexy Latina who understands perfectly well the sexual implications of the song's lyrics.[23]

However, perhaps the most sustained and interesting example of this representation of simultaneous ethnicities is found in the differences between the Spanish and English language versions of the video for 'Ven Conmigo' / 'Come on Over Baby' (2000). Indeed, although elements of the same five performance scenarios feature in both videos, their duration and prominence, as well as the way they are shot and edited in the first place, differ significantly across each video and differ in ways which bear upon the possibilities for reading and determining Aguilera's ethnic identity. To begin with, the English language version, after an initial narrative prologue, is structured around four identifiable, successive dance sequences. Each of these features Aguilera performing a choreographed routine with a group of other dancers. Moreover, each sequence is marked out not only by its distinctive staging, but also by the colour-coordinated clothing worn by Aguilera and the performers. So, as the video progresses, the colour palette moves from its initial concentration on bright blues, to a sequence drenched in yellows and greens, then on to one in brilliant white, the costumes of which provide the accent to the saturated red of the final sequence. What this structure does, especially when one takes into account the exuberance of the dancing and the iridescence of the staging, is to establish Aguilera as part of a group of friends having fun together, an idea set up and reinforced by the narrative prologue in which Aguilera is shown with these same 'friends', chatting to someone on the phone arranging to meet later. The fifth principal performance scenario, one in which Aguilera is alone, performing in a predominantly white environment and singing directly to the camera, is used, in the context of this video, as cut-aways to the main action, as, that is to say, more or less discrete footage which often merely accentuates the vocal capabilities of Aguilera's voice.

It is this latter scenario, however, which is used to structure the video for the Spanish language version of the song. By the same token, the other four scenarios, which were privileged in the COME ON OVER BABY video, are themselves relegated to the status of cut-aways, deployed this time without the motivation of the narrative prologue. In short, what we get this time is an extended solo performance directly to the camera intercut with snippets of apparently random dance routines variously featuring Aguilera herself, Aguilera and other dancers, or individual or groups of anonymous dancers. The most obvious implication of this shift is that Aguilera is separated from the other performers in the video. Far greater attention is focused on her as the sole object of scrutiny, and indeed such attention and scrutiny seems to be invited through aspects of her appearance and performance, as well as through the stylistic properties of the shots which put her on display.

In this performance scenario, Aguilera's hair, clothes, make-up and jewellery are very different to those featured in the other four. For instance, the deliberately sculpted blonde hair of these latter segments is replaced by a tousled mane embellished with streaks of crimson red. Moreover, unlike the untouched neatness of the other hairstyles Aguilera wears, this hair is blown, swished, swept and stroked; in other words, while in constant motion, it momentarily rests to frame her face, emphasise her expression, and display her large hooped earrings. Indeed, the ornamentation of the body is a crucial aspect in the redetermination of Aguilera's on-screen ethnicity. The ordinary, everyday girliness of the wristband, hairgrip, name-necklace, and the blue and green eyeshadow is replaced by heavy kohl eyes, an elaborate hand-bracelet, and a stomach decorated with a mehndi-like design in glitter and jewels. Moreover, the 'exotic' nature of the design is foregrounded and framed by the cut and style of her clothing. For in this sequence, performing in front of a wall of shimmering white silk, she wears, not the acid green or the electric blue of the dance sequences, but rather a white, bejewelled, cropped top and skin-tight, white, hipster trousers laced at each side. The exoticised nature of her appearance is introduced and consistently reinforced through the sensuous nature of her performance. Rather than the predetermined athleticism of the rigidly choreographed dance routines, what we are presented with here is an erotically tactile display in which Aguilera is seen to constantly touch her body: fondling her hair, stroking her shoulders, moving her hands down her body to find her hips. This not only emphasises the ornamentation of her appearance but also fixes her body and its sexualised performance as the focus of attention. Indeed, this process is inaugurated in the first shot of the video. Gone is any narrative pretext to the action, replaced instead by a close-up of Aguilera's embellished midriff as it turns towards the camera, her fingers moving to clasp her hips, guiding the eye towards her navel, her 'torrid zone'. Close-ups of Aguilera's hips and stomach are, in fact, a constant refrain throughout the video and, moreover, the sheer presence and frequency of close-ups is yet another key mileage marker in the distance between the Spanish language version and the English language version of the video. Time and again in VEN CONMIGO, the space between us and Aguilera's face and body, most usually the hips and midriff, seems to disappear and we are allowed a physical closeness to her body which we are simply not afforded in COME ON OVER BABY. Taken together, therefore, Aguilera's appearance and performance, as well as the formal properties of the video, combine to produce a particularised gendered ethnicity across and through her body, one that can be read as exotic in a number of ways but which is, in the final instance, anchored as Latina by the fact that she is performing in Spanish to an intended Hispanic audience.

A number of interesting observations emerge from this. In the first place, in the English language version of each video there is a striking consistency in the way that Anglophone-Aguilera is represented as an innocent, fun-loving teenager with an emerging sexuality, but who still enjoys 'hanging out' with a group of friends. This is signalled most clearly through the centrality of collective dance routines, a focus on teenage dress codes, and the youthful energy of her performance. However, there is a marked difference between this 'bubblegum pop' Aguilera and the Aguilera found in the Spanish language videos. Indeed, while it is not possible to attribute the same level of specificity or coherence to this latter Aguilera, the identity she inhabits in these videos is no less consistent inasmuch as it is *consistently not*, and *consistently distinct* from, Anglophone-Aguilera. In other words, although there are clear differences between the Aguileras of GENIO ATRAPADO and VEN CONMIGO, they, in the end, operate in a similar discursive space precisely in so far as they are the Other to Anglophone-Aguilera. So while appearance and performance function to define Anglophone-Aguilera, in deploying different configurations of these codes they also come to define the Other Aguilera. In terms of VEN CONMIGO, this takes the form of a generalised exoticisation of the female image, but in GENIO ATRAPADO, the exotic is located in a much more readily identifiable image of Latina identity, what Aparicio and Chavez-Silverman have called the tropicalised image. They argue that, in a process analogous to Said's notion of orientalism, tropicalisation is descriptive of socio-cultural practices in which specific tropes, that is to say, 'sets of images and attributes', are 'superimposed onto both Latin American and U.S. Latino subjects' either from above, in a top-down process, or from the bottom-up.[24] Either way, tassel-fringed cropped tops, laced trousers, elaborate jewellery and intimate performances work to destabilise, and potentially undercut, the wholesome security of Anglophone-Aguilera and relocate meaning variously in the tropicalised and exoticised image of the eroticised female Other. While the precise formulation of that eroticisation differs between GENIO ATRAPADO and VEN CONMIGO, this identity-shift is nevertheless enacted, and shored up, through the stylistic consistencies of framing, shot composition and duration, and editing. In short, Aguilera's image is sexualised and eroticised in the Spanish language videos ultimately not through appearance and performance alone, but rather through the much more intimate relationship we are permitted with her body through the formal properties of both individual shots and each video as a whole. Indeed, her more sexualised appearance and the intimacy of her performance are, in the end, secondary to the sense of physical closeness instigated through the proximity of the camera to her body and the frequent use of close-up.

The crucial point here, however, is that even if this more eroticised version of Aguilera is not reducible at the level of the image alone to any one gendered ethnicity, it nevertheless remains the case that it is ultimately linked with, and readable as, Latina precisely to the extent that that image is anchored by the oral/lyrical. As such, the non-Anglophone Aguilera, that is, the Other(ed) Aguilera, is located as Latina not only through the erotic/tropical image that is presented but also by the presentation of that image in the context of the Spanish language. Or more precisely, it is not the performance of the song per se, but rather the authentic performance of the Spanish language which serves, in these videos, to fix her identity as Latina.

While music video remains a central mechanism through which identities are produced and circulated – and in this case Aguilera's official/commercial celebrity identities take shape – it is only one thread in a much broader web of textuality in which identities are negotiated and defined. Indeed, Aguilera's relationship to, and performance of, the Spanish language is not just played out in the videos for 'Genio Atrapado' and 'Ven Conmigo', but, in fact, across a range of interdiscursive spaces, spaces in which the music videos circulate alongside a whole host of other texts and in which the videos are not necessarily privileged as evidence of an authentic identity. For example, depending on which texts one reads, Aguilera 'is fluent in Spanish', 'speaks a little bit of Spanish', 'is steadily improving [her Spanish]', 'understands Spanish', or alternatively, 'is not fluent in Spanish', 'can barely speak Spanish', or 'can't speak Spanish' at all.[25] By the same token, her recordings in Spanish are said to demonstrate 'her love for the Spanish language', her 'comfortableness in singing in Spanish', or, by contrast, that 'she doesn't know how to sing the words', and that she had to 'learn the lyrics phonetically' in order to 'make sure her Spanish language fans understand' the words.[26] Crucial here, of course, is the way in which Aguilera's relationship to Spanish is being mobilised to construct her identity as either inside or outside of authentic Latina culture. On the one hand, this leads to a tropicalised claim of closeness to the language which, for Torres, creates 'more passion and showmanship' in her performances and, according to a reviewer for *Time* magazine, the discovery of 'new fires within'.[27] On the other hand, for reviewers such as a number of those who posted opinions about the release of Aguilera's album *Mi Reflejo* (2000) on Amazon.com, this closeness is inauthentic, described at best as 'an obvious marketing ploy', and, at worst, simply as 'fake', 'phony', 'pretentious' and 'show offy'.[28] These disagreements over the authenticity of Aguilera's ethnic identity are also played out in a number of online discussion forums. In one of these, the 'Cultura' forum on the *Latina* magazine website, the notions of roots, culture, language and parentage are evoked, to argue on the one hand that Aguilera 'is Latino [*sic*] because she is of Latin descent' and, on the other, that because 'Christina's mom is white and she doesn't have a relationship with her Latino dad', she has 'no Latin roots' to come from or 'get in touch with'.[29]

In these ways, then, language, or more precisely, the putatively authentic command and performance of Spanish, is crucial, depending on one's position, in either reinforcing or undermining Aguilera's Latina credentials. However, while language is a privileged marker of identity, especially as it seems to provide evidence of shared culture and ancestry, that is to say, evidence of one's ethnicity, in terms of Aguilera's simultaneous identities it is only one node in a far more complex intertextual circuit. In 2000, for example, Aguilera was nominated for, and received, a number of mainstream music awards: the Grammy Award for 'Best New Artist', the Billboard Music Award for 'Female Artist of the Year', the Teen Magazine Awards for 'Most Stylish Female Artist' and 'Best Girl Power Song', the Latina Magazine Award for 'Entertainer of the Year', and the ALMA Award for 'Best New Artist'. In this process, Aguilera's success was being acknowledged in a range of different contexts. Those contexts, however, imply a very different understanding of her ethnic identity. While the first three awards do not imply, or even require, recognition of a particularised ethnic identity, the latter two are predicated precisely on such a recognition. Indeed, the American Latino Media Arts (ALMA) Award is explicitly designed 'to promote fair, accurate, and balanced portrayals of Latinos in television, film, and music' and is awarded to 'honor Latino performers for their outstanding artistic achievement, impact, and enhancement of the image of Latinos'.[30] Moreover, by the following year, Aguilera had been awarded not only a Latin Grammy and a Billboard Latin Music Award, but also the Lo Nuestro Award for 'Best Female Artist of the Year', as well as a host of other awards not tied to specific ethnic identity.

What analysis of Aguilera's complex and often controversial identity throws into relief is that ethnic identity, like all forms of identity, is apprehendable only through forms of representation and can only adhere to the body through, and as, representation. Her ability to defy and flout identities – or, more exactly, to invent and inhabit a number of simultaneous gendered ethnicities – is a powerful demonstration of the way in which identity is always a product of discourse. And, more importantly, the process of recognising and exposing identity formation as a discursive procedure is a key step towards short-circuiting those social power relations which depend for their survival on myths of origin. Another way of putting this would be to say that while Shakira's hips may not lie, neither is there a truth of Latina identity to which they can bear testimony.

NOTES

1. Richard Dyer, 'White', *Screen*, vol. 29, no. 4 (1988), p. 45.
2. Edward Said, *Orientalism: Western Conceptions of the Orient*, 25th Anniversary Edition (London: Penguin, 2003).
3. Said, *Orientalism*, p. 331.
4. Said, *Orientalism*, p. 332.
5. Betty Clarke, 'Christina Aguliera: Stripped', *Guardian*, 25 October 2002, http://www.guardian.co.uk/arts/fridayreview/story/0,,818206,00.html (25/07/2005); Joe D'Angelo, '"Dirrty" Christina Aguilera Video Thai-ed To Sex Industry', *MTV News*, 18 October 2002, http://www.mtv.com/news/articles/1458223/10182002/nullaguilera_christina.jhtml (20/07/2005).
6. Christopher O'Connor, 'Christina Aguilera Tops Puff Daddy With #1 Album in U.S.', *VH1.com*, 1 September 1999, http://www.vh1.com/artists/news/517097/09011999/aguilera_christina.jhtml (05/07/2005).
7. Eric Boehlert, 'Christina Aguilera, Puff Daddy Displace Backstreet Boys, Limp Bizkit', *Rolling Stone*, September 1999.
8. Jacqueline Hodges, 'Stripped' (no date), http://www.bbc.co.uk/music/pop/reviews/aguilera_stripped.shtml#review (03/07/2005).
9. Juan Mendez, 'Unbottled and Unleashed: Christina Aguilera', *Latina*, December 1999, pp. 78, 80.
10. Myra Mendible, 'Embodying Latinidad', in Myra Mendible (ed.), *From Bananas to Buttocks: The Latina Body in Popular Film and Culture* (Austin: University of Texas Press, 2007), p. 9.
11. Said, *Orientalism*, p. 332.
12. Nira Yuval-Davis, 'Ethnicity, Gender Relations and Multiculturalism', in P. Werbner and T. Modood (eds), *Debating Cultural Hybridity: Multi-cultural Identities and the Politics of Anti-Racism* (London: Zed Books, 1997), pp. 193–4.
13. Alberto Sandoval-Sánchez, 'De-Facing Mainstream Magazine Covers: The New Faces of Latino/a Transnational and Transcultural Celebrities', *Encrucijada/Crossroads: An Online Academic Journal*, vol. 1, no. 1 (2003), p. 23.
14. Angharad Valdivia, 'Is Penélope to J.Lo as Culture is to Nature? Eurocentric approaches to "Latin" Beauties', in Mendible (ed.), *From Bananas to Buttocks*, p. 140.
15. Clara E. Rodríguez, *Latin Looks: Images of Latinas and Latinos in the U.S. Media* (Boulder: Westview Press, 1997), p. 6; Valdivia, 'Is Penélope to J.Lo as Culture is to Nature?', p. 135.
16. Wilfred Sellars, *Science and Metaphysics* (London: Routledge and Kegan Paul, 1968).
17. Sandoval-Sánchez, 'De-Facing Mainstream Magazine Covers', p. 23.
18. Jennifer L. Willis, '"Latino Night": Performance of Latino/a Culture in Northwest Ohio', *Communication Quarterly*, vol. 45, no. 4 (1997), pp. 335–50.
19. Judith Ortiz Cofer, *The Latin Deli: Prose and Poetry* (New York: W. W. Norton and Company, 1995), p. 150.
20. Maria Elena Cepeda, 'Mucho Loco For Ricky Martin: Or the Politics of Chronology, Crossover and Language Within the Latin(o) Music "Boom"', *Popular Music and Society*, vol. 24, no. 3 (2000), p. 57; Shari Roberts, '"The Lady in the Tutti-Frutti Hat": Carmen Miranda, a Spectacle of Ethnicity', *Cinema Journal*, vol. 32, no. 3 (1993), p. 11.
21. Shari Roberts, '"The Lady in the Tutti-Frutti Hat"', p. 11.
22. David E. Thigpen, 'Christina's World', *Time*, vol. 154, no. 7 (1999).
23. While it is now commonplace to assert that textual interpretation of any kind of

language is always an imprecise process, it is nevertheless possible to discern a fairly obvious sexual narrative in Aguilera's 'Genie in a Bottle' (RCA, 1999). The song begins with Aguilera claiming to 'feel like I've been locked up tight / For a century of lonely nights / Waiting for someone to release me'. And while she warns the person to whom the lyrics are directed that she is not 'gonna give it away' or that 'it might not be tonight', she nevertheless makes it clear that her 'body's saying let's go' and that 'if you want to be with [her]' then 'you gotta rub [her] the right way'.

24. Frances R. Aparicio and Susana Chavez-Silverman (eds), *Tropicalizations: Transcultural Representations of 'Latinidad'* (Hanover: University Press of New England, 1997), p. 12.

25. *Disney Channel Magazine*, 'Christina Aguilera Biography' (no author, no date), http://www.christinamultimedia.com/newssource/index.php?date=1993–00&articleID=57 (23/06/2005); Laura Jamison, 'Heavy Weight', *Teen People*, December 1999; Leila Cobo, 'Christina Aguilera Prepares Spanish Debut', *Billboard Magazine*, 7 August 2000, http://www.billboard.com/bb/search/article_display.jsp?vnu_content_id=1314735 (12/06/2005); Jane Gardner, 'What a Chica Wants!', *Popstar*, September 2000, http://www.christinamultimedia.com/newssource/index.php?date=2000–00&articleID=6909 (23/07/2005); Teri van Horn, 'Christina Aguilera Delves Into Latin Roots On Spanish LP', *MTV News*, 16 August 2000, http://www.mtv.com/news/articles/1424794/20000816/story.jhtml (23/06/2005); *Yahoo News*, 'Costa del Christina', 9 September 2000, http://uk.news.yahoo.com//dotmusic_news/15328.html (23/06/2005); *Hispanic Business*, 'Hispanic Boom Yet to Arrive', 24 June 2003, http://www.christinamultimedia.com/newssource/index.php?articleID=4692 (03/07/2005).

26. Rex Rutkoski, 'Multi-Platinum Blond: Christina Aguilera Finds Success In A Genie Bottle', *The Inside Connection* (2000), http://www.insidecx.com/interviews/archive/christina.html (23/06/2005); Richard Torres, 'Sonidos Latinos Latin Sounds: A True Talent, in English and Spanish', *Newsday*, 17 September 2000, p. 27; *Yahoo News*, 'Costa del Christina', 9 September 2000, http://uk.news.yahoo.com//dotmusic_news/15328.html (23/06/2005); Steve Huey, 'Christina Aguilera: Biography', *Yahoo Music* (no date), http://music.yahoo.com/ar-293441-bio--Christina-Aguilera (20/07/2005); *LA Times*, 'Aguilera Releases Spanish Album', September 2000, http://www.christinamultimedia.com/newssource/index.php?articleID=1276 (23/07/2005).

27. Torres, 'Sonidos Latinos Latin Sounds', p. 27; Christopher John Farley, 'Inner Visions: A Teen Pop Vocalist Rediscovers Her Latin Side', *Time*, vol. 156, no. 13 (2000), p. 101.

28. Customer Reviewers, 'Mi Reflejo: Customer Reviews', *Amazon.com* (no date), http://www.amazon.com/gp/product/customer-reviews/B00004WJDG/ref=cm_cr_dp_2_1/104–9909223–9983150?%5Fencoding=UTF8&s=music (14/07/2005).

29. thescarletweasel, 'Is A Non-Latino Latino?', in 'Cultura Discussion Forum' (posted 8 April 2005) *Latina.com*, http://forums.prospero.com/n/mb/message.asp?webtag=latcultura&msg=465.1 (20/07/2005); bstn57, 'Is A Non-Latino Latino?', in 'Cultura Discussion Forum' (posted 8 April 2005) *Latina.com*, http://forums.prospero.com/n/mb/message.asp?webtag=latcultura&msg=465.1 (20/07/2005).

30. *ALMA Awards.com*, 'About ALMA Awards: Background and Purpose' (no date), http://www.almaawards.com/wmspage.cfm?parm1=45 (23/07/2005).

6. MASCULINITY AND THE ABSENT PRESENCE OF THE MALE BODY

The previous two chapters have explored the ways in which feminine identities are both presented and represented, produced and reproduced, in and through the codes and conventions of music video and how, in turn, these codes and conventions are embedded within wider networks of representations which enable and circumscribe the limits of their intelligibility. More specifically, we have argued that these identities cannot be understood as ontological givens, as the result of genetic biology, material physicality and deep psychology, but are rather enactments of being, imitations of behaviour and reiterations of selfhood that are constructed and sustained by discursive means. In this respect, the position we have been developing chimes with the work of Judith Butler and her now well-established notion of performativity, the idea that the gendered body has 'no ontological status apart from the various acts which constitute its reality' and, as such, gender itself is always 'tenuously constituted in time, instituted in an exterior space through a *stylized repetition of acts*'.[1]

This is not to say, however, that gendered identity can be reworked and remade at will in a kind of radical dressing-up game, that identity operates merely as a symbolic deception or corporeal simulation. Neither is it to suggest that all subject positions and possibilities are equally available to all people at all times, nor that identities conceived as performative are any less subject to regimes of symbolic and social power than those conceived ontologically. Indeed, to say that gender is performative, that it is as much written on the body as it is lived through the body, is not the same thing as saying that it is possible to transcend or deny the body, nor that identity has wriggled free of external regulation, supervision and control. In other words, there are always limits to just how malleable and amenable identity can be. For there are not only very real constraints on what identity can be 'performed' by whom, but also normative restrictions placed on the terms of its realisation and materialisation. This holds both for the way identities are lived and enacted in the real world by real people and for the way identities are constituted in forms of cultural representation. Indeed, the two cannot be cleanly separated.

This position frames the now commonplace assertion of many theories of gender that masculinity is every bit as discursive, contingent, constructed and performed as femininity. What is more, the question of how male identity is variously inscribed in popular culture, as well as the processes by which cultural representations operate as a resource for the lived enactment of 'being masculine', offers critics one way of unmaking the category of universal masculinity and destabilising its presumed unity, coherence and security. However, just as the claim that men are no less gendered than women is not the same as saying that women are no more oppressed than men, to claim that masculinity is discursively constructed is not to claim that all men have equal access to discourses of masculinity and their attendant regimes of power. Connell's concept of 'hegemonic masculinity' is useful here in so far as it acknowledges not only that masculinity is historically constituted within social practice but also that it is plural, dynamic and complex.[2] Moreover, the cash value of this concept is that, on the one hand, it focuses attention on the practices by which men maintain their dominance over women while, on the other hand, stressing that masculinity is not monolithic but rather internally fractured and organised hierarchically. In this respect, hegemonic masculinity 'is always constructed in relation to various subordinated masculinities as well as in relation to women' and, thus, operates as a particular configuration of gendered identity which positions both.[3] As such, hegemonic masculinity is not descriptive of particular powerful people, social groups, or even specific acts, but is better understood as certain 'currently accepted' cultural ideals, or exemplars of masculinity, that work to preserve 'the legitimacy of patriarchy'.[4] Patriarchy, therefore, is achieved, not by force, violence or coercion, but through strategies of persuasion. Or more precisely, hegemonic masculinity seduces both men and women into compliance, even if the consequences of such compliance are worse for women than for men.

In a more recent article, written with James W. Messerschmidt, Connell has returned to hegemonic masculinity in order to re-examine the concept in light of developments in the field and to reformulate it in contemporary terms.[5] Of particular interest, here, is the article's concern with the idea, or possibility, of multiple hegemonic masculinities. What emerges from this is not only a more complex model of gender hierarchy – of men's relationship to women as well as their relationship to other men – but, perhaps more interestingly, the idea of 'the geography of masculine configurations', a model for analysing 'empirically existing hegemonic masculinities' in terms of their geographic and social location.[6] Connell and Messerschmidt suggest adopting an analytical framework geared around three geographic levels, the local, the regional and the global, a tripartite distinction which reveals the importance of place in the construction of gendered identity. Glossing Connell's original formulation of hegemonic masculinity in this way impels us to recognise that masculinities, like femininities, are constructed in specific locations and are thus framed within local discourses. However, these local contexts always exist within, and interact with, wider discursive fields that operate at regional and global levels. So, while the global level does not determine the totality of local hegemonic masculinities it nevertheless cannot be ignored. Indeed, this observation goes some way towards explaining both the existence of, and need for, multiple hegemonic masculinities. Simply put, patriarchy, in order to be effective, must adapt to its local context.

Connell and Messerschmidt's geographical model for analysing empirically existing hegemonic masculinities is useful, *mutatis mutandis*, for thinking through the plurality of ways in which men are represented in popular culture generally, and in music video specifically. Indeed, at the level of representation, music video sets in motion a complex interplay between the local, the regional and the global. In the first instance, music video makes a range of local hegemonic masculinities available at a global level. So while any one video will present a specific geo-cultural masculinity, on a general level the complex generic context which frames the production and reception of music videos, as well as the heterogeneous context of their broadcast and dissemination, means that multiple masculine subject positions are on offer. Even though it is tempting to simply map these different subject positions onto different genres of music and, by extension, their associated music video channels, this is far too reductive. Not only can the same video feature in the schedules of two or more channels of different generic identity, but it is important to acknowledge that multiple subject positions may coexist and compete in any single generic configuration. Most obviously, for example, Kanye West's GOLD DIGGER (2005) regularly featured, and continues to feature, on general pop-oriented channels such as VH1, TMF, The Box and Smash Hits while also appearing on 'black music' channels such as MTV Base, Kiss and Flava. The important point, here, is that while the image of masculinity articulated by West's video is clearly different to the one embodied by such TMF staples as James Blunt or Take That, it is also very different from other high-profile black performers such as Snoop Dogg, Mystikal or 50 Cent. Indeed, it is West's difference from what Patricia Hill Collins calls the controlling image of black men as 'aggressive thugs or as promiscuous hustlers' that allows Athena D. Mutua to argue that West is 'one of the more interesting hip hop artists' inasmuch as he not only offers 'a more nuanced understanding of [racial] oppression' but also embodies 'the twin concepts of *progressive blackness* and *progressive masculinity*'.[7]

If in the first instance music video makes a range of local hegemonic masculinities available at a global level, then in the second instance, and precisely through exalting the diversity of local masculinities, this global display of difference tends to disguise the pernicious work of global hegemonic masculinity. And, of course, this is where the real political rub is felt. For, in discussions of differences between modes of masculinity, it is too easy to lose sight of the idea that the primary function of hegemonic masculinity (regardless of whether it is conceived as a singular or a plural concept) is to maintain a sex-role system that privileges men over women. On this view, even if at one level West's performance of the progressive black masculine self can be seen, as Mutua suggests, as 'unique and innovative', at another level it is yet one more iteration of global hegemonic masculinity.[8] Put simply, while it is important that there are a range of masculine subject positions made available through popular culture – something that we explore in the context of music video below – what remains all important is that, with very few exceptions, they are constructed and operate within the rigid constraints of heteronormative discourse. In this context, even performances of masculinity which at first sight seem to be questioning the unity and fixity of masculine subjectivity very often end up not only leaving the power dynamics between men and women untouched, but worse, also extend the range of ways of being a man who 'acceptably' oppresses women.

What follows, then, is an exploration of some of the principal ways in which music video attempts to solve what, in a different context, Ina Rae Hark has called the 'dilemma of masculine subjectivity', a situation in which male identity is dependent on the material and/or symbolic subjugation of another for its definition and power.[9] And of course, as Connell suggests, while that 'other' can be other men, it is also always other(ed) women. In this respect, music video offers a range of local solutions to this dilemma, solutions that are articulated through, and in relation to, the various genres of popular music and their related subcultures. Indeed, at this point it is useful to recast Connell and Messerschmidt's tripartite geography of hegemonic masculinities into a form that helps us describe the interrelationships between the global, the regional and the local as it relates specifically to the operation and analysis of music video. In this context, the local is descriptive of the many different representations of masculinity portrayed in music video and accounts for the fact that, on a cursory inspection, the image of Kanye West in GOLD DIGGER is very different to the image of 50 Cent in CANDYSHOP (2003). The regional operates on the level of music genre and relates to how generic conventions regulate the ways of being masculine. This explains why both GOLD DIGGER and CANDYSHOP's representations of masculinity strike us as quite different to those contained in James Blunt's YOU'RE BEAUTIFUL (2005) or Take That's PATIENCE

(2006). It is worth stressing in light of what we discuss below that these differences are not simply a result of the former being black men and the latter being white men. Rather, it is because these artists are working within different genres of popular music (respectively, hip hop and pop) that are themselves empirically and symbolically raced. The global, then, is constructed in the transnational arenas of globalised business and celebrity culture, and refers not only to the ways in which different masculinities are raced but also to the way that popular music as a form is gendered. This is not to imply a straightforward unidirectional flow of power from the global to the local. Indeed, as the conclusion to this chapter discusses, the local can, in certain instances, pose a challenge to the sovereignty of the global. It is to say, however, that these instances tend to be the exception rather than the rule to the extent that the corporate and cultural discourses that frame the global usually have the power to shape local hegemonic masculinities. Adopting this analytical framework, an approach which is sensitive to the different sexed and raced masculine subject positions available to men, allows us not only to identify and interrogate individual manifestations of local hegemonic masculinities but also to situate these local masculinities within both regional and global contexts, which is to say, of course, to situate them in relation to women and femininities. As such, we will begin by discussing a particularly interesting example of a local black masculinity.

Black Masculinity and Women's Bodies

The representation of black masculinity in D'Angelo's UNTITLED (HOW DOES IT FEEL?) (1999) is simultaneously typical and atypical of the way in which tropes of raced and sexed identity are inscribed on the black male body. It is typical in so far as its aestheticisation and eroticisation of the naked black male body is typical of what Kobena Mercer calls 'certain ways in which white people "look" at black people and how, in this way of looking, black male sexuality is perceived as something different, excessive, Other'.[10] The context in which Mercer says this is in his discussion of the images of black men in Robert Mapplethorpe's *The Black Book* and *Black Males*. Keith M. Harris has made a similar comparison between UNTITLED and Mapplethorpe's work in suggesting that the 'austerity of the video renders the visualization of the song as one more within a photographic tradition than a video one'.[11] Indeed, in many ways it is profitable to think about UNTITLED as an animated version of those photographs, images which not only deploy the conventions of Western art to sculpt and fetishise the black male body into an erotic object of contemplation and fascination, but also to fragment and dissect that body into an object of scrutiny and curiosity. For, like Mapplethorpe's photographs, the video's sole focus is the naked black male body, a body posed on a revolving pedestal and displayed against a solid black background. Shot in a single take, the video works through a combination of static medium-long-shots which frame the singer from the hips up – or perhaps more precisely from just above the base of the penis – and slow zooms which, at their destination, frame parts of the body in extreme close-up. It begins, however, with a slow track across the side of D'Angelo's head revealing not only the sculpture of the ear but also the fine detail of his tightly cornrowed hair. Eventually his body turns on its plinth to meet the camera's gaze face-to-face in an extreme close-up of his closed eyes. As his eyes flick open we tilt down to a close-up of his mouth and then embark on a deliberate zoom out to reveal his face, neck, shoulders, chest and torso. In this way, the opening of the video establishes that its subject is not simply D'Angelo but rather blackness and the black male body as site of erotic fantasy. The initial focus on the cornrows is crucial in this respect in so far as hair itself is an important marker of raced identity. Brenda Dixon Gottschild argues that even though 'carefully constructed cornrows may have signified order and adherence to communal values in traditional African cultures' in their transposition to Western culture they have come to signify 'raunchy radicalism' and 'primitive sexuality'.[12] Moreover, the brilliance of the whites of the eyes and enamel of the teeth and their contrast to the black of the backdrop and the dark tones of D'Angelo's skin make it clear that this primitive sexuality is raced, that it is black male sexuality that is being scrutinised, aestheticised, fetishised.[13]

The series of zooms and close-ups which then follow not only crop and fragment the black body into ever more intense images of fascination but, in combination with a lighting scheme which enhances the sculpted musculature of D'Angelo's body, fix attention on the shining surface of the black skin itself. And, of course, it is skin which is 'the alpha and omega of racial difference'.[14] For as Stuart Hall argues, skin colour functions as the most visible 'ethnic signifier', and is 'the most visible of fetishes' according to Homi K. Bhabha.[15] Indeed, as Mercer states, one of the functions of shiny, glistening black skin is not simply to indicate the 'physical exertion of powerful bodies' but also to 'suggest intense sexual activity'.[16] As the camera zooms back in towards D'Angelo's body we see sweat rolling down past his navel, its downward course suggesting just such intense sexual activity occurring out of sight, just beneath the bottom of the frame. In fact, it is what remains out of sight that is the true focus of the video; not the implied sexual activity but the locus of this activity – the black penis. So even if, on the one hand, UNTITLED is unlike many of Mapplethorpe's photographs inasmuch as the black penis remains literally unrevealed, on the other hand the video's tantalising framing and D'Anglelo's own performance constantly direct our eyes to the bottom of the frame and thus reinscribe the hidden penis as 'the forbidden totem of colonial fantasy'.[17] Therefore, with D'Angelo, as with Mapplethorpe's images, 'what we *see* is only [his] *sex* as the essential sum total of the meanings signified around blackness and maleness'.[18] In other words, even though the penis is not on display, the sexualised image of a black male body 'becomes reduced to a focus on the Black male penis as a distillation of the essence of Black masculinity'.[19] The political point here, of course, is that in fixing black masculinity around what Robyn Wiegman calls a 'super phallic imago' and thus locating the 'essence' of black masculinity in the domain of sexuality, black men become 'confined and defined in their very *being* as sexual and nothing but sexual, hence hypersexual'.[20] In this sense, then, the image of hypersexual black masculinity replayed in UNTITLED can be understood as a very specific form of racial fetish, one built around a pull between envy and fear, attraction and repulsion, admiration and threat.

Even if the video is typical of raced and racist patterns of looking, it is, however, atypical in so far as, in the context of music video, black men's sexuality is overwhelmingly defined not through the display of the male body itself but rather in terms of access to the bodies of women, and more often than not black women. This notion of access is instigated and played out in a number of ways. Firstly, some videos establish a one-on-one relationship between a black man and a (usually black) woman, a relationship which is nearly always geared around her sexualised performance for him. For instance, Wayne Wonder's NO LETTING GO (2003), Cassidy's HOTEL (2004), Sean Paul's EVER BLAZIN' (2005), and Akon's BELLYDANCER (BANANZA) (2005) are all staged performance videos which feature black women explicitly desiring the black male performer – often despite his apparent indifference to her – and expressing this desire through highly provocative and overtly sexualised dance moves. Indeed, even in videos where black men are not the performer of the song, videos such as Beyoncé Knowles's CRAZY IN LOVE (2003) and DÉJÀ VU (2006), Ashanti's ROCK WIT U (2003), and Kelis's BLINDFOLD ME (2006), the female artists, through similar dance routines, make themselves available to the scrutinising gaze and physical touch of an (often unnamed) black man. A variant of this mode is the narrative video, or generic hybrids which feature a strong narrative element, in which access to the woman's body is motivated by the story's conceit. So, the scenes of Usher and his ex-lover in LET IT BURN (2004), Nelly's liaison with girl-next-door Kelly Rowland in DILEMMA (2002), Ne-Yo's infidelity in BECAUSE OF YOU (2006) and Akon's secret romance in DON'T MATTER (2007) are all activated by the video's narrative premise and enacted within a fictional diegesis. Either way, the sexualised imagery makes it clear that the woman is available to be looked at and to be touched. And it is precisely this evident availability that both confirms the desirability of the black man and confers sexual power on him.

The second main mode of access to women's bodies afforded to black men in music video also works to communicate the desirability of a potent black male sexuality but, instead of being played out around individual and individuated women, is signalled by the casual availability of seemingly any and all women. Whatever the genre of the video, this casual availability usually entails a social situation – the street, the neighbourhood, a beach or house party, and so forth – involving groups of black men and women. Perhaps the most common of these situations, however, is 'the club'. Redman's LET'S GET DIRTY (2000), Nelly's HOT IN HERRE (2002), R Kelly's IGNITION (2003), 50 Cent's IN DA CLUB (2003) and Little Brother's LOVIN IT (2005), for example, all use the setting of 'the club' not only to sanction a sexualised gaze directed towards women's bodies, but also as a way of apparently justifying the touching, groping and fondling of those bodies as they variously dance, stand at the bar, or simply walk by. Indeed, the third main way in which access to women's bodies is granted to black men in music videos is through the formalisation of this kind of casual availability into an economic contract. In other words, videos such as Dr Dre's THE NEXT EPISODE (2000), N.E.R.D'.s LAP DANCE (2001), Ludacris's PUSSY POPPIN' (2003), and 50 Cent's CANDYSHOP (2005) all make the unlimited access to women's bodies dependent on the ability to pay for that access. Put simply, these videos deploy the trappings of the commercial sex industry – lap dancing, pole dancing and prostitution – as a means of articulating black male sexuality around the ownership of women's bodies rather than the black male body itself. As Patricia Hill Collins argues, 'those African American men who rely upon ideas of Black sexual prowess to define Black masculinity, especially Black heterosexual prowess, typically need women in order to actualize this type of masculinity'.[21] Indeed, in general, black male sexuality in music videos is not represented as a phallic, corporeal male body, but is rather displaced onto the visible bodies of black women. Here, the black female body, or more specifically, the ability to have black women's bodies put on display for the (black) male gaze, becomes both the symbolic stand-in for, and the projection of, omnipotent black male sexuality.

Masculinity and the Absence of the Body

Disavowing the sex of the male body by displacing it on to the hypervisible bodies of women is one strategy, particularly associated with representations of black artists, for disguising the somatic nature of masculinity. It is, however, only one strategy amongst many, all of which have a long history in Western traditions of representation. Indeed, Susan Bordo argues that 'male scientists and philosophers have created a nearly unbroken historical stream of tracts – philosophical, religious, scientific – on women's bodies . . . [b]ut they have been remarkably good at forgetting that men have a sex'.[22] Similarly, Maxine Sheets-Johnstone has argued that 'within cultural practice . . . a male's body is not anatomized nor is it ever made into an object of study in the same way as female bodies'.[23] This is perhaps not surprising given that, to paraphrase de Beauvoir, man, defined as the absolute human, never has to present himself as a sexed being with glands, hormones and testicles – for 'it goes without saying that he is a man'.[24] With one important qualification: this line of thinking tends to assume a white man and a white male body. For, as we have seen in relation to D'Angelo's UNTITLED, there is a history of scientific and artistic representation that has sought to scrutinise and particularise the black male body, even if more recent traditions efface that body by covering it or projecting its sexuality on to women. Either way, what analysis of UNTITLED, and to a lesser extent videos such as CANDYSHOP, HOT IN HERRE and LET'S GET DIRTY, achieves is, if nothing else, to throw into relief the absent presence of the white male body in representation. In other words, when it comes to the white male body, and the sex of that body, music video overwhelmingly tends to confirm Bordo, Sheets-Johnstone and de Beauvoir's thinking in so far as it is de-sexed, de-anatomised and forgotten. This disavowal of the male body is achieved through a combination of deletion, disguise and displacement.

The Deleted Male Body

While the commercial imperatives of music video make it uncommon for the bodies of male artists to be completely absent from their music videos, the examples that do exist can nevertheless be seen as one extreme of a continuum of representational strategies that conspire to elide the male body from vision. Some examples, which tend to work within the generic conventions of the art music video, entirely delete the male body through techniques of abstraction or semi-abstraction. For instance, the videos for Funki Porcini's 'Atomic Kitchen' (2002), Coldcut's 'Sound Mirrors' (2006), and Sigur Ros's 'Hljómalind' (2007) all pretermit the masculine performer of the song from the visual performance of the video by ignoring the human form and, instead, focusing on the play of light, colour, shape and motion. Other videos realise the same ends by different means. Benny Benassi's SATISFACTION (2002), Boogie Pimps' SOMEBODY TO LOVE (2003), Narcotic Thrust's I LIKE IT (2004), Alex Gaudino's DESTINATION CALABRIA (2006) and MSTRKRFT's EASY LOVE (2006) are representative of an increasing number of videos where the music is produced by male artists, often the organising figure of the DJ, but the video exclusively features women and women's bodies.

Another tactic that erases the corporeal male body is to assign it a graphic stand-in which, depending on the individual video, operates at varying degrees of difference from both the anatomical composition of the human male form in general and the image of the respective male performer(s) specifically. For example, the bovine and porcine protagonists in the video for Radiohead's '2+2=5' (2003) are not only anthropomorphically narrativised into a story about the brutal consequences of capitalism, but are also clearly gendered. Here, a combination of 2D and 3D animation is used to depict the proletariat male body as, somewhat paradoxically, a horned cow while their bourgeois masters are rendered as fat snarling pigs. Gigi D'Agostino's BLA, BLA, BLA (2000) and THE RIDDLE (2000) also use animation to absent actual photographic male bodies and replace them with virtual graphic ones. Both feature the same rudimentary character, rendered using primitive white marks against a single-colour background (black and green respectively), to tell a simple story of his journey along an unbroken white line. To borrow from de Beauvoir once again, in consisting entirely of basic geometric shapes, points and squiggles these videos superbly ignore the fact of male anatomy while simultaneously making it clear not only that the character is male, but also that masculinity is not predicated on the particularities of the body. In this respect, BLA, BLA, BLA and THE RIDDLE can be seen as a literalisation of de Beauvoir's claim that 'the fact of being a man is no peculiarity'.[25]

There are some useful comparisons to be made between D'Agostino's videos and Robbie Williams's LET LOVE BE YOUR ENERGY (2001) that point us towards some of the ways in which the facticity of the male body is obfuscated even when its representation appears to correspond more directly to identifiable male performers. LET LOVE BE YOUR ENERGY, like BLA, BLA, BLA and THE RIDDLE, is based around a simple quest-oriented plot and depicts its male protagonist running through various environments, encountering a range of characters, and overcoming a series of obstacles in search of resolution, in this case uniting with 'the woman of his dreams' atop a mountain. The main point here, however, is that, despite using 3D computer animation, being rendered in far more detail, and even despite the fact that its protagonist is clearly a Robbie Williams cartoon avatar, the male body is still absent even if it appears to have a greater presence than in the videos discussed above. So, while the character *is* immediately recognisable as Williams, this has less to do with the particular caricature and more to do with the song/voice. Moreover, as the video progresses Williams's identity is further deferred to a series of synechdochic facial gestures, the raising of an eyebrow, a cheeky grin, and a knowing glance at the camera. Put simply, we know that the video's protagonist is Williams, not strictly speaking because it 'looks' like him (in fact the caricature is in many ways quite weak), but because it 'sounds' like he does and 'does' what he does. In this sense, masculinity literally becomes a performance, but, of course, one not predicated on a sexed body. Indeed, the sexing of the avatar is achieved not through representing the peculiarities of the male body but, quite the contrary, through representing the peculiarities of the female body in the other characters he meets on his journey. As such, the performance of masculinity in LET LOVE BE YOUR ENERGY becomes dematerialised and disembodied in three ways: defined by action, in the sense of being at the centre of a quest; defined as certain traits and mannerisms, such as a cocksure swagger and an impertinent flirtatiousness; and defined against what it is not, the image of sexed female bodies. In the end, therefore, these three strategies function not only to instil considerable distance between the real embodied Robbie Williams and the representation of him in the music video, but also to effect a break between masculinity and the (sexed) male body. It is in this sense, then, that the presence of masculinity is predicated on, or necessitates, the absence or deletion of the male body.

The Displaced Male Body

Notwithstanding what we have said above about attempts to entirely eradicate the male body from the frame, it is true to say that the majority of music videos contain images of the 'real' male body. It is also true to say, however, that access to that body is managed in such a way as to render it neither sexed nor sexual. Indeed, just as in LET LOVE BE YOUR ENERGY, it is the actions of the performers, rather than their bodies, that serve to define their masculinity. In other words, by objectifying action and activity, these videos uncouple masculinity from the sex of the body and locate it elsewhere. More often than not this is accomplished by displacing it onto either the skills of musicianship or onto a hyperbolic portrayal of emotional sincerity. In both cases, the result is to desexualise male physicality and, in doing so, reinforce the long-standing equation between the male body and the 'absolute human' body.

The Strokes's REPTILIA (2004) is exemplary of the first of these strategies in so far as its formal and aesthetic composition dislocates the masculinity of the band members from their bodies and instead invests it in the fetishised performance of their musical abilities. The video is comprised exclusively of a series of close-up shots cut together in rapid succession which showcase the particular skill, style and artistry of each band member. Indeed, it is perhaps more accurate to say that the band members are reduced to the markers of their virtuosity. So, the singer, Julian Casablancas, becomes a face behind a microphone, a hand gripping its stand, and feet in scuffed white loafers at its base. The drummer becomes Converse hi-top sneakers working the pedals, drumsticks hitting the skins and cymbals, and a dense thicket of black hair that bounces as he pounds out the beat. And it is fingers moving along the fretboards of guitars, picking or strumming at their strings, and the image of a battered trainer marking out the rhythm of the song on the floor that substitute for the band's three guitarists. The effect of this fragmentation is to abstract masculinity from the flesh of the body and reposition it in a series of actions that come to stand for that body, actions that entail not only mastery of the instrument but, by extension, control of the world itself. This process offers a striking example of the way in which the male body operates as an absent presence in forms of cultural representation, present as a series of tropes of universal masculinity yet absented from a particularising and scrutinising gaze. The moment in REPTILIA that best exemplifies this tendency comes towards the end of the video when the frame divides first into a two-way then into a four-way split-screen sequence. Each quartern offers a distillation of the representational strategies that define the video in so far as the image of Casablancas's disembodied face, partially obscured by his microphone, is accompanied by a trio of close-ups of the three guitarists' fingers forming the song's chords on their frets. In a single image, therefore, masculinity is defined by what the body does, its purposeful actions, rather than the body itself, its manifest physicality. Even though REPTILIA presents a particularly concentrated instance of this strategy at work, it can nevertheless be found in videos for songs as musically diverse as Jamie Cullum's jazz-inspired 'All at Sea' (2003), Zac Brown Band's country hit 'Chicken Fried' (2008), and Pantera's post-thrash groove metal track 'Five Minutes Alone' (1994).

The second strategy which works to de-sexualise the male body does so by displacing masculinity onto exaggerated displays of emotional sincerity. In other words, in constructing masculine identity around the sentiments, and in particular romantic sentiments, the sex of the male body becomes obscured by its association with a set of traditionally feminine discourses – sensitivity, vulnerability, wistfulness and a general softheartedness in matters of love and life. Indeed, the body's primary role, here, is to make internal emotional states available externally by recourse to representational strategies that, to a greater or lesser extent, feminise the male performers. This is achieved by using a variety of techniques. In the first instance, the body is isolated in the sense that it is very often entirely alone, physically disconnected, represented as a singular and solitary body. This is commonly achieved by staging the video in domestic space, very often the bedroom, and using that environment to represent the emotional isolation of the performer. Moreover, in videos such as James Blunt's GOODBYE MY LOVER (2005), Keith Urban's MAKING MEMORIES OF US (2005), James Morrison's BROKEN STRINGS (2008), and HEY THERE DELILAH (2006) by Plain White T's, what is already coded as a feminine setting is deployed alongside a range of other techniques which function to render the male body variously vulnerable and sensitive. To put it crudely, though in truth not that crudely, on the evidence of videos such as these it appears that walking barefoot around your apartment wearing a white vest or shirt, sitting melancholically on the edge of your bed staring meaningfully into the middle distance, and occasionally picking up an acoustic guitar to express your pent up feelings is sufficient to communicate masculine emotional sincerity.

While locating the male body in a domestic space is one strategy by which masculinity is displaced onto the emotions, perhaps a more common strategy is to situate it in a bleak and barren landscape, isolating it in nature, and rendering it vulnerable to the threat posed by the elements. James Blunt's YOU'RE BEAUTIFUL (2005) offers one example of this in so far as the camera focuses solely on Blunt himself as he sings the words which tell of an unattainable love. Staged on a cliff top and shot against a backdrop of a blank snowy sky, Blunt ritualistically removes his coat, then his shirt, and finally his shoes to expose his bare torso and feet to the wind and the rain. The anguish and emotional torment expressed in the lyrics thus becomes visualised through the physical vulnerability of his body. Indeed, the video's conclusion sees Blunt choosing to leap from the cliff's edge into the ocean below, an image in which the male body is literally sacrificed in an exaggerated display of emotional sincerity.

Even though Blunt is a solo artist this technique of isolating the male body in a threatening landscape in order to articulate inner individual emotional states is nevertheless deployed in a number of videos for songs recorded by bands. In the case of Coldplay's YELLOW (2000) and Snow Patrol's CHASING CARS (2006), all members of the band except the singer are absented from the video thus individualising and personalising the sentiments of the song. By contrast, Boyzone's WORDS (1996), Westlife's YOU RAISE ME UP (2005) and Take That's PATIENCE (2006) do feature all band members but in adopting a *mise en scène* and editing style which serves to physically separate them from each other these videos nevertheless also invest the feelings expressed in the lyrics in individual members of the band. The use of close-ups of the faces of band members is one key technique for achieving this. So, not only is PATIENCE set in a barren, windswept landscape, in a similar fashion to YELLOW and CHASING CARS, with the four performers individuated within the diegesis, but the audience is afforded access to their emotional distress through regular close-ups of pained expressions and angst-ridden faces. Importantly, these close-ups are not necessarily focused on the singer or, in fact, on the act of singing. Indeed, a significant proportion of the shots that comprise videos such as YOU RAISE ME UP, WORDS and PATIENCE feature the wistful faces of one member of the band while another sings in the background. The function of this type of close-up, and indeed of close-ups of singers emoting the lyrics, is quite different to that discussed earlier in relation to The Strokes's REPTILIA. While the latter serves to direct attention to Casablancas's skill as the vocalist of a band, the former's abundance of sentimentality confers emotional integrity onto the performance. Either way, however, the result is a displacement of the male body onto something else which absents it symbolically and often literally from the frame.

The Disguised Male Body

The third, and perhaps most obvious, tactic used to manage access to the male body in music video is to disguise it by variously hiding it beneath clothes or obscuring it behind instruments. While the latter tends to be associated with certain genres of music more than others, the former is, to all intents and purposes, ubiquitous. Although on the one hand such a claim *is* obvious at the level of common-sense, on the other hand its analytical import lies in the comparison it prompts with the representation of women's bodies. This is not simply to say that women's bodies are displayed and sexualised more than men's per se, but that this situation seems normal, and is indeed normalised, even in videos in which one would expect such a contrast to appear ridiculous. The video I WANNA LOVE YOU (2006) serves to illustrate what characterises many videos in so far as the bodies of the song's two performers, Akon and Snoop Dogg, are hidden beneath layers of oversized clothing while the bodies of the female dancers are not only underdressed but emphasised by under-sized clothing. So, whereas Akon is seen variously wearing a red velvet suit, loose-fitting jeans with a leather jacket zipped to the neck, and, later, a heavy woollen coat with its collar turned up, and Snoop wears baggy jeans but swaps between a Cincinnati Reds baseball jacket and cap and a bulky black fur coat with grey fur collar, the dancers perform in items of underwear incongruously embellished with high-heeled shoes, jewellery and, most oddly of all, a long sleeved, polo neck sweater cropped at the level of the armpits. Put crudely, not only do the men appear dressed for wintry outdoor conditions despite being indoors while the women appear in various stages of undress more suited to the privacy of the bedroom, but neither the men's nor the women's clothes fit, the difference being that, in contrast to the female bodies that are squeezed and moulded into exaggerated shape by tight, skimpy garments, the male body is lost beneath the sheer bulk of its capacious clothing. Indeed, though glib, it is accurate to say that the video literalises the lyric sung by Snoop, 'You can't see me but I can see you' inasmuch as it is the women's bodies that are par-ticularised in their visibility whilst those of the men remain unanatomised and shapeless in their sartorial disguise.

Neither the fact that I WANNA LOVE YOU is a staged performance video set in the abstracted spaces of a studio nor the fact that the song it promotes is a hybrid of R&B and rap explains this situation. Quite the contrary, this pattern of representation is neither generically specific in terms of music or music video, nor necessarily motivated by the lyrical content of the song or the particular performance or narrative scenario of any given video. Despite being from quite different music genres, country and pop respectively, both Trace Adkins's HOT MAMA (2003) and Fountains of Wayne's STACY'S MOM (2003) feature male sexual fantasies which show their female protagonists in various stages of undress performing to fully clothed men. However, while it is just about possible to identify a narrative pretext for these representations in the lyrical content of both songs, a similar representation can be found in the videos for Destiny's Child's 'Cater 2 U' and Sasha Dith's 'Russian Girls' which contain no such pretext. In the same way that this strategy operates relatively independently of music genres, it also seems to be able to occupy different genres of music video. So while, for instance, CATER 2 U (2005) and RUSSIAN GIRLS (2005) are both squarely staged performance videos, and STACY'S MOM is organised around the song's narrative, all, nevertheless, obfuscate male corporeality while putting women's bodies on display. Even videos which evidence many conventions associated with the art music video, such as Kanye West's LOVE LOCKDOWN (2008), Make the Girl Dance's BABY, BABY, BABY (2009) and Rocco DeLuca and the Burden's COLORFUL (2006), can use their artistic conceit to justify a gaze at the female form, thus directing it way from the male body.

Either way, the important thing in this context is not simply the lack of clothing on the bodies of women, but rather the inaccessibility of the male body itself. So, for example, while both the bodies of Jay Z and Alicia Keys are predominantly covered in EMPIRE STATE OF MIND (2009) it is the differing ways that their clothes present their bodies which direct us towards the political point, the latter's contoured into exaggerated feminine shape in stark contrast to the amorphous corporeality of the former. Indeed, the comparative element merely serves to throw into relief the ways in which our perceptions of the male body, and by extension definitions of masculinity more generally, are highly regulated by normative cultural and aesthetic codes, those which in the context of music video function to variously delete, displace or disguise the male body. Indeed, in the exceptional cases where the flesh of the male body is made visible it is overwhelmingly for comic purposes. In their own ways Armand van Helden's MY MY MY (2004) and Blink 182's WHAT'S MY AGE AGAIN? (1999) only reveal the flesh of the male body in order to ridicule, mock or poke fun at exposed masculinity. For in dealing with what Lawrence R. Schehr calls 'the taboo on the representation of male nudity', what videos such as these do is make it clear that undressed male bodies, or more precisely men without their clothes on, are, more often than not, simply funny, certainly not sexual.[26] To put this another way, it is difficult, if not impossible, to conceive of a serious mirror version of Benny Benassi's SATISFACTION (2002) in which men take the role of fetish object occupied by the women. Or rather, the only framework in which it is possible to conceive it is a comic one, something borne out by Kelly Llorenna's THIS TIME I KNOW IT'S FOR REAL (2004). For regardless of whether the video is supposed to be funny, that is the effect it achieves.

Perhaps a more interesting example of the exposed male body in music video is provided by Robbie Williams's ROCK DJ (2000). The video features Williams, positioned on a central podium, performing to a women-only audience in a highly stylised roller disco. As the skaters circle him and the DJ busies herself selecting which record to play next, Williams becomes increasingly desperate to attract their attention. In the face of their complete indifference to his dancing, he embarks on a striptease believing this will secure their interest. When this fails, and he stands naked amidst the impervious crowd, he resorts to stripping down to his bare skeleton by literally tearing off his skin, muscles, organs and remaining flesh. Indeed, the more of the body he removes the more interest he manages to garner from the women until, finally, the DJ is convinced to dance with what is left of the skinned and eviscerated Williams. Tara Brabazon reads this as a deconstructive performance capable of disrupting 'the power held by men in phallocentrism'.[27] She argues that ROCK DJ plays 'with the symbols of masculine performance' and in so doing 'attacks the new subjectivities of the male body, by generating not only self-surveillance but humour through the removal of clothes, skin and muscle'.[28] However, while we would agree with Brabazon that Williams is useful to 'theories of masculine representation' in so far as he is good 'to think with', we would disagree with the idea that his strip in ROCK DJ 'reveals the predictability of masculinity and the ordinariness of the male body'.[29] Quite the contrary, for Brabazon's understandable desire to reconnect masculine subjectivity to the male body, in other words to re-embody masculinity for political ends, is simply not borne out in the video itself. Indeed, using similar tactics to those videos discussed above, ROCK DJ's striptease is not only justified by the comic sensibilities that frame the video, but perhaps more importantly, its entire conceit turns on the idea that the male body in its presence and visibility is unattractive, undesirable, and unwanted. Following this logic, it is only when that body is discarded and represented as an absence that consummate masculinity is achieved. It is in this sense that, if the video reveals anything of what is predictable about masculinity it is that, in cultural representation, the male body ordinarily has very little to do with it.

At this point it is worthwhile returning to D'Angelo's UNTITLED in so far as its representation of a stripped male body offers an instructive comparison to ROCK DJ, one which reveals some of the more complex workings of hegemonic masculinity. For, despite a number of obvious superficial similarities, each video constructs masculinity quite differently in relation to the body. In other words, even though both videos are organised around the pedestalled performance of their respective male stars, and even though both of their bodies are put on display, it is here that the comparison ends. Although important, it is not just the different 'race' of the performers, the different colours of their skin, that serves to differentiate the performances. Indeed, the very different sense of raced identity produced by each video emerges from a much more subtle set of differences of genre and register. In the first place, the fact that one is a staged performance video and one is an art music video bears significantly on how we can read them. Operating firmly within the conventions of the staged performance genre, a genre which not only legitimates the skills of its performer but also authenticates an image of that performer that pre-dates the video itself, ROCK DJ thus reconfirms Williams as a knowing hijacker of popular culture's lexicon of former masculinities. So, Williams's performance as a hapless Jackie Stewart-esque, 1960s racing driver in SUPREME (2000), and the inept, Sean Connery inspired, James Bond character he adopts in MILLENNIUM (1998) is reworked in ROCK DJ as an ineffectual cabaret singer working in a 1970s-style roller disco. In each case, Williams's failed attempts to achieve hegemonic masculinity nevertheless function to sanction its nostalgic return in the first place.

UNTITLED also comes with a history. However, its self-reflexive relationship to Mapplethorpe's work serves to uncouple it from the conventions of the staged performance video and shift it into the category marked out as art music video. This is important not only because it authenticates D'Angelo's performance as an intentional, creative art work, but also because it encourages us to read the video's interrogation of the black male body as an historically aware political statement. Indeed, D'Angelo's re-performance of myths of the black male body is every bit as knowing as Williams's pick-and-mix masculinity, but, of course, without the nostalgia. Rather, D'Angelo's co-option of the slave gaze rewrites the history of a look which has traditionally served to regulate and oppress the black male body. It is in this sense that UNTITLED recasts an anonymous peripheral masculinity as a self-authored, non-hegemonic subject position. In fact, it is precisely these generic distinctions, and the different political cultural heritages which each video reactivates, that explain how Williams is able to distance his masculine identity from the fact of the body but D'Angelo ultimately cannot escape its limitations. This idea is reinforced by the different mode of address established by each video. ROCK DJ's ironic register disrupts any straightforward reading of Williams's strip as a sexual display and, in fact, ultimately functions to instil a gap between his identity and his body. UNTITLED, on the other hand, does not have recourse to a similar ironic vocabulary and even though it, too, displays a sophisticated consciousness about the history of its own imagery it cannot open up a similar ironic gap between D'Angelo's identity and body and thus leaves his masculinity firmly rooted in corporeality (D'Angelo frequently looks down his body to what hangs below the frame with obvious pleasure and pride; when Robbie looks down to what is inside his pants, however, it is with a cheeky indifference). It is in this sense that the videos reveal the structured, asymmetrical, relations among masculinities constitutive of the hegemonic model. Put simply, D'Angelo cannot discard his body in the same way as Williams because of the different discursive regimes available to them. By the same token, both masculinities are able to co-exist in the hegemonic model but are positioned in hierarchical relation. As such, while ROCK DJ reiterates and re-circulates a dominant model of masculinity, UNTITLED engages in a re-writing of an imposed peripheral black non-identity as a self-authored position, but one which is nevertheless a marginal one within the hegemonic scheme.

It is in this sense, then, that far from expanding 'the popular cultural vocabulary of masculinity', as Brabazon reads it, Williams's performance of masculinity in ROCK DJ and other videos is actually a re-articulation of an already existing vocabulary.[30] What is novel, and often pleasurable, in Williams's videos is the fluency with which he utilises this lexis in order to inhabit, or resuscitate, extant masculine tropes, images and subjectivities. As such, the ambivalence that Brabazon finds in Williams's performance of masculinity is perhaps more apparent than real inasmuch as it is so often derived from sentimental representations which anchor it to a set of historical certainties. The political result of this is to make nostalgic masculinity part of contemporary quotidian experience. Quite ironically, therefore, the rewritten and re-authored marginal black masculinity of UNTITLED is perhaps more aesthetically complex and politically important than hegemonic masculinity's continual reiteration of its own past successes.

NOTES

1. Judith Butler, *Gender Trouble: Feminism and the Subversion of Identity* (London: Routledge, 1990), pp. 136, 140.
2. Robert W. Connell, *Gender and Power: Society, the Person and Sexual Politics* (Cambridge: Polity Press, 1987); Robert W. Connell, *Masculinities* (Cambridge: Polity Press, 1995); Robert W. Connell and James W. Messerschmidt, 'Hegemonic Masculinity: Rethinking the Concept', *Gender and Society*, vol. 19, no. 6 (2005).
3. Connell, *Gender and Power*, p. 183.
4. Connell, *Masculinities*, p. 77.
5. Connell and Messerschmidt, 'Hegemonic Masculinity'.
6. Connell and Messerschmidt, 'Hegemonic Masculinity', pp. 847, 849.
7. Patricia Hill Collins, *Black Sexual Politics: African Americans, Gender, and the New Racism* (London: Routledge, 2004), p. 189; Athena D. Mutua, 'Theorizing Progressive Black Masculinities', in Athena D. Mutua (ed.), *Progressive Black Masculinities* (London: Routledge, 2006), pp. 3, 4–5.
8. Mutua, 'Theorizing Progressive Black Masculinities', p. 4.
9. Ina Rae Hark, 'Animals or Romans: Looking at Masculinity in *Spartacus*', in Steven Cohan and Ina Rae Hark (eds), *Screening the Male: Exploring Masculinities in Hollywood Cinema* (London: Routledge, 1993), p. 153.
10. Kobena Mercer, *Welcome to the Jungle* (London: Routledge, 1994), p. 173.
11. Keith M. Harris, ' "Untitled": D'Angelo and the Visualization of the Black Male Body', *Wide Angle*, vol. 21, no. 4 (1998), p. 67.
12. Brenda Dixon Gottschild, *The Black Dancing Body: A Geography from Coon to Cool* (New York: Palgrave Macmillan, 2003), p. 207.
13. Dixon Gottschild argues that 'when a brown-skinned person smiles, his white teeth are more clearly delineated against the skin than the smile of a lighter-skinned individual' (Dixon Gottschild, *The Black Dancing Body*, pp. 191–2).
14. Dixon Gottschild, *The Black Dancing Body*, p. 190.
15. Stuart Hall, 'Pluralism, Race and Class in Caribbean Society', in (no editor), *Race, Class and Postcolonial Society* (Paris: UNESCO, 1977); Homi K. Bhabha, 'The Other Question: The Stereotype and Colonial Discourse', *Screen*, vol. 24, no. 8 (1983).

16. Mercer, *Welcome to the Jungle*, p. 184.
17. Mercer, *Welcome to the Jungle*, p. 183.
18. Mercer, *Welcome to the Jungle*, p. 174.
19. Hill Collins, *Black Sexual Politics*, p. 207.
20. Robyn Wiegman, 'Feminism, "The Boyz", and Other Matters Regarding the Male', in Steven Cohan and Ina Rae Hark (eds), *Screening the Male* (London: Routledge, 1993), p. 185; Mercer, *Welcome to the Jungle*, p. 174.
21. Hill Collins, *Black Sexual Politics*, p. 208.
22. Susan Bordo, *The Male Body: A New Look at Men in Public and in Private* (New York: Farrar, Straus and Giroux, 1999), p. 19.
23. Maxine Sheets-Johnstone, *Roots of Power: Animate Form and Gendered Bodies* (Chicago: Open Court, 1994), p. 93.
24. Simone de Beauvoir, *The Second Sex*, trans. H. M. Parshley (New York: Vintage Books, 1989), p. xxi.
25. de Beauvoir, *The Second Sex*, p. xxi.
26. Lawrence R. Schehr, *Parts of an Andrology: On Representations of Men's Bodies* (Stanford: Stanford University Press, 1997), p. 22.
27. Tara Brabazon, 'Robbie Williams: A Better Man?', *International Journal of Cultural Studies*, vol. 5, no.1 (2002), p. 57.
28. Brabazon, 'Robbie Williams: A Better Man?', p. 58.
29. Brabazon, 'Robbie Williams: A Better Man?', p. 57.
30. Brabazon, 'Robbie Williams: A Better Man?', pp. 56, 62.

AFTERWORD: MUSIC VIDEO GOES GAGA

During the writing of this book, Lady Gaga has emerged as a significant global star. Her debut album, *The Fame* (2008), spawned six singles and has so far sold more than 12 million copies worldwide.[1] The second of these, 'Poker Face', was the best-selling digital track of 2009, selling a total of 9.8 million units globally.[2] A further four tracks have been released from her second album, *The Fame Monster* (2009), which topped the album chart in the UK and has to date sold more than 4 million copies. Moreover, MTV recently reported that the online viewing figure for her music videos has now exceeded one billion, the first artist whose work has done so.[3] Visible Measures, a company specialising in calculating internet video reach, documents that three of Lady Gaga's videos, JUST DANCE (2008), BAD ROMANCE (2009) and POKER FACE (2009), have been viewed in excess of 250 million times each. Indeed, these videos occupy three of the top twenty positions in their '100 Million Views Club' – the only music video by a female artist to have been watched more times than these is Beyoncé's SINGLE LADIES (PUT A RING ON IT), which has attracted an audience of more than 500 million.[4] This situation might go some way towards explaining both the cultural success and critical controversy that attended the release in March 2010 of the video for Lady Gaga's 'Telephone', a collaboration with Beyoncé.

A number of critics have referred to the release of TELEPHONE as an 'event'. For example, James Montgomery commented on MTV that 'you will remember where you were when you first saw it' and Armond White claimed in the *New York Press* that it is 'more exciting than any feature-length American film released so far this year'.[5] Moreover, Montgomery hailed the video as a 'medium landmark' and White suggested that its release was her passport to 'the rarest of pop stratospheres, up there with the Madonnas and the, gasp, Michael Jacksons'.[6] Indeed, the film stills posted on Lady Gaga's website more than a month before the official premiere of the video triggered significant initial speculation about its content and the eighteen-second teaser for the video that was subsequently released on the internet was viewed over 5 million times on YouTube and its associated Vevo channel. TELEPHONE itself has, at the time of writing, now been watched more than 120 million times on YouTube alone. The sheer scale of this cultural 'event' was matched not only by the scale of the critical response to it, but also by the passions it incited in the critics who clamoured to respond to it in the press and on the internet. On the one hand, Bridget Barrett declared that 'Gaga is pushing new boundaries in the art of making music videos' and that TELEPHONE is 'an astonishing achievement'.[7] Even more approving was the critic Sady who, writing on the *Feministe* blog, claimed that TELEPHONE was 'the most important film of the year' and operates as the latest contribution to Lady Gaga's 'ongoing project of unpacking female sexuality'.[8] On the other hand, the video has been described as 'a sign of cultural decline', the epitome of 'the insanity of the contemporary pop mainstream [which] celebrates a heedless refusal to communicate; to mindlessly, heartlessly indulge pop culture'.[9] This latter response was perhaps most forcefully expressed by Sandy Rios in an interview with Megyn Kelly on *Fox News* where she described the video as 'disgusting', 'poison for the minds of our kids and our minds too' which 'should be outlawed, it should be banned'.[10]

In this afterword we consider how several ideas explored in the book may be of assistance in understanding this furore which accompanied the release and reception of TELEPHONE and suggest that such phenomena might jump-start critical interest in music video as an important form of contemporary popular culture. Indeed, if the initial burst of interest in music video was very much wedded to a particular socio-historic moment (the emergence of a putatively new form of television) and a specific critical trend in the arts and humanities (a concern with the theory and culture of postmodernism), then the present moment offers us a new set of circumstances and concerns with which it is both possible and desirable to rethink music video as a particular kind of product that implies a multifarious set of cultural practices and operates as a complex form of cultural representation. In other words, if we grant Jason Middleton and Roger Beebe the point that, notwithstanding its 'initial period of relative productivity', the study of music video has tended to remain 'a marginal subfield within television studies', then it is perhaps time to slough off that incipient critical vocabulary and stop seeing music video as merely a form of television.[11] Indeed, as a few critics have begun to suggest, music video's association with television may well turn out to be a pre-historical anomaly, a prototypical blip in the development of the form. For instance, A. J. Ramirez argues that the internet and sites such as YouTube and Vevo are 'so much more a fitting vehicle for the music video medium than any cable network'.[12] So, it is not just the exponential growth, sheer size and geographical reach of sites such as YouTube that is significant, but the fact that the products themselves are increasingly designed for dissemination on multiple platforms, platforms which both imply and impel different modes of consumption. This notion of difference is important not simply because of the sense of *change* it signals from models of consumption developed to describe the encounter with television, but because it captures the idea that the same product is now very often consumed, and is consumable, in a variety of ways. Most obviously, the distinction between the video as a promotional tool for the song and the song proper is increasingly giving way. With the inexorable shift to digital music and the cultural impact of Apple's iPod and iTunes on the music market, sound and image are now frequently welded together in the very acts of purchase and consumption. For a small premium, iTunes's customers can now buy the video rather than just the audio track, a shift in retailing acknowledged by the Official Charts Company in January 2007 with their decision to include music video downloads in the UK singles chart. An allied development has seen a number of artists producing videos for album tracks which are never released as singles in the traditional sense of the term.[13] The clear implication of this practice is an assumption that when listening to a piece of music on devices such as iPods, mobile phones and other portable music platforms there will be an image-track to accompany it. Indeed, both the evolution of the iPod and the design of the current generation of such devices to incorporate high-resolution colour screens imply this.

A second difference relates directly to the impact that the internet has had on the distribution and consumption of music video. Not only does it enable the consumer to select which videos they want to watch and when they want to watch them, but they get to choose from pretty much the entire corpus – facilities not available to the viewer of MTV, a figure which dominated so much of the early theorising of music video as a distinctly postmodern form. Moreover, while that MTV viewer had the record, pause and rewind functions of the VCR at their disposal, such editing functions are redoubled for the internet user who can now literally deconstruct a video, fragment it, reassemble it and, in effect, re-author it on run-of-the-mill software. One result of this is that fans are now able to remake and re-edit music videos to their own design and then redistribute and recirculate these new products. YouTube contains innumerable examples of this kind of fan activity which ranges from homage to parody, prequel to sequel, remake to reassemblage. TELEPHONE, for instance, has been parodied by Key of Awesome, remade by Nofiih, remixed by thehouseofgagamusik, re-edited by rogaga96, and reassembled using footage from previous videos by Shawwtiie.[14] These examples are by no means exceptional. Searching YouTube using the criteria 'telephone fan video' returns nearly 3,000 results; 'telephone parody' returns over 1,500; 'telephone remake' produces over 220; and using 'telephone sims' gets you 152 'movies' which use the production capabilities embedded in the computer game *The Sims 2* to produce replicas of or homages to the video.

Indeed, TELEPHONE offers a particularly fascinating perspective on the relationship between the internet, digital music culture and contemporary patterns of music video production, distribution and consumption. As the blog critic Sady notes, perhaps the most interesting aspect of the video is precisely 'how very internet it is' at the levels of both form and content. She argues that it is 'not *designed* to be shown on television . . . It is ten minutes long, and it has more dialogue than music, and it has the "fuck" word and naked breasts and vaginas and girl-on-girl action and basically everybody gets murdered.'[15] Moreover, she suggests that the specificities of the computer/internet as a platform have penetrated the form of the video in the sense that 'you can tell [it] was meant to be turned into nine million animated GIFs, for example, because there are several parts of it that are shot to look like animated GIFs'.[16] While there is a risk of overstating this impact in any one isolated instance (TELEPHONE is after all a narrative video intercut with aspects of staged-performance), it is nevertheless the case that, on a more general level, this configuration of form, content and platform presents some serious challenges to the traditional models established to conceptualise the way the viewer/user engages with the text and the pleasures derived from doing so. In fact, two of the standard metaphors for describing these processes – the cinematic gaze and the televisual glance – fail to adequately capture the inherent complexity, radical heterogeneity and potential instability of this situation.[17] Put simply, while the notion of the gaze was conceived to account for a relatively controlled encounter between film text and spectator, and the notion of the glance attempted to incorporate more fluidity into the model in order to describe the domestic encounter with televisual texts, we have since entered a moment where cultural texts of all genres can be owned and stored on the same device, easily manipulated and personalised, and transported either physically or digitally from one location to another. And it is these potentialities – the adaptability and the portability of the digital text generally, and music videos specifically – that might go some way towards explaining the recent re-emergence of both public concern over the consumption of videos and an academic response geared around the attempt to gauge their effects on the individual and society.

In their narrative review of the research undertaken into the influence and effects of music video, Atkin and Abelman unearthed 'little in the way of longitudinal, externally valid findings that can establish a "smoking gun" with media influences as potent causal agents with human behaviour'. Moreover, they criticise a number of such studies for conflating and confusing political rhetoric and methodological rigour.[18] They point out that 'in trying to select a compelling stimulus, the researchers typically rely on "worst case" stimuli . . . and present them as "representative" stimuli for a subgenre of music video'.[19] More generally, the severe methodological and conceptual shortcomings of the entire tradition of research into media effects have been thoroughly rehearsed elsewhere.[20] Nevertheless, this has not stood in the way of either the UK or US governments commissioning recent reports into the sexualisation of young people. Both reports subsequently argued that music video plays a causal role in this process. In the case of the former, the report's author, Dr Linda Papadopoulos, deemed there to be sufficient evidence of a damaging link between the content of music videos and the psychological and sexual development of young people to recommend that broadcasters should be compelled to restrict the viewing of videos which contain sexualised imagery.[21] In the case of the latter, the American Psychological Association found that music videos instigated a process of 'adultification' of young girls' sexuality which had consequences for their self-esteem and identity formation, and, by extension, held potential links to the sexual exploitation of them. As a result of its investigations, the APA recommends not only a reduction in the production of such problematic imagery, but also a programme of public education and awareness-raising designed to counteract the putative negative effects of music video.[22]

This 'effects' approach has also found a public voice not only through the national press, but also, and perhaps more curiously, through the work of public intellectuals. Written and narrated by Sut Jhally, professor of communication at the University of Massachusetts and founder of America's Media Education Foundation, *Dreamworlds 3* (an educational documentary) argues that music videos present a 'male dream world' and suggests that even if their 'images of women cannot directly cause sexual and violent assault they do rob women of their humanity and create an environment where attacks against them are not treated seriously'.[23] So while it is not necessarily surprising that newspapers such as the *Daily Mail* should run stories declaring 'Children at Risk From Pop Charts Porn' which condemn music videos as soft pornography, it is more worrying that a cultural scholar of Jhally's standing uses what is essentially teaching material as an opportunity to proselytise on the 'pornographic imagination' that he claims defines 'the system of music video as a whole'.[24] However, perhaps the most surprising thing about this state of affairs is not the one-dimensional and over-generalised analysis that fuels this kind of critical approach, but the lack of a sustained feminist response to it. In other words, if music videos tell 'a consistent story about masculinity and femininity' that is 'based on the degradation and control of women', and if such 'images and stories have worked their way into the inner identities of young women who view their own sexuality through the eyes of the male authors of that culture', then one might have expected some level of reaction.[25] This might have taken the form of a critique of a socio-cultural formation that frames the production of such videos, as well as an analysis of the videos themselves. Alternatively, it might have directed itself towards offering an interrogation of crude effects-based work and providing a more fine-toothed analysis of viewer-text relations. One avenue this latter possibility opens up is the potential identification of videos in which women have worked to resist what Jhally calls 'the visual language that has already been established as the norm' and thus extend the range of representational possibilities available to them and the culture more broadly.[26]

It is here, of course, that TELEPHONE is of particular interest. For it offers a deliberately ambiguous and playfully perverse image of femininity that defies normative conceptions of female sexuality. In its absurdist bricolage of lesbian prison films, female revenge fantasy, feminist road movie, and TV cooking shows it activates a number of complex sex-gender discourses and reworks and repositions them in an indeterminate aesthetic space somewhere between high art and trash culture. Indeed, it is this indeterminacy that also characterises a number of the critical responses to the video. On the one hand, some critics have read the video as presenting 'community between women as [a] very powerful, dangerous, thrilling space'.[27] Adopting a similarly positive approach, another critic reads the image of a naked Lady Gaga wrapped in crime scene tape as a radical comment on a culture in which women's bodies are regularly 'raped, abused, and sexually assaulted' and are thus often literally the physical scene of a crime. Moreover, 'Gaga's body is also a "crime scene" when it comes to crimes of sexual transgression' in so far as her refusal to fulfil traditional expectations of femininity operates as 'a crime against heteronormativity'.[28] On the other hand, other critics have seen this very differently and criticised the video for the way it exploits some female sexualities for commercial notoriety. While not entirely dismissive of the video's fast and loose representation of female sexuality, Sady nevertheless argues that TELEPHONE has 'given misogynist audiences an eyeful of skinny white women dancing in g-strings'.[29] Ms Wizzle takes a similar view in suggesting that 'there are a lot (lot) of problems with this video, from sexual objectification of women to feeding lesbian fetishism to excessive violence'.[30] The blog critic gudbuy t'jane is even more scathing in her condemnation of the video in arguing that the fact that Lady Gaga 'uses trans women and drag queens to exoticize her videos doesn't defer from the cissupremacist stance that women=vagina, and trans women are therefore not real women . . . This is transmisogyny.'[31]

This kind of polarised critical response to a video, and more broadly to the work of a female artist, resonates with the critical debate that surrounded the work of Madonna in the late 1980s and early 1990s and which culminated in the publication of *The Madonna Connection*, *Madonnarama*, and *Deconstructing Madonna* in 1993.[32] For instance, E. Ann Kaplan's description of the capacity for Madonna's videos to engage in a 'blurring of the hitherto sacrosanct boundaries and polarities such as male/female, high art/pop art, film/TV, fiction/reality, private/public' could have been written to describe TELEPHONE's own border crossings.[33] Similarly, despite her scathing reading of Lady Gaga as 'the exhausted end of the sexual revolution', Camille Paglia's assertion that Madonna's JUSTIFY MY LOVE (1990) is 'a deliciously decadent sarabande of transvestite and sadomasochistic personae' could equally apply to Lady Gaga's BAD ROMANCE (2009) or ALEJANDRO (2010).[34] Moreover, Cathy Schwichtenberg's reading of Madonna's 'strategies of simulation' that transform 'the "truth" of gender into drag' that is capable of destabilising gender identity and advancing 'a prodigious sexual plurality' could just as easily be used to interpret any number of Lady Gaga videos.[35] Indeed, given the seismic impact that Judith Butler's work has had on the way identity is theorised in the humanities, and in particular the role that the concept of performativity has played in undermining essentialist notions of sex and gender, one might have expected that the emergence of Lady Gaga would have presented a golden opportunity for Butler-inspired scholars. As yet, however, there is little evidence that this opportunity is being seized. In fact, the most obvious difference between the critical responses to Madonna and to Lady Gaga is that the latter has yet to find its way into the academy. This lacuna is especially surprising when viewed in the context of the recent interest in postfeminist culture and the development of a brand of postfeminist theory which has attempted to analyse its implications. For contemporary feminism, and theorists of popular culture more generally, it perhaps matters less if Lady Gaga turns out to be more 'material girl' than 'postfeminist icon' in the long run than that the debate occasioned by her videos finds a path from the blog to the academy. Indeed, it is our intention in writing this book to offer a contribution to such a debate.

NOTES

1. *CBS News*, 'Lady Gaga Opens Up', 3 August 2010, http://www.cbsnews.com/stories/2010/08/03/earlyshow/leisure/celebspot/main6739115.shtml (09/08/2010).
2. *IFPI Digital Music Report 2010* (International Federation of the Phonographic Industry, 2010), p. 11.
3. Jocelyn Vena, 'Lady Gaga Breaks Records in Sales, Video Viewings', *MTV.com*, 25 March 2010, http://www.mtv.com/news/articles/1634663/20100325/lady_gaga.jhtml (09/08/2010).
4. 'The 100 Million Views Club', *Visible Measures*, 23 March 2010, http://www.visiblemeasures.com/hundred (09/08/2010).
5. James Montgomery, 'Lady Gaga Premieres Epic, Outrageous "Telephone" Video', *MTV.com*, 11 March 2010, http://www.mtv.com/news/articles/1633772/20100311/lady_gaga.jhtml (10/09/2010); Armond White, 'Going

Gaga', *New York Press*, 16 April 2010, http://www.nypress.com/article-21128-going-gaga.html (10/08/2010).

6. Montgomery, 'Lady Gaga Premieres Epic, Outrageous "Telephone" Video'; White, 'Going Gaga'.

7. Bridget Barrett, 'Lady Gaga – Telephone – Music Video Review', *Uprising*, 1 April 2010, http://thecollectivereview.com/uprising/lady-gaga-telephone-music-video-review.html (10/08/2010).

8. Sady, 'Nothing That Happened This Week Was Ever Going To Be As Important As The "Telephone" Video', *Feministe*, 13 March 2010, http://www.feministe.us/blog/archives/2010/03/13/weekend-arts-section-nothing-that-happened-this-week-was-ever-going-to-be-as-important-as-the-telephone-video (10/08/2010).

9. White, 'Going Gaga'.

10. Sandy Rios, Interview with Megyn Kelly, *Fox News*, 15 March 2010, http://video.foxnews.com/v/4106192/lady-gaga-has-gone-too-far (10/08/2010).

11. Jason Middleton and Roger Beebe, 'Introduction', in Roger Beebe and Jason Middleton (eds), *Medium Cool: Music Videos From Soundies to Cellphones* (Durham, NC: Duke University Press, 2007), p. 5.

12. A. J. Ramirez, 'Answering Lady Gaga's "Telephone" Call', *PopMatters*, 2 April 2010, http://www.popmatters.com/pm/post/123236-answering-lady-gagas-telephone-call (10/08/2010).

13. For example, Beck's *The Information* and Beyoncé Knowles's *B'Day* are examples of albums by performers, working in very different genres, who have both produced videos for tracks which were never released as stand-alone singles in the traditional sense.

14. See respectively, http://www.youtube.com/watch?v=XvOucvTpKrE (11/08/2010); http://www.youtube.com/watch?v=vJ6dtLlRNKo (10/08/2010); http://www.youtube.com/user/thehouseofgagamusik#p/u/8/at2AwZMQGv0 (11/08/2010); http://www.youtube.com/watch?v=W4U7sitDYho&feature=fvsr (10/08/2010); http://www.youtube.com/watch?v=K1Z3uuM3d1o (11/08/2010).

15. Sady, 'Nothing That Happened This Week'.

16. Sady, 'Nothing That Happened This Week'.

17. For an account of the cinematic gaze and the televisual glance, see John Ellis, *Visible Fictions: Cinema, Television, Video*, rev. edn (London: Routledge, 1992).

18. D. Atkin and R. Abelman, 'Assessing Social Concerns Over the Impact of Popular Music and Music Video: A Review of Scholarly Research', *The Open Social Science Journal*, vol. 2 (2009), p. 47.

19. Atkin and Abelman, 'Assessing Social Concerns Over the Impact of Popular Music and Music Video', p. 46.

20. See, for example, David Gauntlett, 'Ten Things Wrong With the Media "Effects" Model', in Roger Dickinson, Ramaswami Harindranath and Olga Linné (eds), *Approaches to Audiences: A Reader* (London: Arnold, 1998).

21. Linda Papadopoulos, *Sexualisation of Young People Review* (London: Home Office Publication, 2010).

22. American Psychological Association, Task Force on the Sexualization of Girls, *Report of the APA Task Force on the Sexualization of Girls* (Washington, DC: American Psychological Association, 2007).

23. Sut Jhally, *Dreamworlds 3* (Northampton, MA: Media Education Foundation, 2007).

24. Ben Todd, 'Children at Risk From Pop Charts Porn', *Daily Mail*, 8 September 2010, p. 7; Jhally, *Dreamworlds 3*.

25. Jhally, *Dreamworlds 3*.

26. Jhally, *Dreamworlds 3*.

27. Sady, 'Nothing That Happened This Week'.
28. Emily, 'Why Lady Gaga is a Feminist – Part 3 – Telephone', *Jukebox Heroines*, 15 March 2010, http://jukeboxheroines.wordpress.com/2010/03/15/why-lady-gaga-is-a-feminist-part-3-telephone (09/08/2010).
29. Amy Littlefield, 'Visuality and Feminism(?) in Lady Gaga's "Telephone" Video', *Gender Across Borders*, 16 April 2010, http://www.genderacrossborders.com/2010/04/16/visuality-and-feminism-in-lady-gagas-telephone-video (10/08/2010).
30. Ms Wizzle, 'Telephone: Lady Gaga's Latest Controversy', *feministhemes.com*, 14 March 2010, http://feministhemes.com/telephone-lady-gaga (10/08/2010).
31. gudbuy t'jane, 'Lady Gaga Sets the Record Straight', 12 March 2010, http://gudbuytjane.wordpress.com/2010/03/12/lady-gaga-sets-the-record-straight/ (10/08/2010).
32. Cathy Schwichtenberg (ed.), *The Madonna Connection: Representational Politics, Subcultural Identities, and Cultural Theory* (Boulder: Westview Press, 1993); Lisa Frank and Paul Smith (eds), *Madonnarama: Essays on Sex and Popular Culture* (San Francisco: Cleis Press, 1993); Fran Lloyd (ed.), *Deconstructing Madonna* (London: Batsford, 1993).
33. E. Ann Kaplan, *Rocking Around the Clock: Music Television, Postmodernism, and Consumer Culture* (London: Methuen, 1987), p. 126.
34. Camille Paglia, 'What's Sex Got to do With it?', *Sunday Times*, Magazine Supplement, 12 September 2010, p. 18; Camille Paglia, 'Madonna II: Venus of the Radio Waves', in Camille Paglia, *Sex, Art, and American Culture* (New York: Vintage Books, 1992), p. 11.
35. Cathy Schwichtenberg, 'Madonna's Postmodern Feminism', in Schwichtenberg (ed.), *The Madonna Connection*, p. 141.

BIBLIOGRAPHY

Adaso, Henry, 'A Guide to Hip-Hop Genres and Styles', *Henry's Rap / Hip-Hop Blog* (no date), http://rap.about.com/od/genresstyles/tp/HipHopGenreGuide.htm (22/06/2009).

ALMA Awards.com, 'About ALMA Awards: Background and Purpose' (no date), http://www.almaawards.com/wmspage.cfm?parm1=45 (23/07/2005).

American Psychological Association, Task Force on the Sexualization of Girls, *Report of the APA Task Force on the Sexualization of Girls* (Washington, DC: American Psychological Association, 2007).

Andsager, Julie L. and Kimberley Roe, 'Country Music Video in Country's Year of the Woman', *Journal of Communication*, vol. 49, no. 1 (1999), pp. 69–82.

Ang, Ien and Joke Hermes, 'Gender and/in Media Consumption', in James Curran and Michael Gurevitch (eds), *Mass Media and Society*, 2nd edn (London: Arnold, 1996).

Aparicio, Frances R. and Susana Chavez-Silverman (eds), *Tropicalizations: Transcultural Representations of 'Latinidad'* (Hanover: University Press of New England, 1997).

Atkin, D. and R. Abelman, 'Assessing Social Concerns Over the Impact of Popular Music and Music Video: A Review of Scholarly Research', *The Open Social Science Journal*, vol. 2 (2009), pp. 37–49.

Auslander, Paul, 'Seeing is Believing: Live Performance and the Discourse of Authenticity in Rock Culture', *Literature and Psychology*, vol. 44, no. 4 (1998), pp. 1–26.

Austerlitz, Saul, *Money for Nothing: A History of the Music Video From the Beatles to the White Stripes* (London: Continuum, 2007).

Austin, Thomas and Martin Barker (eds), *Contemporary Hollywood Stardom* (London: Hodder Arnold, 2003).

Barker, Martin, 'Introduction', in Thomas Austin and Martin Barker (eds), *Contemporary Hollywood Stardom* (London: Hodder Arnold, 2003), pp. 1–24.

Barrett, Bridget, 'Lady Gaga – Telephone – Music Video Review', *Uprising*, 1 April 2010, http://thecollectivereview.com/uprising/lady-gaga-telephone-music-video-review.html (10/08/2010).

Bartky, Sandra Lee, *Femininity and Domination: Studies in the Phenomenology of Oppression* (London: Routledge, 1990).

Beebe, Roger, 'Paradoxes of Pastiche: Spike Jonze, Hype Williams, and the Race of the Postmodern Auteur', in Roger Beebe and Jason Middleton (eds), *Medium Cool: Music Videos From Soundies to Cellphones* (Durham, NC: Duke University Press, 2007), pp. 303–27.

Beebe, Roger and Jason Middleton (eds), *Medium Cool: Music Videos From Soundies to Cellphones* (Durham, NC: Duke University Press, 2007).

Bhabha, Homi K., 'The Other Question: the Stereotype and Colonial Discourse', *Screen*, vol. 24, no. 6 (1983), pp. 18–36.

Binelli, Mark, 'U.K. Rock Kings Arctic Monkeys', *Rolling Stone*, 10 March 2006, http://www.rollingstone.com/news/newfaces/story/9447897/uk_rock_kings_arctic_monkeys (08/04/2006).

Blake, Andrew (ed.), *Living Through Pop* (London: Routledge, 1999).

Boehlert, Eric, 'Christina Aguilera, Puff Daddy Displace Backstreet Boys, Limp Bizkit', *Rolling Stone*, September 1999.

Boorstin, Daniel J., *The Image: A Guide to Pseudo-Events in America* (New York: Atheneum, 1971).

Bordo, Susan, *The Male Body: A New Look at Men in Public and in Private* (New York: Farrar, Straus and Giroux, 1999).

Bordwell, David and Kristin Thompson, *Film History* (London: McGraw-Hill, 1994).

Bowie, Robart Pahlavi, 'Rock Video "According to Fredric Jameson"', *Continuum: The Australian Journal of Media & Culture*, vol. 1, no. 2 (1987), pp. 122–9.

Brabazon, Tara, 'Robbie Williams: A Better Man?', *International Journal of Cultural Studies*, vol. 5, no.1 (2002), pp. 45–88.

Brooks, Ann, *Postfeminisms: Feminism, Cultural Theory and Cultural Forms* (London: Routledge, 1997).

Brothers, Robyn, 'Time to Heal, "Desire" Time: The Cyberprophesy of U2's "Zoo World Order"', in Kevin J. H. Dettmar and William Richey (eds), *Reading Rock and Roll: Authenticity, Appropriation, Aesthetics* (New York: Columbia University Press, 1999), pp. 237–68.

Brown, Stephen, 'Material Girl or Managerial Girl? Charting Madonna's Brand Ambition', *Business Horizons*, vol. 46, no. 4 (2003), pp. 2–10.

Brownmiller, Susan, *Femininity* (London: Paladin, 1986).

Brunsdon, Charlotte, *Screen Tastes: Soap Opera to Satellite Dishes* (London: Routledge, 1997).

Brunsdon, Charlotte, 'The Feminist in the Kitchen: Martha, Martha, and Nigella', in Joanne Hollows and Rachel Moseley (eds), *Feminism in Popular Culture* (Oxford: Berg, 2006), pp. 41–56.

bstn57, 'Is A Non-Latino Latino?', Cultura Discussion Forum, *Latina.com*, 8 April 2005, http://forums.prospero.com/n/mb/message.asp?webtag=latcultura&msg=465.1 (20/07/2005).

Burns, Gary, 'Formula and Distinctiveness in Movie-Based Music Videos', *Popular Music and Society*, vol. 18, no. 4 (1994), pp. 7–18.

Butler, Judith, *Gender Trouble: Feminism and the Subversion of Identity* (London: Routledge, 1990).

Carroll, Noel, *Theorizing the Moving Image* (Cambridge: Cambridge University Press, 1996).

CBS News, 'Lady Gaga Opens Up', 3 August 2010, http://www.cbsnews.com/stories/2010/08/03/earlyshow/leisure/celebspot/main6739115.shtml (09/08/2010).

Cepeda, Maria Elena, 'Mucho Loco For Ricky Martin: Or the Politics of Chronology,

Crossover and Language Within the Latin(o) Music "Boom"', *Popular Music and Society*, vol. 24, no. 3 (2000), pp. 55–72.

Chen, Kuan-Hsing, 'MTV: The (Dis)Appearance of Postmodern Semiosis, or the Cultural Politics of Resistance', *Journal of Communication Inquiry*, vol. 10, no. 1 (1986), pp. 66–9.

Christgau, Robert, 'Dear Mr President', *Village Voice*, 18 April 2006.

Clarke, Betty, 'Christina Aguliera: Stripped', *Guardian*, 25 October 2002, http://www.guardian.co.uk/arts/fridayreview/story/0,,818206,00.html (25/07/2005).

Cobo, Leila, 'Christina Aguilera Prepares Spanish Debut', *Billboard Magazine*, 7 August 2000, http://www.billboard.com/bb/search/article_display.jsp?vnu_content_id=1314735 (12/06/2005).

Cofer, Judith Ortiz, *The Latin Deli: Prose and Poetry* (New York: W. W. Norton and Company, 1995), pp. 148–54.

Cohan, Steven and Ina Rae Hark (eds), *Screening the Male: Exploring Masculinities in Hollywood Cinema* (London: Routledge, 1993).

Cohen, Sara, *Rock Culture in Liverpool: Popular Music in the Making* (Oxford: Clarendon Press, 1991).

Cole, Sheri Kathleen, 'I am the Eye, You are my Victim: The Pornographic Ideology of Music Video', *Enculturation*, vol. 2, no. 2 (1999), http://enculturation.gmu.edu/2_2/cole/index.html (10/10/2008).

Collins, Jim, *Architectures of Excess: Cultural Life in the Information Age* (London: Routledge, 1995).

Connell, Robert W., *Gender and Power: Society, the Person and Sexual Politics* (Oxford: Polity Press, 1987).

Connell, Robert W., *Masculinities* (Cambridge: Polity Press, 1995).

Connell, Robert W. and James W. Messerschmidt, 'Hegemonic Masculinity: Rethinking the Concept', *Gender and Society*, vol. 19, no. 6 (2005), pp. 829–59.

Cooke, Rachel, 'Katie Roiphe: The Interview', *Observer*, Review, 1 June 2008.

Coyle, Michael and Jon Dolan, 'Modelling Authenticity, Authenticating Commercial Models', in Kevin J. H. Dettmar and William Richey (eds), *Reading Rock and Roll: Authenticity, Appropriation, Aesthetics* (New York: Columbia University Press, 1999), pp. 17–35.

Culler, Jonathan, *Structuralist Poetics: Structuralism, Linguistics and the Study of Literature* (London: Routledge, 1975).

Curran, James and Michael Gurevitch (eds), *Mass Media and Society*, 2nd edn (London: Arnold, 1996).

Customer Reviewers, 'Mi Reflejo: Customer Reviews', *Amazon.com* (no date), http://www.amazon.com/gp/product/customer-reviews/B00004WJDG/ref=cm_cr_dp_2_1/104-9909223-9983150?%5Fencoding=UTF8&s=music (14/07/2005).

D'Angelo, Joe, '"Dirrty" Christina Aguilera Video Thai-ed To Sex Industry', *MTV News*, 18 October 2002), http://www.mtv.com/news/articles/1458223/10182002/nullaguilera_christina.jhtml (20/07/2005).

Darley, Andrew, *Visual Digital Culture: Surface Play and Spectacle in New Media Genres* (London: Routledge, 2000).

de Beauvoir, Simone, *The Second Sex*, trans. H. M. Parshley (New York: Vintage Books, 1989).

Dettmar, Kevin J. H. and William Richey (eds), *Reading Rock and Roll: Authenticity, Appropriation, Aesthetics* (New York: Columbia University Press, 1999).

Dibben, Nicola, 'Representations of Femininity in Popular Music', *Popular Music*, vol. 18, no. 3 (1999), pp. 331–55.

Dickinson, Roger, Ramaswami Harindranath and Olga Linné (eds), *Approaches to Audiences: A Reader* (London: Arnold, 1998).

Dines, Gail and Jean M. Humez, *Gender, Race, and Class in the Media*, 2nd edn (London: Sage, 2003).

Disney Channel Magazine, 'Christina Aguilera Biography' (no author, no date), http://www.christinamultimedia.com/newssource/index.php?date=1993–00&articleID=57 (23/06/2005).

Dixon, Lynda Dee and Patricia A. Washington, 'Rap Music Videos: The Voices of Organic Intellectuals', *Transcultural Music Review*, no. 4 (1999), http://www.sibetrans.com/trans/trans4/dee.htm (15/12/2005).

Doherty, Thomas, 'MTV and the Music Video: Promo and Product', *Southern Speech Communication Journal*, vol. 52, no. 4 (1987), pp. 349–61.

Donald, James and Ali Rattansi (eds), *'Race', Culture and Difference* (London: Sage/The Open University, 1992).

Douglas, Susan J., 'Manufacturing Postfeminism', *In These Times*, 26 April 2002.

Dow, Bonnie J., *Prime-Time Feminism: Television, Media Culture, and the Women's.*
Movement since the 1970s (Philadelphia: University of Pennsylvania Press, 1996).

Dyer, Richard, *Stars* (London: BFI, 1979).

Dyer, Richard, 'White', *Screen*, vol. 29, no. 4 (1988), pp. 44–64.

Dyer, Richard, *The Matter of Images: Essays on Representations* (London: Routledge, 1993).

Dyer, Richard, *White* (London: Routledge, 1997).

Ellen, Barbara, 'Up Front', *Observer*, Magazine, 4 March 2007.

Ellis, John, *Visible Fictions: Cinema, Television, Video*, rev. edn (London: Routledge, 1992).

Ellsworth, Elizabeth, Margot Kennard Larson and Albert Selvin, 'MTV Presents: Problematic Pleasures', *Journal of Communication Inquiry*, vol. 10, no. 1 (1986), pp. 55–63.

Emerson, Rana A. ' "Where My Girls At?": Negotiating Black Womanhood in Music Videos', *Gender and Society,* vol. 16, no. 1 (2002), pp. 115–35.

Emily, 'Why Lady Gaga is a Feminist – Part 3 – Telephone', *Jukebox Heroines*, 15 March 2010, http://jukeboxheroines.wordpress.com/2010/03/15/why-lady-gaga-is-a-feminist-part-3-telephone (09/08/2010).

Erlewine, Stephen Thomas, 'I'm not Dead: Review', *allmusic.com*, http://www.allmusic.com/cg/amg.dll?p=amg&sql=10:3pfyxqrdldke (24/08/2007).

Fabbri, Franco, 'Browsing Music Spaces: Categories and the Musical Mind', conference paper, IASPM (1999), http://www.tagg.org/others/ffabbri9907.html (15/11/2006).

Faith, Karlene, *Madonna: Bawdy & Soul* (Toronto: University of Toronto Press, 1997).

Faludi, Susan, *Backlash: The Undeclared War Against Women* (London: Chatto & Windus, 1991).

Faludi, Susan, 'I'm Not a Feminist but I Play One on TV', *Ms*, March/April 1995.

Farley, Christopher John, 'Inner Visions: A Teen Pop Vocalist Rediscovers Her Latin Side', *Time*, vol. 156, no. 13 (2000), p. 101.

Firestone, Shulamith, *The Dialectic of Sex: The Case for Feminist Revolution* (New York: Bantam Books, 1970).

Fiske, John, 'MTV: Post-Structural Post-Modern', *Journal of Communication Inquiry*, vol. 10, no. 1 (1986), pp. 74–9.

Foucault, Michel, 'Technologies of the Self', in Luther H. Martin, Huck Gutman and Patrick H. Hutton (eds), *Technologies of the Self: A Seminar with Michel Foucault* (Amherst, MA: University of Massachusetts Press, 1988), pp. 16–49.

Foucault, Michel, *The History of Sexuality Volume Two: The Use of Pleasure*, trans. R. Hurley (Harmondsworth: Penguin, 1992).

Fouz-Hernández, Santiago and Freya Jarman-Ivens (eds), *Madonna's Drowned Worlds:*

New Approaches to her Cultural Transformations 1983–2003 (Aldershot: Ashgate, 2004).

Fox Keller, Evelyn, 'How Gender Matters, or, Why it's so Hard for us to Count Past Two', in Gill Kirkup and Laurie Smith Keller (eds), *Inventing Women: Science, Technology and Gender* (Cambridge: Polity Press/The Open University, 1992), pp. 42–56.

Frank, Lisa and Paul Smith (eds), *Madonnarama: Essays on Sex and Popular Culture* (San Francisco: Cleis Press, 1993).

Frith, Simon, *Music For Pleasure* (Cambridge: Polity Press, 1988).

Frith, Simon, *Performing Rites: Evaluating Popular Music* (Oxford: Oxford University Press, 1996).

Frith, Simon, Andrew Goodwin and Lawrence Grossberg (eds), *Sound and Vision: The Music Video Reader* (London: Routledge, 1993).

Gamman, Lorraine and Margaret Marshment (eds), *The Female Gaze: Women as Viewers of Popular Culture* (London: Women's Press, 1988).

Gardner, Jane, 'What a Chica Wants!', *Popstar*, September 2000, http://www.christinamultimedia.com/newssource/index.php?date=2000–00&articleID=6909 (23/07/2005).

Gauntlett, David, 'Ten Things Wrong With the Media "Effects" Model', in Roger Dickinson, Ramaswami Harindranath and Olga Linné (eds), *Approaches to Audiences: A Reader* (London: Arnold, 1998).

Gauntlett, David, 'Madonna's Daughters: Girl Power and the Empowered Girl-Pop Breakthrough', in Santiago Fouz-Hernández and Freya Jarman-Ivens (eds), *Madonna's Drowned Worlds: New Approaches to her Cultural Transformations 1983–2003* (Aldershot: Ashgate, 2004), pp. 161–75.

Gaut, Berys, 'Film Authorship and Collaboration', in Richard Allen and Murray Smith (eds), *Film Theory and Philosophy* (Oxford: Oxford University Press, 1997), pp. 149–72.

Genz, Stéphanie, 'Third Way/ve: The Politics of Postfeminism', *Feminist Theory*, vol. 7, no. 3 (2006), pp. 333–53.

Genz, Stéphanie and Benjamin A. Brabon, *Postfeminism: Cultural Texts and Theories* (Edinburgh: Edinburgh University Press, 2009).

Geraghty, Christine, 'Re-examining Stardom: Questions of Texts, Bodies, and Performance', in Christine Gledhill and Linda Williams (eds), *Reinventing Film Studies* (London: Arnold, 2000), pp. 183–201.

Gill, Rosalind, 'From Sexual Objectification to Sexual Subjectification: The Resexualisation of Women's Bodies in the Media', *Feminist Media Studies*, vol. 3, no. 1 (2003), pp. 100–6.

Gilman, Sander L. 'Black Bodies, White Bodies: Toward an Iconography of Female Sexuality in Late Nineteenth-Century Art, Medicine, and Literature', *Critical Inquiry*, vol. 12, no. 1 (1985), pp. 204–42.

Gilman, Sander L. *Difference and Pathology: Stereotypes of Sexuality, Race, and Madness* (Ithaca, NY: Cornell University Press, 1985).

Giroux, Henry A., 'Racial Politics and the Pedagogy of Whiteness', in Mike Hill (ed.), *Whiteness: A Critical Reader* (New York: New York University Press, 1997), pp. 294–315.

Gledhill Christine, 'Rethinking Genre', in Christine Gledhill and Linda Williams (eds), *Reinventing Film Studies* (London: Arnold, 2000), pp. 221–43.

Gledhill, Christine and Linda Williams (eds), *Reinventing Film Studies* (London: Arnold, 2000).

Goodwin, Andrew, *Dancing in the Distraction Factory: Music Television and Popular Culture* (London: Routledge, 1993).

Gottschild, Brenda Dixon, *The Black Dancing Body: A Geography from Coon to Cool* (New York: Palgrave Macmillan, 2003).

Gow, Joe, 'The Relationship Between Violent and Sexual Images and the Popularity Of Music Videos', *Popular Music And Society*, vol. 14, no. 4 (1990), pp. 1–9.

Gow, Joe, 'Music Video as Communication: Popular Formulas and Emerging Genres', *The Journal of Popular Culture*, vol. 26, no. 2 (1992), pp. 41–70.

Greer, Germaine, *The Female Eunuch* (London: Paladin, 1971).

Greig, Charlotte, *Will You Still Love Me Tomorrow? Girl Groups from the 50s on* (London: Virago, 1989).

gudbuy t'jane, 'Lady Gaga Sets the Record Straight', 12 March 2010), http://gudbuyt-jane.wordpress.com/2010/03/12/lady-gaga-sets-the-record-straight/ (10/08/2010).

Guilbert, Georges-Claude, *Madonna as Postmodern Myth: How One Star's Self-Construction Rewrites Sex* (London: McFarland, 2002).

Gunn, Joshua, 'Gothic Music and the Inevitability of Genre', *Popular Music and Society*, vol. 23, no. 1 (1999), pp. 31–50.

Hacking, Ian, 'Why Race Still Matters', *Daedalus*, vol. 134 (2005), pp. 102–16.

Hall, Stuart, 'Pluralism, Race and Class in Caribbean Society', in (no editor), *Race, Class and Post-colonial Society* (Paris: UNESCO, 1977), pp. 150–82.

Hall, Stuart, 'New Ethnicities', in James Donald and Ali Rattansi (eds), *'Race', Culture and Difference* (London: Sage, 1992), pp. 252–9.

Hanna, Suzie, 'Composers and Animators – The Creation of Interpretative and Collaborative Vocabularies', *Journal of Media Practice*, vol. 9, no. 1 (2008), pp. 29–41.

Hark, Ina Rae, 'Animals or Romans: Looking at Masculinity in *Spartacus*', in Steven Cohan and Ina Rae Hark (eds), *Screening the Male: Exploring Masculinities in Hollywood Cinema* (London: Routledge, 1993), pp. 151–72.

Harker, Dave, 'Taking Fun Seriously', *Popular Music*, vol. 15, no. 1 (1996), pp. 108–21.

Harris, Keith M., ' "Untitled": D'Angelo and the Visualization of the Black Male Body', *Wide Angle*, vol. 21, no. 4 (1998), pp. 62–83.

Hertz, Noreena, 'A Fond Farewell', *Guardian*, 29 January 2004.

Hill Collins, Patricia, *Black Sexual Politics: African Americans, Gender, and the New Racism* (London: Routledge, 2004).

Hill, Mike (ed.), *Whiteness: A Critical Reader* (New York: New York University Press, 1997).

Hispanic Business, 'Hispanic Boom Yet to Arrive', 24 June 2003, http://www.christina-multimedia.com/newssource/index.php?articleID=4692 (03/07/2005).

Hodges, Jacqueline, 'Stripped' (no date), http://www.bbc.co.uk/music/pop/reviews/aguilera_stripped.shtml#review (03/07/2005).

Holdstein, Deborah H., 'Music Video: Messages and Structure', *Jump Cut*, vol. 29 (1984), pp. 1–13.

Hollows, Joanne, *Feminism, Femininity and Popular Culture* (Manchester: Manchester University Press, 2000).

Hollows, Joanne and Rachel Moseley (eds), *Feminism in Popular Culture* (Oxford: Berg, 2006).

hooks, bell, *Black Looks: Race and Representation* (Boston: South End Press, 1992).

Horne, John and Scott Fleming (eds), *Masculinities: Leisure Cultures, Identities and Consumption* (Eastbourne: Leisure Studies Association, 2000).

Huey, Steve, 'Christina Aguilera: Biography', http://music.yahoo.com/ar-293441-bio--Christina-Aguilera (23/06/2005).

Huff, Quentin B., 'Far From Buried, But Don't Call it a Comeback', *Popmatters*, 17 May 2006, http://www.popmatters.com/pm/review/pink-im-not-dead (13/04/2008).

Hurley, Jennifer M., 'Music Video and the Construction of Gendered Subjectivity (Or How Being a Music Video Junkie Turned Me into a Feminist)', *Popular Music*, vol. 13, no. 3 (1994), pp. 327–38.

Hutcheon, Linda, *The Politics of Postmodernism* (London: Routledge, 1989).

Huyssen, Andreas, *After the Great Divide: Modernism, Mass Culture, Postmodernism* (Bloomington: Indiana University Press, 1986).

Hye, Jin Lee and Wen Huike, 'Where the Girls are in the Age of New Sexism: An Interview With Susan Douglas', *Journal of Communication Inquiry*, vol. 33, no. 2 (2009), pp. 93–103.

IFPI Digital Music Report 2010 (International Federation of the Phonographic Industry, 2010).

Jamison, Laura, 'Heavy Weight', *Teen People*, December 1999.

Jhally, Sut, *Dreamworlds 3* (Northampton, MA: Media Education Foundation, 2007).

Jones, Amelia (ed.), *The Feminism and Visual Culture Reader* (London: Routledge, 2003).

Jones, Steve, 'Cohesive But Not Coherent: Music Videos, Narrative and Culture', *Popular Music and Society*, vol. 12, no. 4 (1988), pp. 15–29.

Jonze, Tim, 'Arctic Monkeys: Whatever People Say I am, That's What I'm Not', *NME* (no date), http://www.nme.com/reviews/arctic-monkeys/7837 (08/04/2006).

Kaplan, E. Ann, *Rocking Around the Clock: Music Television, Postmodernism, and Consumer Culture* (London: Methuen, 1987).

Kaplan, E. Ann, 'Madonna Politics: Perversion, Repression or Subversion? Or Masks and/as Mastery', in Cathy Schwichtenberg (ed.), *The Madonna Connection: Representational Politics, Subcultural Identities, and Cultural Theory* (Boulder: Westview Press, 1993), pp. 149–65.

Karlyn, Kathleen Rowe, '*Scream*, Popular Culture, and Feminism's Third Wave: "I'm Not My Mother"', *Genders*, no. 38 (2003), http://www.genders.org/g38/g38_rowe_karlyn.html (04/07/2005).

Kavka, Misha, 'Feminism, Ethics, and History, or What Is the "Post" in Postfeminism?', *Tulsa Studies in Women's Literature*, vol. 21, no. 1 (2002), pp. 29–44.

Keightly, Keir, 'Reconsidering Rock', in Simon Frith, Will Straw and John Street (eds), *The Cambridge Companion to Pop and Rock* (Cambridge: Cambridge University Press, 2001), pp. 109–42.

Kellner, Douglas, *Media Culture: Cultural Studies, Identity, and Politics Between the Modern and the Postmodern* (London: Routledge, 1995).

Kirkup, Gill and Laurie Smith Keller (eds), *Inventing Women: Science, Technology and Gender* (Cambridge: Polity Press/The Open University, 1992).

LA Times, 'Aguilera Releases Spanish Album', September 2000, http://www.christina-multimedia.com/newssource/index.php?articleID=1276 (23/07/2005).

Lewis, Lisa A., *Gender Politics and MTV: Voicing the Difference* (Philadelphia: Temple University Press, 1990).

Lewis, Lisa A., 'Being Discovered: The Emergence of Female Address on MTV', in Simon Frith, Andrew Goodwin and Lawrence Grossberg (eds), *Sound and Vision: The Music Video Reader* (London: Routledge, 1993), pp. 129–52.

Littlefield, Amy, 'Visuality and Feminism(?) in Lady Gaga's "Telephone" Video', *Gender Across Borders*, 16 April 2010, http://www.genderacrossborders.com/2010/04/16/visuality-and-feminism-in-lady-gagas-telephone-video (10/08/2010).

Lloyd, Fran (ed.), *Deconstructing Madonna* (London: Batsford, 1993).

Lloyd, Genevieve, *The Man of Reason: 'Male' and 'Female' in Western Philosophy* (Minneapolis: University of Minnesota Press, 1984).

Lotz, Amanda D., 'Postfeminist Television Criticism: Rehabilitating Critical Terms and

Identifying Postfeminist Attributes', *Feminist Media Studies*, vol. 1, no. 1 (2001), pp. 105–21.

Love, Meredith A. and Brenda M. Helmbrecht, 'Teaching the Conflicts: (Re)Engaging Students with Feminism in a Postfeminist World, *Feminist Teacher*, vol. 18, no. 1 (2007), pp. 41–58.

Lynch, Joan D., 'Music Videos: From Performance to Dada-Surrealism', *Journal of Popular Culture*, vol. 18, no. 1 (1984), pp. 53–7.

McClintock, Anne, *Imperial Leather: Race, Gender, and Sexuality in the Colonial Contest* (London: Routledge, 1995).

McDonnell, Evelyn, 'What a Girl Wants – Singer Christina Aguilera Discusses Her Career', *Interview*, April 2000.

McRobbie, Angela (ed.), *Zoot Suits and Second Hand Dresses: An Anthology of Fashion and Music* (Boston: Unwin and Hyman, 1988).

McRobbie, Angela, 'Postfeminism and Popular Culture', *Feminist Media Studies*, vol. 4, no. 3 (2004), pp. 255–64.

Mapplethorpe, Robert, *Black Males* (Amsterdam: Galerie Jurka, 1980).

Mapplethorpe, Robert, *The Black Book* (New York: Griffin, 1988).

Martin, Luther H., Huck Gutman and Patrick H. Hutton (eds), *Technologies of the Self: A Seminar with Michel Foucault* (Amherst, MA: University of Massachusetts Press, 1988).

Mendez, Juan, 'Unbottled and Unleashed: Christina Aguilera', *Latina*, December 1999, pp. 78–80.

Mendible, Myra (ed.), *From Bananas to Buttocks: The Latina Body in Popular Film and Culture* (Austin: University of Texas Press, 2007).

Mendible, Myra, 'Embodying Latinidad', in Myra Mendible (ed.), *From Bananas to Buttocks: The Latina Body in Popular Film and Culture* (Austin: University of Texas Press, 2007), pp. 1–28.

Mercer, Kobena, *Welcome to the Jungle* (London: Routledge, 1994).

Middleton, Jason and Roger Beebe, 'Introduction', in Roger Beebe and Jason Middleton (eds), *Medium Cool: Music Videos From Soundies to Cellphones* (Durham, NC: Duke University Press, 2007), pp. 1–12.

Millett, Kate, *Sexual Politics* (London: Virago, 1989).

Minh-ha, Trinh T., 'The Totalizing Quest of Meaning', in Michael Renov (ed.), *Theorizing Documentary* (London: Routledge, 1993), pp. 90–107.

Montgomery, James, 'Lady Gaga Premieres Epic, Outrageous "Telephone" Video', *MTV.com*, 11 March 2010, http://www.mtv.com/news/articles/1633772/20100311/lady_gaga.jhtml (10/09/2010).

Moore, Allan, 'Authenticity as Authentication', *Popular Music*, vol. 21, no. 2 (2002), pp. 209–23.

Moseley, Rachel and Jacinda Read, ' "Having it *Ally*": Popular Television (Post-)Feminism', *Feminist Media Studies*, vol. 2, no. 2 (2002), pp. 231–49.

Ms Wizzle, 'Telephone: Lady Gaga's Latest Controversy', *feministhemes.com*, 14 March 2010), http://feministhemes.com/telephone-lady-gaga (10/08/2010).

Mutua, Athena D. (ed.), *Progressive Black Masculinities* (London: Routledge, 2006).

Mutua, Athena D., 'Theorizing Progressive Black Masculinities', in Athena D. Mutua (ed.), *Progressive Black Masculinities* (London: Routledge, 2006), pp. 3–42.

Neale, Stephen, *Genre* (London: BFI, 1980).

Nicholson, Linda (ed.), *Feminism/Postmodernism* (London: Routledge, 1990).

Nicholson, Linda (ed.), *The Second Wave: A Reader in Feminist Theory* (London: Routledge, 1997).

O'Connor, Christopher, 'Christina Aguilera Tops Puff Daddy With #1 Album in U.S.',

VH1.com, 1 September 1999, http://www.vh1.com/artists/news/517097/09011999/aguilera_christina.jhtml (05/07/2005).

O'Grady, Lorraine, 'Olympia's Maid: Reclaiming Black Female Subjectivity', in Amelia Jones (ed.), *The Feminism and Visual Culture Reader* (London: Routledge, 2003), pp. 174–87.

Paglia, Camille, 'What's Sex Got to do With it?', *Sunday Times*, Magazine Supplement, 12 September 2010, pp. 14–21.

Paglia, Camille, 'Madonna II: Venus of the Radio Waves', in Camille Paglia, *Sex, Art, and American Culture* (New York: Vintage Books, 1992), pp. 6–13.

Papadopoulos, Linda, *Sexualisation of Young People Review* (London: Home Office Publication, 2010).

Peeters, Heidi, 'The Semiotics of Music Videos: It Must be Written in the Stars', *Image [&] Narrative*, no. 8 (2004), http://www.imageandnarrative.be/issue08/heidipeeters.htm (25/06/2005).

Perry, Imani, 'Who(se) Am I?: The Identity and Image of Women in Hip-Hop', in Gail Dines and Jean M. Humez (eds), *Gender, Race, and Class in The Media*, 2nd edn (London: Sage, 2003), pp. 136–48.

Peterson, Richard A., *Creating Country Music: Fabricating Authenticity* (Chicago: University of Chicago Press, 1997).

P!nk's Page, http://www.pinkspage.com/uk/node/19515 (24/08/2007).

Pough, Gwendolyn D., *Check It While I Wreck It: Black Womanhood, Hip-Hop Culture, and the Public Sphere* (Boston: Northeastern University Press, 2004).

Projansky, Sarah, *Watching Rape: Film and Television in Postfeminist Culture* (New York: New York University Press, 2001).

Railton, Diane, 'Somebody to Love: The Complex Masculinities of "Boy Band" Pop', in John Horne and Scott Fleming (eds), *Masculinities: Leisure Cultures, Identities and Consumption* (Eastbourne: Leisure Studies Association, 2000).

Railton, Diane and Paul Watson, 'Naughty Girls and Red Blooded Women: Representations of Female Heterosexuality in Music Video', *Feminist Media Studies*, vol. 5, no. 1 (2005), pp. 51–63.

Railton, Diane and Paul Watson, 'The Pornification of a Music Video: Sexed Authorship and Pornographic Address in Khia's "My Neck, My Back (Lick It)"', in Kaarina Nikunen, Susanna Paasonen and Laura Saarenmaa (eds), *Pornification: Sex and Sexuality in Media Culture* (Oxford: Berg Publishers, 2007).

Railton, Diane and Paul Watson, '"She's So Vein": Madonna and the Drag of Ageing', in Josie Dolan and Estella Tinknell (eds), *Ageing Femininities: Representation, Identities, Feminism* (Newcastle: Cambridge Scholars Press, 2011).

Railton, Diane and Paul Watson, 'Rebel Without a Pause: The Continuity of Controversy in Madonna's Contemporary Music Videos', in Abigail Gardner and Ros Jennings (eds), *Rock On: Women, Ageing and Popular Music* (Aldershot: Ashgate Publishing, 2012, forthcoming).

Ramirez, A. J., 'Answering Lady Gaga's "Telephone" Call', *PopMatters*, 2 April 2010, http://www.popmatters.com/pm/post/123236-answering-lady-gagas-telephone-call (10/08/2010).

Regev, Motti, 'Producing Artistic Value: The Case of Rock Music', *Sociological Quarterly*, vol. 35, no. 1 (1994), pp. 85–102.

Reiss, Steve and Neil Feineman, *Thirty Frames Per Second: The Visionary Art of the Music Video* (New York: Harry N. Abrams, 2000).

Renov, Michael (ed.), *Theorizing Documentary* (London: Routledge, 1993).

Repass, Scott, 'Review', *Film Quarterly*, vol. 56, no. 1 (2002), pp. 29–36.

Rios, Sandy, Interview with Megyn Kelly, *Fox News*, 15 March 2010, http://video.foxnews.com/v/4106192/lady-gaga-has-gone-too-far (10/08/2010).

Roberts, Robin, '"Ladies First": Queen Latifah's Afrocentric Feminist Music Video', *African American Review*, vol. 28 (1994), pp. 245–57.

Roberts, Shari, '"The Lady in the Tutti-Frutti Hat": Carmen Miranda, a Spectacle of Ethnicity', *Cinema Journal*, vol. 32, no. 3 (1993), pp. 3–23.

Robertson, Pamela, *Guilty Pleasures: Feminist Camp from Mae West to Madonna* (Durham, NC: Duke University Press, 1996).

Rock, S., 'P!nk Pink Posters Encourage Women To Be Smart and Sexy – Not Stupid Girls', *EzineArticles.com*, 9 May 2006, http://ezinearticles.com/?P!nk-Pink-Posters-Encourage-Women-To-Be-Smart-and-Sexy---Not-Stupid-Girls&id=194099 (24/08/2007).

Rodríguez, Clara E., *Latin Looks: Images of Latinas and Latinos in the U.S. Media* (Boulder: Westview Press, 1997).

Rojek, Chris, *Celebrity* (London: Reaktion, 2001).

Roman, Leslie G. and Linda Eyre, *Dangerous Territories: Struggles for Difference and Equality in Education* (London: Routledge, 1997).

Rose, Tricia, *Black Noise: Rap Music and Black Culture in Contemporary America* (Hanover: Wesleyan Press, 1994).

Rothenberg, Paula S. (ed.), *Race, Class, and Gender in the United States*, 3rd edn (New York: St. Martins Press, 1995).

Rutkoski, Rex, 'Multi-Platinum Blond: Christina Aguilera Finds Success in a Genie Bottle', *The Inside Connection* (2000), http://www.insidecx.com/interviews/archive/christina.html (23/06/2005).

Sady, 'Nothing That Happened This Week Was Ever Going to be as Important as The "Telephone" Video', *Feministe*, 13 March 2010, http://www.feministe.us/blog/archives/2010/03/13/weekend-arts-section-nothing-that-happened-this-week-was-ever-going-to-be-as-important-as-the-telephone-video/ (10/08/2010).

Said, Edward, *Orientalism: Western Conceptions of the Orient*, 25th Anniversary Edition (London: Penguin, 2003).

Sandoval-Sánchez, Alberto, 'De-Facing Mainstream Magazine Covers: The New Faces of Latino/a Transnational and Transcultural Celebrities', *Encrucijada/Crossroads: An Online Academic Journal*, vol. 1, no. 1 (2003), pp. 13–24.

Sawyer, Miranda, 'Why It's A Man's World', *Observer*, Observer Music Monthly, 20 June 2004, http://observer.guardian.co.uk/omm/story/0,,1240294,00.html (02/04/2007).

Sawyer, Miranda, 'Here Come the Girls', *Observer*, Magazine, 20 July 2008, p. 7.

Schehr, Lawrence R., *Parts of an Andrology: On Representations of Men's Bodies* (Stanford: Stanford University Press, 1997).

Schulze, Laurie, Anne Barton White and Jane D. Brown, '"A Sacred Monster in her Prime": Audience Construction of Madonna as Low-Other', in Cathy Schwichtenberg (ed.), *The Madonna Connection: Representational Politics, Subcultural Identities, and Cultural Theory* (Boulder: Westview Press, 1993), pp. 15–38.

Schwichtenberg, Cathy (ed.), *The Madonna Connection: Representational Politics, Subcultural Identities, and Cultural Theory* (Boulder: Westview Press, 1993).

Schwichtenberg, Cathy, 'Madonna's Postmodern Feminism', in Cathy Schwichtenberg (ed.), *The Madonna Connection: Representational Politics, Subcultural Identities, and Cultural Theory* (Boulder: Westview Press, 1993), pp. 129–45.

Scott, Ronald B., 'Images of Race and Religion in Madonna's Video *Like a Prayer*: Prayer and Praise', in Cathy Schwichtenberg (ed.), *The Madonna Connection: Representational Politics, Subcultural Identities, and Cultural Theory* (Boulder: Westview Press, 1993), pp. 57–77.

Segal, Lynne, 'A Fond Farewell', *Guardian*, 29 January 2004.

Seidman, Steven A., 'Revisiting Sex Role Stereotyping in MTV Videos', *International Journal of Instructional Media*, vol. 6, no. 1 (1999), pp. 11–22.

Sellars, Wilfred, *Science and Metaphysics* (London: Routledge and Kegan Paul, 1968).

Sexton, Adam, *Desperately Seeking Madonna: In Search of the Meaning of the World's Most Famous Woman* (New York: Delta, 1992).

Shaviro, Steven, 'The Erotic Life of Machines', *Parallax*, vol. 8, no. 4 (2002), pp. 21–31.

Sheets-Johnstone, Maxine, *Roots of Power: Animate Form and Gendered Bodies* (Chicago: Open Court, 1994).

Shuker, Roy, *Key Concepts in Popular Music* (London: Routledge, 1998).

Shusterman, Richard, 'The Fine Art of Rap', *New Literary History*, vol. 22, no. 3 (1991), pp. 613–32.

Shusterman, Richard, *Pragmatist Aesthetics: Living Beauty, Rethinking Art*, 2nd edn (Oxford: Rowman & Littlefield, 2000).

Skeggs, Beverley, 'Two Minute Brother: Contestation Through Gender, "Race" and Sexuality', *Innovations*, vol. 6, no. 3 (1993), pp. 299–321.

Sommers-Flanagan, Rita, John Sommers-Flanagan and Britta Davis, 'What's Happening On Music Television?: A Gender Role Content Analysis', *Sex Roles*, vol. 28, nos 11–12 (1993), pp. 545–83.

Spence, D., 'I'm not Dead: Review', *ign.com*, http://uk.music.ign.com/articles/700/700279p1.html (24/08/2007).

Stevenson, Jane, 'Christina Aguilera Carving Out Her Own Niche', *Toronto Sun*, 29 September 1999·

Stockbridge, Sally, 'Music Video: Questions of Performance, Pleasure, and Address', *Continuum*, vol. 1, no. 2 (1987), http://wwwmcc.murdoch.edu.au/ReadingRoom/1.2/Stockbridge.html (11/05/2004).

Straw, Will, 'Systems of Articulation, Logics of Change: Communities and Scenes in Popular Music', *Cultural Studies*, vol. 5, no. 3 (1991), pp. 368–88.

Talbot, Margaret, 'Little Hotties', *The New Yorker*, 4 December 2006, pp. 74–6.

Talbot, Margaret, 'Spoilt Bratz', *Daily Telegraph*, 28 January 2007, http://www.telegraph.co.uk/fashion/stellamagazine/3358500/Spoilt-Bratz.html (02/04/2007).

Tasker, Yvonne and Diane Negra (eds), *Interrogating Postfeminism* (London: Duke University Press, 2007).

Tasker, Yvonne and Diane Negra, 'Introduction: Feminist Politics and Postfeminist Culture', in Yvonne Tasker and Diane Negra (eds), *Interrogating Postfeminism* (London: Duke University Press, 2007), pp. 1–26.

thescarletweasel, 'Is A Non-Latino Latino?', Cultura Discussion Forum, *Latina.com*, 8 April 2005, http://forums.prospero.com/n/mb/message.asp?webtag=latcultura&msg=465.1 (12/08/2008).

Thigpen David E., 'Christina's World', *Time*, vol. 154, no. 7 (1999).

Todd, Ben, 'Children at Risk from Pop Charts Porn', *Daily Mail*, 8 September 2010, p. 7.

Torres, Richard, 'Sonidos Latinos Latin Sounds: A True Talent, in English and Spanish', *Newsday*, 17 September 2000.

Tsitso, William, 'Rules of Rebellion: Slamdancing, Moshing and the American Alternative Scene', *Popular Music*, vol. 18, no. 3 (1999), pp. 397–414.

Tudor, Andrew, 'Genre: Theory and Mispractice in Film Criticism', *Screen*, vol. 11, no. 6 (1970), pp. 34–43.

Tudor, Andrew, *Theories of Film* (London: Secker and Warburg, 1973).

Turner, Graeme, *Understanding Celebrity* (London: Sage, 2004).

Tyler, Imogen, ' "Who Put the 'Me' in Feminism?": The Sexual Politics of Narcissism', *Feminist Theory*, vol. 6, no. 1 (2005), pp. 25–44.

Valdivia, Angharad, 'Is Penélope to J.Lo as Culture is to Nature? Eurocentric

Approaches to "Latin" Beauties', in Myra Mendible (ed.), *From Bananas to Buttocks: The Latina Body in Popular Film and Culture* (Austin: University of Texas Press, 2007), pp. 129–48.

van Horn, Teri, 'Christina Aguilera Delves into Latin Roots on Spanish LP', *MTV News*, 16 August 2000, http://www.mtv.com/news/articles/1424794/20000816/story.jhtml (23/06/2005).

Vena, Jocelyn, 'Lady Gaga Breaks Records in Sales, Video Viewings', *MTV.com*, 25 March 2010, http://www.mtv.com/news/articles/1634663/20100325/lady_gaga.jhtml (09/08/2010).

Vernallis, Carol, *Experiencing Music Video: Aesthetics and Cultural Context* (New York: Columbia University Press, 2004).

Visible Measures, 'The 100 Million Views Club', 23 March 2010, http://www.visible-measures.com/hundred (09/08/2010).

Walter, Natasha, *The New Feminism* (London: Virago, 1999).

Walters, Barry, 'Music Reviews: Pink: I'm not Dead', *Rolling Stone*, 4 April 2006, http://www.rollingstone.com/artists/pink/albums/album/9558059/review/9580060/im_not_dead (24/08/2007).

Ware, Vron, *Beyond the Pale: White Women, Racism, and History* (London: Verso, 1992).

Weber, Max, 'Objectivity in Social Science and Social Policy', *The Methodology of the Social Sciences*, ed. Edward Shils and Henry H. Finch (New York: Free Press, 1949).

Weeks, Jeffrey, *Sexuality* (London: Routledge, 2003).

Weitz, Rose (ed.), *The Politics of Women's Bodies: Sexuality, Appearance and Behaviour*, 2nd edn (Oxford: Oxford University Press, 2003).

Weitz, Rose, 'A History of Women's Bodies', in Rose Weitz (ed.), *The Politics of Women's Bodies: Sexuality, Appearance and Behaviour*, 2nd edn (Oxford: Oxford University Press, 2003), pp. 3–11.

Wells, Paul (ed.), *Art and Animation* (London: Academy Group, 1998).

Wells, Paul, ' "Animation is the Most Important Art Form of the Twentieth Century" Discuss', in Paul Wells (ed.), *Art and Animation* (London: Academy Group, 1998), pp. 2–3.

Werbner, Pnina and Tariq Modood (eds), *Debating Cultural Hybridity: Multi-cultural Identities and the Politics of Anti-Racism* (London: Zed Books, 1997).

Whelehan, Imelda, *Modern Feminist Thought: From the Second Wave to 'Post-Feminism'* (Edinburgh: Edinburgh University Press, 1995).

Whelehan, Imelda, *Overloaded: Popular Culture and the Future of Feminism* (London: Women's Press, 2000).

Whelehan, Imelda, *The Feminist Bestseller: From Sex and the Single Girl to Sex and the City* (Basingstoke: Palgrave Macmillan, 2000).

White, Armond, 'Going Gaga', *New York Press*, 16 April 2010, http://www.nypress.com/article-21128-going-gaga.html (10/08/2010).

Whiteley, Sheila, *Women and Popular Music: Sexuality, Identity and Subjectivity* (London: Routledge, 2000).

Wiegman, Robyn, 'Feminism, "The Boyz", and Other Matters Regarding the Male', in Steven Cohan and Ina Rae Hark (eds), *Screening the Male* (London: Routledge, 1993), pp. 173–93.

Wignall, Alice, 'Can a Feminist Really Love Sex and the City?', *Guardian*, 16 April 2008.

Williams, Alan, 'Is a Radical Genre Theory Possible?', *Quarterly Review of Film Studies*, vol. 9, no. 2 (1984), pp. 121–5.

Willis, Jennifer L., ' "Latino Night": Performance of Latino/a Culture in Northwest Ohio', *Communication Quarterly*, vol. 45, no. 4 (1997), pp. 335–50.

Wollen, Peter, 'Ways of Thinking About Music Video (and Post-Modernism)', *Critical Quarterly*, vol. 28, nos. 1–2 (1986), pp. 167–70.

Yahoo Music (no date), http://music.yahoo.com/ar-293441-bio--Christina-Aguilera (20/07/2005).

Yahoo News, 'Costa del Christina', 9 September 2000, http://uk.news.yahoo.com//dotmusic_news/15328.html (23/06/2005).

Yuval-Davis, Nira, 'Ethnicity, Gender Relations and Multiculturalism', in Pnina Werbner and Tariq Modood (eds), *Debating Cultural Hybridity: Multi-cultural Identities and the Politics of Anti-Racism* (London: Zed Books, 1997), pp. 193–208.

VIDEOGRAPHY

50 Cent, CANDYSHOP (dir. Dr Dre, 2005).

50 Cent, IN DA CLUB (dir. Phil Atwell, 2003).

A Perfect Circle, COUNTING BODIES LIKE SHEEP TO THE RHYTHM OF THE WAR DRUMS (dirs Steven Grasse, Nick Paparone, Paul Thie, 2005).

Adams, Bryan (EVERYTHING I DO) I DO IT FOR YOU (dir. Julien Temple, 1991).

Adkins, Trace, HOT MAMA (dir. Michael Salomon, 2003).

Adkins, Trace, HONKY TONK BADONKADONK (dir. Michael Salomon, 2005).

Aguilera, Christina, GENIO ATRAPADO (dir. Diane Martel, 1999).

Aguilera, Christina, GENIE IN A BOTTLE (dir. Diane Martel, 1999).

Aguilera, Christina, VEN CONMIGO (SOLAMENTE TÚ) (dirs Lorin Finkelstein and Paul Hunter, 2000).

Aguilera, Christina, COME ON OVER BABY (ALL I WANT IS YOU) (dir. Paul Hunter, 2000).

Aguilera, Christina, featuring Redman, DIRRTY (dir. David LaChapelle, 2002).

Aguilera, Christina featuring Lil' Kim, CAN'T HOLD US DOWN (dir. David LaChapelle, 2003).

Akon, BELLYDANCER (BANANZA) (dir. Erik White, 2005).

Akon, I WANNA LOVE YOU (dir. Benny Boom, 2006).

Akon, DON'T MATTER (dir. Gil Green, 2007).

Aphex Twin, COME TO DADDY (dir. Chris Cunningham, 1997).

Aphex Twin, WINDOWLICKER (dir. Chris Cunningham, 1999).

Arctic Monkeys, I BET YOU LOOK GOOD ON THE DANCEFLOOR (dir. Huse Monfaradi, 2005).

Arctic Monkeys, WHEN THE SUN GOES DOWN (dir. Fraser Scrimshaw, 2006).

Ashanti, ROCK WIT U (dir. Paul Hunter, 2003).

Audioslave, SHOW ME HOW TO LIVE (dir. A/V Club, 2003).

Beck, DEAD WEIGHT (dir. Michel Gondry, 1997).

Beck, CELLPHONE'S DEAD (dir. Michel Gondry, 2006).

Beenie Man, KING OF THE DANCEHALL (dir. Little X, 2004).

Benassi, Benny, SATISFACTION (dir. Dougal Wilson, 2002).

Benassi, Benny, WHO'S YOUR DADDY? (dir. Kalimera, 2005).

Beyoncé featuring Jay-Z, CRAZY IN LOVE (dir. Jake Nava, 2003).

Beyoncé featuring Sean Paul, BABY BOY (dir. Jake Nava, 2003).

Beyoncé featuring Jay-Z, DÉJÀ VU (dir. Sophie Muller, 2006).

Beyoncé featuring Shakira, BEAUTIFUL LIAR (dir. Jake Nava 2007).

Beyoncé, GREEN LIGHT (dirs Milena and Beyoncé Knowles, 2007).

Beyoncé, SINGLE LADIES (PUT A RING ON IT) (dir. Jake Nava, 2008).

Beyoncé featuring Lady GaGa, VIDEO PHONE (dir. Hype Williams, 2009).

Björk, HUMAN BEHAVIOUR (dir. Michel Gondry, 1993).

Björk, BACHELORETTE (dir. Michel Gondry, 1997).

Blink 182, WHAT'S MY AGE AGAIN? (dir. Marco Siega, 1999).

Blunt, James, GOODBYE MY LOVER (dir. Sam Brown, 2005).

Blunt, James, YOU'RE BEAUTIFUL (dir. Sam Brown, 2005).

Boogie Pimps, SOMEBODY TO LOVE (dirs Simon & Jon, 2003).

Boyzone, WORDS (dir. Greg Masuak, 1996).

Bratz, ME AND MY GIRLS (dir. Nick Rijgersberg, 2006).

Cassidy, HOTEL (dir. Little X, 2004).

Cave, Nick, and Kylie Minogue, WHERE THE WILD ROSES GROW (dir. Rocky Schenck, 1995).

Coldcut, SOUND MIRRORS (dir. Up The Resolution, 2006).

Coldplay, YELLOW (dir. James & Alex, 2000).

Coldplay, FIX YOU (dir. Sophie Muller, 2005).

Cullum, Jamie, ALL AT SEA (dir. Unknown, 2003).

D'Agostino, Gigi, BLA, BLA, BLA (dirs Andreas Hykade and Ged Haney, 2000).

D'Agostino, Gigi, THE RIDDLE (dirs Andreas Hykade and Ged Haney, 2000).

D'Angelo, UNTITLED (HOW DOES IT FEEL?) (dirs Paul Hunter and Dominique Trenier, 1999).

De Souza, GUILTY (dir. Unknown, 2007).

Destiny's Child, BOOTYLICIOUS (dir. Matthew Rolston, 2001).

Destiny's Child, LOSE MY BREATH (dir. Mark Klasfeld, 2004).

Destiny's Child, CATER 2 U (dir. Jake Nava, 2005).

Dido, DON'T LEAVE HOME (dir. Jake Nava, 2004).

Dith, Sasha, RUSSIAN GIRLS (dir. Jure Matjazic, 2005).

DJ Peran, WE WANT TO BE FREE (dir. Unknown, 2003).

Dr Dre featuring Snoop Dogg, THE NEXT EPISODE (dir. Paul Hunter, 2000).

Elvis vs JXL, A LITTLE LESS CONVERSATION (dirs Scott Lyon and Toby Hyde, 2002).

Eminem, LOSE YOURSELF (dirs Eminem, Paul Rosenberg and Phillip G. Atwell, 2002).

Eminem, MOSH (dir. Ian Inaba, 2004).

Evans, Sara, SUDS IN THE BUCKET (dir. Peter Zavadil, 2004).

Fountains of Wayne, STACY'S MOM (dir. Chris Applebaum, 2003).

Fratellis, The, FLATHEAD (dir. James Sutton, 2007).

Funki Porcini, ATOMIC KITCHEN (dir. Funki Porcini, 2002).

Gabriel, Peter, SLEDGEHAMMER (dir. Stephen R Johnson, 1986).

Gaudino, Alex, DESTINATION CALABRIA (dir. Eran Creevy, 2006).

Goldfrapp, STRICT MACHINE (dir. Jonas Odell, 2004).

Goldfrapp, NUMBER 1 (dir. Dawn Shadforth, 2005).

Goldfrapp, OOH LA LA (dir. Dawn Shadforth, 2005).

Green Day, AMERICAN IDIOT (dir. Samuel Bayer, 2004).

Guns 'N' Roses, PARADISE CITY (dir. Nigel Dick, 1988).

Guns 'N' Roses, YOU COULD BE MINE (dirs Jeffrey Abelson, Andy Morahan and Stan Winston, 1991).

Horrors, The, SHEENA IS A PARASITE (dir. Chris Cunningham, 2006).

Houston, Whitney, I WILL ALWAYS LOVE YOU (dir. Alan Smithee, 1992).

Jay Z and Alicia Keys, EMPIRE STATE OF MIND (dir. Hype Williams, 2009).

Jet, ARE YOU GONNA BE MY GIRL? (dir. Robert Hales, 2003).

Junior Jack, STUPIDISCO (dir. Charles Devens, 2004).

Junior Senior, MOVE YOUR FEET (dir. Shynola, 2004).

Keith, Toby, GET DRUNK AND BE SOMEBODY (dir. Michael Salomon, 2006).

Kelis, TRICK ME (dir. Little X, 2004).

Kelis featuring Nas, BLINDFOLD ME (dir. Mark Klasfeld, 2006).

Khia, MY NECK MY BACK (LICK IT) (dir. Diane Martel, 2002).

Khia, MY NECK MY BACK (LICK IT) (dir. Andreas Tibblin, 2004).

Kweli, Talib, featuring Mary J Blige, I TRY (dir. Steven Murashige, 2004).

Lady Gaga, BAD ROMANCE (dir. Francis Lawrence, 2009).
Lady Gaga, ALEJANDRO (dir. Steven Klein, 2010).
Lady Gaga, TELEPHONE (dir. Jonas Åkerlund, 2010).
Leftfield featuring Afrika Bombaata, AFRIKA SHOX (dir. Chris Cunningham, 1999).
Limp Bizkit, RE-ARRANGED (dir. Fred Durst, 1999).
Limp Bizkit, TAKE A LOOK AROUND (dir. Fred Durst, 2000).
Little Brother, LOVIN IT (dir. Joey the Greek, 2005).
Llorenna, Kelly, THIS TIME I KNOW IT'S FOR REAL (dir. Unknown, 2004).
Ludacris, PUSSY POPPIN' (dir. Fat Cats, 2003).
Madonna, EXPRESS YOURSELF (dir. David Fincher, 1989).
Madonna, LIKE A PRAYER (dir. Mary Lambert, 1989).
Madonna, JUSTIFY MY LOVE (dir. Jean-Baptiste Mondino, 1990).
Madonna, VOGUE (dir. David Fincher, 1990).
Madonna, FROZEN (dir. Chris Cunningham, 1998).
Make the Girl Dance, BABY, BABY, BABY (dir. Pierre Mathieu, 2009).
Melanie G, WORD UP (dir. W.I.Z., 1999).
Metallica, NOTHING ELSE MATTERS (dir. Adam Dubin, 1992).
Mind, Michael, BLINDED BY THE LIGHT (dir. Unknown, 2007).
Minogue, Dannii, PUT THE NEEDLE ON IT (dir. Miikka Lommi, 2002).
Minogue, Kylie, CAN'T GET YOU OUT OF MY HEAD (dir. Dawn Shadforth, 2001).
Minogue, Kylie, I BELIEVE IN YOU (dir. Vernie Young, 2005).
Morrison, James, BROKEN STRINGS (dir. Micah Meisner, 2008).
MSTRKRFT, EASY LOVE (dir. Sean Turrell, 2006).
Narcotic Thrust, I LIKE IT (dir. Andreas Tibblin, 2004).
Nelly featuring Kelly Rowland, DILEMMA (dir. Benny Boom, 2002).
Nelly, AIR FORCE ONES (dir. David Palmer, 2002).
Nelly, HOT IN HERRE (dir. Bille Woodruff, 2002).
Nelly, TIP DRILL (dir. Benny Boom, 2002).
N.E.R.D. featuring Lee Harvey, LAP DANCE (dir. Diane Martel, 2001).
Ne-Yo, BECAUSE OF YOU (dir. Melina, 2006).
Nickelback, HERO (dir. Nigel Dick, 2002).
Nirvana, IN BLOOM (dir. Kevin Kerslake, 1992).
Pantera, FIVE MINUTES ALONE (dir. Wayne Isham, 1994).
Paul, Sean, EVER BLAZIN' (dir. Anthony Mandler, 2005).
Pink, STUPID GIRLS (dir. Dave Meyers, 2006).
Plain White T's, HEY THERE DELILAH (dir. Jay Martin, 2006).
Prodigy, The, BREATHE (dir. Walter Stern, 1996).
Prodigy, The, SMACK MY BITCH UP (dir. Jonas Åkerlund, 1997).
Prydz, Eric, CALL ON ME (dir. Huse Monfaradi, 2004).
R Kelly, IGNITION (dir. Bille Woodruff, 2003).
Radiohead, KNIVES OUT (dir. Michel Gondry, 2001).
Radiohead, 2+2=5 (dir. Gastón Viñas, 2003).
Redman, LET'S GET DIRTY (I CAN'T GET IN DA CLUB) (dir. David Meyers, 2000).
R.E.M., WHAT'S THE FREQUENCY, KENNETH? (dir. Peter Care, 1994).
Rihanna, IF IT'S LOVING THAT YOU WANT (dir. Marcus Raboy, 2005).
Rocco DeLuca and the Burden, COLORFUL (dir. Frank Borin, 2006).
Scissor Sisters, TAKE YOUR MAMA OUT (dir. Andy Soup, 2004).
Shakira, HIPS DON'T LIE (dir. Sophie Muller, 2006).
Shakur, Tupac, BRENDA'S GOT A BABY (dir. Hughes Brothers, 1991).
Shakur, Tupac, featuring the Notorious B.I.G., RUNNING (DYING TO LIVE) (dir. Philip G. Atwell, 2004).
Shanice, TAKE CARE OF U (dir. Gina Prince-Bythewood, 2006).

Sia, BREATHE ME (dir. Daniel Askill and Sia, 2005).

Sigur Ros, HLJÓMALIND (dir. Unknown, 2007).

Simpson, Jessica, featuring Willie Nelson, THESE BOOTS WERE MADE FOR WALKING (dir. Brett Ratner, 2005).

Snoop Dogg featuring Pharrell, DROP IT LIKE IT'S HOT (dir. Paul Hunter, 2004).

Snow Patrol, CHASING CARS (dirs Arni & Kinski, 2006).

Spears, Britney, EVERYTIME (dir. David LaChapelle, 2004).

Stevens, Rachel, SWEET DREAMS MY L.A. EX (dir. Tim Royes, 2003).

Strokes, The, REPTILIA (dir. Jake Scott, 2004).

Take That, PATIENCE (dir. David Mould, 2006).

Timbaland featuring Justin Timberlake, CARRY OUT (dir. Bryan Barber, 2009).

Timberlake, Justin, ROCK YOUR BODY (dir. Francis Lawrence, 2003).

Tritt, Travis, THE GIRL'S GONE WILD (dir. Michael Salomon, 2004).

Twain, Shania, UP (dir. Antti Jokinen, 2003).

Urban, Keith, MAKING MEMORIES OF US (dir. Chris Hicky, 2005).

Usher, LET IT BURN (dir. Jake Nava, 2004).

van Helden, Armand, MY MY MY (dir. unknown, 2004).

West, Kanye, THROUGH THE WIRE (dirs Coodie and Chike, 2003).

West, Kanye, featuring Jamie Foxx, GOLD DIGGER (dir. Hype Williams, 2005).

West, Kanye, LOVE LOCKDOWN (dir. Simon Henwood, 2008).

Westlife, YOU RAISE ME UP (dir. Alex Hemming, 2005).

Wet Wet Wet, LOVE IS ALL AROUND (dir. Marcus Nispel, 1994).

White Stripes, The, FELL IN LOVE WITH A GIRL (dir. Michel Gondry, 2002).

White Stripes, The, SEVEN NATION ARMY (dirs Alex and Martin, 2003).

Williams, Robbie, MILLENNIUM (dir. Vaughan Arnell, 1998).

Williams, Robbie, ROCK DJ (dir. Vaughan Arnell, 2000).

Williams, Robbie, SUPREME (dir. Vaughan Arnell, 2000).

Williams, Robbie, LET LOVE BE YOUR ENERGY (dir. Olly Reid, 2001).

Wonder, Wayne, NO LETTING GO (dir. Little X, 2003).

Zac Brown Band, CHICKEN FRIED (dir. Clifton Collins Jr., 2008).

INDEX